"In the author's characteristically judicious and winsome fashion, this volume makes a timely and welcome contribution to the age-old debate on the relationship between Christian theology and philosophy. In doing so it provides a resolute and compelling case that the basic questions philosophy asks find their fundamental answers only in the Bible, God's written Word. In the midst of so much current confused thinking on these matters, I commend *Redeeming Philosophy* to all concerned with 'taking every thought captive to obey Christ.'"

Richard B. Gaffin Jr., Professor of Biblical and Systematic Theology, Emeritus, Westminster Theological Seminary

"Poythress has again gotten it right. This book contains a great deal of fresh thinking and careful Christian philosophical work. This is Poythress's clearest integration between linguistics, philosophy, and exegesis. Surely this book contains the most incisive analyses of apples and bookmarks you will ever find. The point, of course, is that everything in God's world reflects the richness of the triune God."

John M. Frame, J. D. Trimble Chair of Systematic Theology and Philosophy, Reformed Theological Seminary, Orlando, Florida

"Matters of philosophy are often complex and laden with challenging issues. Christians wonder whether they should avoid philosophy altogether and simply stick with the Bible or if there is something that can be gained from philosophical study. Employing the theological methodology of John Frame, Dr. Poythress has written a useful introductory exploration of the relationship between philosophy and the teachings of Scripture."

J. V. Fesko, Academic Dean and Professor of Systematic and Historical Theology, Westminster Seminary California

T0334974

REDEEMING PHILOSOPHY

REDEEMING PHILOSOPHY

*A God-Centered Approach
to the Big Questions*

VERN S. POYTHRESS

WHEATON, ILLINOIS

Trade paperback ISBN: 978-1-4335-3946-6
PDF ISBN: 978-1-4335-3947-3
Mobipocket ISBN: 978-1-4335-3948-0
ePub ISBN: 978-1-4335-3949-7

Library of Congress Cataloging-in-Publication Data

Poythress, Vern S.
  Redeeming philosophy : a God-centered approach to the big questions / Vern S. Poythress.
     pages cm
  Includes bibliographical references and index.
  ISBN 978-1-4335-3946-6 (tp)
  1. Christian philosophy. I. Title.
BR100.P65   2014
261.5'1—dc23   2014003912

Crossway is a publishing ministry of Good News Publishers.

5L		31	30	29	28	27	26	25	24	23	22	21
14	13	12	11	10	9	8	7	6	5	4	3	2

To John Frame,
my teacher, colleague, and friend

Contents

PART I

Basic Issues in Exploring Big Questions

1

The Big Questions about Life

Life has big questions: Who are we as human beings? What is unique about being human? Does our existence have a purpose, and does the world have a purpose? How should we conduct our lives? What are moral standards, and where do they come from? Why does anything exist? What is the nature of the world? How do we know anything? Is there a God? Are there many gods? Is there an afterlife? What is it like?

In the history of the Western world, *philosophers* have sought to explore some of these big questions about the nature of the world. The word *philosophy* comes from the Greek word *philosophia*, which means "love of wisdom." Philosophers seek wisdom, especially wisdom about the big questions.[1]

Clusters of Big Questions

Philosophers have considered a whole host of big questions. Over the centuries, philosophy has developed a considerable number of subdisciplines that focus on a smaller set of questions. Three of the main subdivisions are metaphysics, epistemology, and philosophi-

---

[1] In the twentieth century a tradition of *analytic philosophy* arose that has focused on analyzing fundamental concepts (like the concept of "good" or the concept of "science") and on analyzing key uses of language in various fields. Some of its practitioners are suspicious of human ability to find answers to "big" questions. Our focus on the big questions leaves these practitioners to one side. See Norman Geisler and Paul D. Feinberg, *Introduction to Philosophy: A Christian Perspective* (Grand Rapids: Baker, 1980), 14–17; Vern S. Poythress, *Logic: A God-Centered Approach to the Foundation of Western Thought* (Wheaton, IL: Crossway, 2013), appendix F2.

cal ethics. (Later, we will briefly consider some other subdivisions as well.)[2]

Metaphysics studies questions about existence: Why does anything exist? And what is the nature of what exists? Epistemology studies the nature of knowledge: What is knowledge? How do we come to know what we know? When can we be sure that we know something (rather than having a mistaken belief)? Philosophical ethics studies issues of right and wrong: What are moral standards? Are they universal? Where do they come from?

Why worry about such questions? Do they matter? Questions about ethics matter because right and wrong affect the well-being of humankind. Is murder wrong? Is theft wrong? Is lying wrong? If so, why? If not, how do we prevent social relations from disintegrating into continual fights? Are moral standards absolute, or do they vary with culture? And how do we find out what is right and wrong? Ethical questions clearly affect how we conduct our lives, and how our lives harmonize or clash with the lives of others.

What about the other two subdivisions of philosophy, namely, metaphysics and epistemology? Do they matter? Or are these two areas only matters of academic interest, without significant impact on ordinary living? Metaphysics considers questions about what exists. That includes the question of God. Does God exist? If he does, what kind of God is he? Does he hold us morally accountable? Our answers can make a big difference.

Metaphysics and epistemology, as they are traditionally studied, can seem like formidable subjects. If ordinary people begin reading some of the more technical discussions in metaphysics, they may find their interest lagging and even disappearing. The discussions may seem to them distant or irrelevant or hard to understand. But some of the issues *are* relevant. As we indicated, the question of God makes a big difference. And even answers to more specialized questions can influence our view of the world as a whole. So it is worthwhile to consider how this area affects our view of the world and our view of life.

---

[2] See part 5. Ethics can be seen as part of a larger subdivision, the theory of value (axiology), which includes aesthetics and political philosophy.

To illustrate, let us consider one kind of metaphysics that has an influence in our day. In the Western world many people among the intelligentsia think that the world consists in matter and motion and energy. According to this view, more complex things, like rocks and trees, animals and people, are built up from complex arrangements and interactions of matter. But the ultimate nature of the world is material. This view is called *materialism*. It is one kind of *metaphysical* position, that is, one view concerning the ultimate nature of things. Philosophers have debated metaphysics for centuries, and materialism in one form or another has been one of the options offered in debate ever since the time of the ancient Greeks.

Does this position make any difference? It does, because when it is held consistently, it tells us about ourselves. It says that each of us is a complex arrangement of atoms in motion. Any personal significance that we want to have, we must invent for ourselves, because the universe as a whole has no purpose. The universe just is. It is matter in motion.

That is a grim picture. And while some people endeavor to follow materialism consistently, others find pure materialism forbidding in its bleakness. With one part of their mind, they may believe that matter and motion are at the foundation of it all, but they endeavor to add extra layers of personal significance on top of the foundational layer. Both the people who follow materialism consistently and the people who add extra layers are thinking *metaphysically*. Both have beliefs about the ultimate nature of the world. The people who add extra layers are implying that these layers do exist within a total metaphysical picture of the nature of things. But are they right to add the extra layers? Hard-nosed materialists might accuse them of living lives of illusion and refusing to face reality.

People who believe in God have yet another form of metaphysical belief. They are saying that matter and motion are not everything. They believe that God exists, and that God created matter and motion—and extra layers as well. They would say that the materialists are ignoring many dimensions of reality, including God himself. And they would say that when people add layers of their own choosing, they are missing God's way and God's meanings by trying to substitute their own notions.

Many other people do not think about metaphysics *explicitly*. They do not worry about it, but just go about living their lives. Still, they are often influenced, even heavily influenced, by metaphysical views that are "in the air," that hover around as part of the intellectual atmosphere of the modern world. Many people who have not *thought through* the philosophy of materialism are influenced by materialism, particularly as it takes shape among people who interpret the theory of evolution as a form of materialistic philosophy.[3]

Ties through Epistemology

Finally, what about epistemology? Epistemology studies how we come to know things. This subdivision of philosophy might seem to be the least relevant. But it has ties with the other two. People disagree about metaphysics—whether God exists, whether everything can be reduced to matter and motion, whether as persons we survive bodily death. The disagreements lead to asking questions about knowledge, such as, how do we *know* whether matter is the ultimate nature of the world? And how do we *know* whether God exists?

Some people worry that maybe we can never know. Some currents within postmodern thought have become radically skeptical. They suggest that we cannot know what is true, but must endeavor to creep along with whatever appears to work best for us.

Moral standards have similar ties with epistemology. Even if absolute moral standards exist, can we *know* that they exist, and can we know what they are? How do we know?

In fact, then, questions about how we come to *know* things interact with the questions about metaphysics and ethics. For example, let us suppose that Sue becomes skeptical in her reflections about knowledge. She may decide that she cannot know the answers to

---

[3] On the distinction between evolution as a narrow theory about biological development and evolution as a form of materialistic philosophy, see Vern S. Poythress, *Redeeming Science: A God-Centered Approach* (Wheaton, IL: Crossway, 2006), 80–81, and chaps. 18–19.

basic questions in metaphysics and ethics. She tells herself that she might as well stop longing for what she can never have. So her epistemological position, namely skepticism, has caused her to give up thinking about metaphysics and ethics.

Suppose, on the other hand, that she has robust confidence in human reason, and she thinks that reason is the main source for knowledge. She may believe that rational reflection or Platonic dialogue can give her the metaphysical and ethical answers that she seeks. She may also hope that rational reflection can clarify the nature of moral standards. In taking this view about the central role of reason in epistemology, she has already tacitly assumed that moral standards are basically rational in character. And the metaphysical nature of the world must be rational in character in order to be accessible through her use of reason. Thus her views of epistemology have affected her expectations about morality and metaphysics.

Or suppose that she thinks that repeated experience, sense experience, is the main source of knowledge. Then she will in some ways treat sense experience as if it were the ultimate metaphysical basis for the world—maybe not the world as it actually is, but the world as she perceives it.

Ties through Metaphysics

Conversely, answers to metaphysical questions have an influence on epistemology and ethics. Suppose that Sue has found what she considers to be fundamental answers about the nature of the world. The world includes her, so she has also arrived at some answers about her own nature as a human being. With answers of this kind, she has come a long way toward answering how she as a human being can interact with the world in such a way that she can obtain knowledge.

For example, if Sue believes, as a metaphysical truth, that God exists, she can reason that God made both her and the world around her, and that God has equipped her with an ability to know this world, because he has given her a mind and has created an intrinsic harmony between her and the world. Or suppose that she has reached materialist conclusions about the nature of the world. She will probably believe that she is a product of purposeless Darwinian evolution. Evolution has equipped her with ability to survive, and ability to know is a subcomponent of the more fundamental ability to survive.

Sue's metaphysical views also have implications for ethics. If she believes that God exists, she can easily conclude that God is the ultimate source for moral standards. If she is a materialist Darwinist, she may conclude that morality is a psychic illusion to restrain us from destroying one another and terminating the race.

Subdivisions of Philosophy as Perspectives

In fact, we can treat metaphysics, epistemology, and ethics as subdivisions that offer perspectives on one another.[4] For example, let us start with metaphysics. Metaphysics answers questions about what exists. A thorough set of answers would include answers about whether knowledge exists and what is its nature. So metaphysics in an expansive sense includes epistemology as a subdivision. Likewise, metaphysics should include answers about whether moral standards exist. If they do, it should specify what relation they have to us as humans who exist. And so metaphysics should actually include answers to ethical questions. Thus, when we use the term *metaphysics* expansively and let it answer all kinds of questions about existence, it becomes a perspective that includes within it the other two subdivisions, epistemology and ethics.

We may also see epistemology as a perspective on the other two subdivisions. If epistemology deals with what we know, it also deals with what we know about the nature of things, and thus includes metaphysics. It includes what we know about moral standards and ethics, and so it includes ethics.

Finally, we can treat ethics as a perspective on the other two subdivisions. Ethics includes questions about what we ought to believe. What we ought to believe about the nature of things is

---

[4] See John M. Frame, *A History of Western Philosophy and Theology: Spiritual Warfare in the Life of the Mind* (Phillipsburg, NJ: P&R, forthcoming), chap. 1; title subject to change.

metaphysics. What we ought to believe about knowledge is epistemology. We cannot really make progress in either metaphysics
or epistemology without standards for how we ought to proceed
in examining these subdivisions. And the standards are ethical
standards. Conversely, we cannot make progress in ethics without
some sense of how we would come to know moral standards. And
this process of coming to knowledge is the domain of epistemology.

Thus all three subdivisions—metaphysics, epistemology, and
ethics—offer perspectives on one another. In many respects they
presuppose one another. Though we may temporarily focus on
only one subdivision within philosophy, the others lurk in the
background. Tentative answers about ethics guide what we do in
metaphysics and epistemology. Similarly, answers in metaphysics
influence epistemology and ethics, and answers in epistemology
influence metaphysics and ethics.

In one book we cannot cover all three of these big areas equally.
So in the bulk of our discussion we will focus on metaphysics. But
we acknowledge the influences of the two other subdivisions on
our work.[5] In addition, what we say in the area of metaphysics has
fruitful implications in epistemology, ethics, and still other subdivisions of philosophy. By working on one area more thoroughly, I
hope to give readers a good idea of what it would be like to work out
the other areas as well. And when we have finished our reflections
on metaphysics, we can also call attention to excellent resources
that already exist in epistemology and ethics—as well as other
philosophical subjects.

---

[5] For epistemology, see John M. Frame, *The Doctrine of the Knowledge of God* (Phillipsburg, NJ: P&R, 1987); for ethics, see Frame, *The Doctrine of the Christian Life* (Phillipsburg, NJ: P&R, 2008).

2

The Bible as a Resource

We want to explore how to obtain answers about the nature of things. But our answers will differ from most of the history of philosophy, because we are seeking answers from the Bible, rather than just trying to reason things out. The Bible's teaching has implications for how we answer big questions.

Why should we listen to the Bible more than any other book? The Bible claims to be the very word of God addressed to us. It makes a most weighty claim. But should we believe it? In our day skeptical voices rise up. We cannot possibly consider all the skeptical questions without a long detour, which would result in another book. I prefer to direct readers to existing works that address the questions of skeptics.[1] Whether or not you accept that the Bible is the word of God, I invite you to see how the Bible supplies answers to big questions.

Summary of Biblical Teaching

When we listen to the Bible, we find out many things. Here we can only summarize a few of the most central teachings. The Bible indicates that there is one God, who created the whole world, including us as human beings. But our first parents rebelled against him. Since then, we have all been deep in rebellion, and it takes God to come and rescue us. At the heart of God's plan for rescue is

---

[1] See Timothy Keller, *The Reason for God: Belief in an Age of Skepticism* (New York: Dutton, 2008).

Jesus Christ. God the Father sent Christ into the world to rescue us from sin and rebellion and their consequences. Christ accomplished his work on earth, died for our sins, and rose from the dead. He now reigns in heaven until the future time when he will inaugurate a new heaven and a new earth, free from sin and its effects (Rev. 21:1).

According to the Bible, Christ is the only Redeemer, and he is the source of redemption for everyone who trusts in him. He accomplished our redemption when he died on the cross and was raised on the third day to new life (Rom. 4:25). On the cross he bore the punishment for our rebellion against God (1 Pet. 2:24) and so accomplished for us reconciliation to God. What he accomplished, he then applies to us as individuals and as a community (the church). Christ sends the Holy Spirit to work a transformation in us. He also instructs us through the Bible, which was written under the inspiration and power of the Holy Spirit, so that it is his word.[2]

The Bible calls on us to place our faith in Christ in order to be saved from God's judgment on our rebellion (Acts 16:31; Rom. 10:9–10). It tells us to follow Jesus Christ, to become his disciples, and to submit to his teaching. (We must leave to books on theology a more extended summary of biblical teaching.)[3]

Following Christ means paying attention to what he says in the Bible. When we follow its teaching, it transforms our thinking: "Do not be conformed to this world, but be transformed by the renewal of your mind, that by testing you may discern what is the will of God, what is good and acceptable and perfect" (Rom. 12:2). This transformation means that our thinking is redeemed, including our thinking about the big questions. Thus, we can say that philosophy is supposed to be redeemed as we receive Christ's instruction and follow his ways.

---

[2] Whole books take up the discussion of the nature of the Bible. For arguments that the Bible is God's word in written form, see especially John Murray, "The Attestation of Scripture," in *The Infallible Word*, ed. Ned B. Stonehouse and Paul Woolley (Philadelphia: Presbyterian and Reformed, 1946), 1–54; Benjamin B. Warfield, *The Inspiration and Authority of the Bible*, ed. Samuel G. Craig (Philadelphia: Presbyterian and Reformed, 1967); John M. Frame, *The Doctrine of the Word of God* (Phillipsburg, NJ: P&R, 2010).

[3] See John M. Frame, *Salvation Belongs to the Lord: An Introduction to Systematic Theology* (Phillipsburg, NJ: P&R, 2006).

But not everyone believes that Jesus Christ is the only Savior and that the Bible's teaching is true and can be trusted. If we do not trust what the Bible says, what is the alternative? Some people follow other religions. Some people try to reason things out on their own. This latter course is the predominant one in Western philosophy. Before we try to answer some of the big questions, we should understand the major differences between the Bible and Western philosophy. But these differences offer us a vast subject and could consume a whole book. We will have to simplify and confine ourselves to a few basic points.[4]

Philosophers Searching in Autonomy

The history of Western philosophy goes back to Greece, and especially to Socrates, Plato, and Aristotle. Prior to these three men there were still earlier philosophers: Thales, Anaximander, Heraclitus, Parmenides, the Sophists, and others. The ancient Greek philosophers varied from one another in their views, but they all sought to obtain *wisdom* about the nature of the world. In this search, they used human reason, but they did not turn to the special divine revelation in the Bible. They wanted to think things through, and they wanted their reasoning to be independent of God or gods. This desire for independence can be called *autonomy*, which means self-law. The Greek philosophers sought to use reason as its own law and guide, independent of God.[5]

They did so partly because Greek culture as a whole was confused about divinity. The Greeks were polytheists, believing in many gods. They thought of Zeus as the supreme god, or the father of the gods, but Zeus was still limited in relation to the other gods. None of these gods could be trusted. So, if a person sought to arrive at rock-bottom truth, what resources did he have except his own wits?

---

[4]An introduction to the history of philosophy from a Christian point of view can be found in W. Andrew Hoffecker, ed., *Revolutions in Worldview: Understanding the Flow of Western Thought* (Phillipsburg, NJ: P&R, 2007). For a more thorough account, see John M. Frame, *A History of Western Philosophy and Theology: Spiritual Warfare in the Life of the Mind* (Phillipsburg, NJ: P&R, forthcoming), title subject to change.

[5]See John Frame, "Greeks Bearing Gifts," in Hoffecker, *Revolutions in Worldview*, 6–7.

Human Beings Knowing God

We can understand why the ancient philosophers gave up on the Greek gods, because these gods were morally unworthy of their allegiance. But the Bible has something more to say. Romans 1:20–23 indicates that all human beings know God:

> For his [God's] invisible attributes, namely, his eternal power and divine nature, have been clearly perceived, ever since the creation of the world, in the things that have been made. So they are without excuse. For although they knew God, they did not honor him as God or give thanks to him, but they became futile in their thinking, and their foolish hearts were darkened. Claiming to be *wise*, they became fools, and exchanged the glory of the immortal God for images resembling mortal man and birds and animals and creeping things.

Human beings know God by virtue of creation. But they suppress the knowledge. They turn to "images," that is, idols. That is what happened in ancient Greece.

When Christ came into the world, he came to redeem people from all their sins, including the sins of serving idols instead of God and the sins of suppressing the truth about God. If we want deliverance, we need to come to him.

The Bible's Role

When Christ works a change in us through the Holy Spirit, we come to believe and understand the Bible better and better. From the Bible, we learn that God created human beings in a state of goodness or innocence (Genesis 1–2). Human beings were not always suppressing the truth and rebelling against God and trying to escape from his lordship.

Even while human beings were innocent, God intended that they should not live independently of him. He created us to have communion with him. He spoke to human beings in Genesis 1:28–30 and 2:16–17. His speeches revealed who he was, and also what were his standards for human actions. He told Adam not to eat from the one special tree in the garden of Eden, the "tree of the knowledge of good and evil" (Gen. 2:17). God also indicated in summary form the tasks in which human beings were to engage (Gen. 1:28–30). God intended that human thinking should pay attention to, digest, and honor what he said in verbal communication.

The first communication was oral. But later God wrote the Ten Commandments in written form (Ex. 24:12; Deut. 5:22). He then commissioned Moses to write much more (Deut. 31:24–26). This early writing was the first portion of a written *canon*, or standard, that was to guide and instruct the people who belonged to God. The Bible is the canon in completed form.[6] Much more could be said, but we need not pursue the details. As the book of God's instruction, the Bible provides important answers for human living and human significance.

---

[6] For further information, see, for example, Herman Ridderbos, *Redemptive History and the New Testament Scriptures* (Phillipsburg, NJ: P&R, 1988); Michael J. Kruger, *Canon Revisited: Establishing the Origins and Authority of the New Testament Books* (Wheaton, IL: Crossway, 2012).

3

Opposite Approaches to Philosophy

We can see a pronounced difference between the way most philosophers have chosen to pursue wisdom and the way we are proposing. In fact, there are several notable points of difference.

Antithesis

First, there is a difference in the heart. The Bible indicates that Christ sends the Holy Spirit to give his chosen people "a new heart" (Ezek. 36:26). As a result, they desire to obey God rather than rebel against him as they did before. They find themselves loving God and understanding and loving what the Bible says rather than feeling that it makes no sense or that its ideas are distasteful to them. God has brought about a fundamental change, a change from heart-level rebellion against God and desire for independence from God to heart-level love for God.

Sometimes people use the expression *born again* to describe a subjective experience of change or renewal. And indeed the Holy Spirit does work renewal (John 3:3–8). But his renewal goes deeper than what we can see or feel. Moreover, people may have religious experiences of change that still fall short of the spiritual renewal that the Bible describes. The Bible is talking about the real change that the Holy Spirit works in a person's heart, not just good feelings or a vague religious experience. Not everyone who claims to have been born again really has been, in the biblical sense. The people who are born again are also called *regenerate* (a virtual synonym for *born again*).

Regenerate people are different from unregenerate people. The difference is fundamental rather than superficial. The one person loves God, while the other is still in rebellion. The one desires to submit to what God says in the Bible, while the other does not. The one desires to obey God, while the other does not. The one believes in Christ for salvation, while the other does not. I will accordingly call the unregenerate people *unbelievers*, meaning that they do not believe in Christ. But they nevertheless believe in *something*—whether another religion, or naturalism, or atheism, or maybe just themselves. There is a radical *antithesis* or contrast between the two types of people. And this antithesis affects how they think and how they reason, because the one person wants to do his thinking in submission to God, and the other does not.

This antithesis is real, but it is combined with inconsistencies and practical failings on both sides. Within this life, regenerate people or believers are not completely free from sin. And the sins that remain include intellectual sins. Neither their thinking nor their attitudes nor their behavior is consistently righteous.

Conversely, unbelievers are not consistent with their heart-level commitment *against* God. They are still made in the image of God, and God still showers good gifts on them, including intellectual gifts. They are not as bad as they could be, while believers are not as good as they could be. In fact, some unbelievers may be very moral and admirable people, from the standpoint of their outward behavior. They may be gracious in speech and upright in action. But their good actions are still contaminated with self-love. Their underlying motive is still corrupt. At heart, they are not serving God but serving themselves—perhaps their pride, perhaps their reputation, perhaps their comfort (e.g., they may want a comfortable conscience).

Except in the medieval period, most Western philosophers have not been thoroughly committed Christians who were trying to "take every thought captive to obey Christ" (2 Cor. 10:5). Some may have called themselves Christian. But our discussion of regeneration makes it clear that true Christianity, which means following Christ as Lord, is not merely a matter of giving oneself the *name* Christian or undergoing the Christian rite of baptism. True Christianity starts with the work of the Holy Spirit in a person's heart.

So the products of philosophers' thinking are mixed. There are some positive insights even from non-Christian philosophers, because they enjoy good gifts from God. They still live in God's world, and they cannot escape the fact that they are made in the image of God. They want to be autonomous, but they cannot succeed, because they are continuously dependent on God. Theirs is a would-be autonomy, a striving for independence that is continually frustrated by the presence of God.

The good products from non-Christians are sometimes called products from *common grace*. The products come from *grace* because all of us are guilty of sin and rebellion, and we do not deserve the good things that we receive from God. The word *common* is used to indicate that God distributes these gifts both to believers and to unbelievers:

> For he [God] makes his sun rise on the evil and on the good, and sends rain on the just and on the unjust. (Matt. 5:45)

> Yet he [God] did not leave himself without witness, for he did good by giving you rains from heaven and fruitful seasons, satisfying your hearts with food and gladness. (Acts 14:17)

We can see that God's common grace includes in principle not only physical gifts like sending rain, but also intellectual gifts. God has given to some people keen insights about the world. So unbelieving philosophy contains good insights. Conversely, philosophers who are Christians produce reflections that are inevitably mixed, because Christians are not yet sinless.

Submission to God's Communication in the Bible

A second major difference between the two types of people is that believers and unbelievers differ in their use of the Bible. Believers are ready to receive its instruction with faith. Unbelievers are not. Again, there are mixtures. Believers may be beset by doubts. Or they may sinfully resist a particular teaching of the Bible for a while, because it is distasteful to them. Unbelievers may see some attractive things in the Bible that they are willing to accept.

But there is still a principial difference. At the root, their attitudes are different. Believers acknowledge that their own hearts and their thinking need redemption from sin and from a desire to be autonomous and to be their own god. They have repudiated the practice of simply following the inclinations of their own minds and lording it over the Bible whenever they wish. They realize that they need the Bible's instruction, and that God has designed the Bible to be a means by which their hearts and minds are progressively renewed. Unbelievers, by contrast, believe that their thinking is already basically all right. They think that they do not need to submit to the Bible. They want to make up their own minds independently of the Bible—they want autonomy.

Normality or Abnormality of Human Thinking

Believers think that the present state of affairs, including the state of human minds, is *abnormal*. It is ruined by the fall into sin, and the effects of sin. Unbelievers, by contrast, think that the present state of the human mind is normal.

These differences affect philosophy. It has become virtually a ground rule for the practice of philosophy in the Western world that one must *not* appeal to the Bible—or any other religious source, for that matter—for authority. One must appeal only to reason. In my opinion, that ground rule exhibits disastrous rebellion against the God of the universe. God's will is that we *should* use the Bible. We are already rebelling if we imply that we know better and refuse to use his guidance.

Tactics in Discussion with Unbelievers

Philosophers who are Christians might say in reply that in their own thinking they want to submit to God, but they are not appealing to the Bible when they do philosophy because *other* people, who are non-Christians, are participating in the conversation.

This situation needs sorting out. We can indeed distinguish short-range tactics for communication from the totality of what we are thinking. But when we engage in conversations with unbelievers, we need to beware of falling into the error of assuming that we are all thinking alike. We are not. The ground rules are different for Christians, because we are under the lordship of Christ. We are never "off duty." Everything we say or think ought to be serving him. We are not religiously neutral part of the time. And neither are unbelievers.

If we know that we are not thinking alike, it makes good sense, somewhere along the line, to make known the differences in the process of our conversation, lest our dialogue partners misunderstand us. In other words, as opportunity affords, we had better talk about the difference that Christ makes in our thinking. And if he makes no difference, we had better go back to consider what Romans 12:2 says about the transformation of our minds.

In addition, if we are concerned for unbelievers as whole people and not just narrowly worried about debating points, we should try to think about how we can explain to them that they will never come to know the truth rightly without communion with God. We should say that such renewed communion comes through Christ. We should indicate the Christ of whom we speak is the Christ who is described in the Bible and who reveals himself in the Bible. So the Bible ought to come into the discussion as we try to rescue unbelieving philosophers from their suppression of the truth and their rebellion against God.

Just continuing the conversation using reason alone can easily be taken by unbelievers to imply that reason is all right when it is *autonomous*, when we are not listening to the Bible. We risk conveying a false impression.

The tradition of presuppositional apologetics, as expounded by Cornelius Van Til, has been particularly helpful to me in understanding these points, and I commend it to those who want to know how to conduct conversations with unbelievers.[1] We cannot pursue every dimension of these apologetic challenges in this book. But I want to make a basic point. Whether we are followers of Christ matters. The orientation of our hearts matters. It matters whether we listen to the Bible. It matters whether we make known our commitments. It matters whether we think of reason as operating autonomously.

We may say it another way. Suppose a Christian wants to participate in a philosophical dialogue in a modern context. He needs to consider two issues. First, he needs to ask whether the ground rules of the discussion in philosophy forbid him from reasoning the way he is committed to reasoning, that is, with God speaking in Scripture as his instructor and guide. Second, he should ask whether he ought not first to take some time and use the Bible to find answers to the big questions that the philosophers raise. Only *after* he has attained some clarity in his own mind—and purity of thinking in communion with the purity of God—is he in a reasonable position to engage in dialogue without compromising his beliefs by falling into the same pattern of autonomous reasoning that the ground rules try to force upon him.

Seeking Answers

Other books in the tradition of presuppositional apologetics have dealt extensively with how we conduct discussions with unbelievers of various kinds. We are not going to go over that ground again here. Rather, we want to seek clarity of mind for ourselves as believers. We want to employ the full resources of the Bible to seek knowledge. The Bible itself encourages a search that seeks God and his instruction, rather than following an autonomous route:

The fear of the LORD is the *beginning of wisdom*. (Ps. 111:10)

---

[1] See, for example, John M. Frame, *Apologetics to the Glory of God: An Introduction* (Phillipsburg, NJ: P&R, 1994); Cornelius Van Til, *Christian Apologetics*, 2nd ed., ed. William Edgar (Phillipsburg, NJ: P&R, 2003); Van Til, *The Defense of the Faith*, 4th ed., ed. K. Scott Oliphint (Phillipsburg, NJ: P&R, 2008). One can find a very accessible, simple introduction in Richard L. Pratt, *Every Thought Captive: A Study Manual for the Defense of Christian Truth* (Phillipsburg, NJ: P&R, 1979).

> The fear of the LORD is the *beginning of knowledge*;
>   fools despise wisdom and instruction. (Prov. 1:7)

Unbelievers may think we are fools, because to them it seems as if they can find wisdom only in autonomy. They do not trust God's word in the Bible, and so they are not confident that we are growing in wisdom rather than forsaking it. In fact, we seem to them to be forsaking it in the very process of submitting without question to what the Bible says. They will say that we are "uncritical" and "dogmatic." But of course they in turn are uncritical and dogmatic about their commitment to autonomy. Let us not be discouraged by criticisms that already presuppose a way of life opposite to what we have found in Christ.

This book, then, is written primarily for Christians. We want to see what the Bible teaches and where God leads us with his teaching, rather than endlessly debating our basic commitments in comparison with the basic commitments of non-Christians. If you are not a Christian, you are still welcome to read, of course. You may learn about what it is like to be a Christian in the pursuit of wisdom. And along the way you may find individual insights that you like, as well as others that you do not like. It may be that God will confront you along the way, and you will be changed. But I am not writing *primarily* with the non-Christian reader in view, and we are going to pursue truth on the basis of Christian presuppositions, which at points are very different from the usual ways of the world.

Are We Fit to Tackle the Big Questions?

Philosophers have been debating the big questions for centuries. For the most part, the debates continue. Individual philosophers may have their own convictions. But in most cases there is no consensus. And given the number of centuries that have passed, there is little hope of consensus. (One exception is the area of logic, where there appears to be a good amount of agreement.) Given the difficulties, can we as Christians hope to make a contribution? Would it not be presumptuous for an ordinary Christian to try to outdo centuries of philosophy, conducted by some of the brightest minds in the Western world?

It would be presumptuous if a Christian proceeded to work by the same ground rules as everyone else. But we do not have the same ground rules. We can go and study the Bible.

I believe that the time is ripe for Christians to do significant rethinking of philosophy—a *redemption* of philosophy, if you will. In the last few decades a number of Christians who are professional philosophers and apologists have called for a distinctively Christian approach to doing philosophy.[2] But more remains to be done.

In 1987 John Frame already indicated the direction to take when he briefly discussed philosophy in his work *The Doctrine of the Knowledge of God*. There he says:

> It is difficult for me to draw any sharp distinction between a Christian theology and a Christian philosophy. Philosophy generally is understood as an attempt to understand the world in its broadest, most general features. It includes metaphysics, or ontology (the study of being, of what "is"), epistemology (the study of knowing), and the theory of values (ethics, aesthetics, etc.). If one seeks to develop a truly Christian philosophy, he will certainly be doing so under the authority of Scripture and thus will be applying Scripture to philosophical questions. As such, he would be doing theology, according to our definition. Christian philosophy, then, is a subdivision of theology. Furthermore, since philosophy is concerned with reality in a broad, comprehensive sense, it may well take it as its task to "apply the Word of God to all areas of life." That definition makes philosophy identical with, not a subdivision of, theology.[3]

John Frame goes on to indicate that there might still be a difference in focus. A philosopher might focus more on revelation from God through nature, while the theologian focuses more on the special revelation in Scripture. Yet each should take account of both

---

[2] Among Christian philosophers Alvin C. Plantinga is prominent, and after him, Nicholas Wolterstorff. Others include William Lane Craig, Norman L. Geisler, J. P. Moreland, Paul Helm, Garrett J. DeWeese, K. Scott Oliphint, William Edgar, Al Wolters, David K. Naugle, Esther L. Meek, Steven Cowan, and James Spiegel. Still others are too numerous to mention.

[3] John M. Frame, *The Doctrine of the Knowledge of God* (Phillipsburg, NJ: P&R, 1987), 85.

kinds of revelation. There is no sharp distinction between Christian philosophy and Christian theology.

This striking overlap implies that the Bible has a lot to say that is pertinent to the questions that philosophers have traditionally asked. The main problem is that many philosophers are not paying attention! Or, rather, it may be that they have ceased paying attention because they do not have confidence in what the Bible says.

Inconsistencies among Christians

Now let us return to the issue of inconsistencies. Christians, we have said, are inconsistent at times with their most basic commitments. This principle applies to me as I write this book. I still struggle with sins, some of which are subtle and some of which I am not aware of. These can affect my thinking as well as my heart and my behavior. So, though the Bible is the infallible word of God, my thoughts are not. Like all human products, what I write needs to be weighed and sifted.

Ideally, the weighing and sifting take place through comparison with the Bible as our standard for evaluation (Acts 17:11). I hope to make progress because I am listening to the Bible. But I also endeavor to build on the insights and gifts of believers living around me, as well as those from previous generations. I pay attention to unbelievers as well, because they have received insights through common grace. If I do well, those who read this book may continue to build on and improve what I have done. They can thus move beyond it. And if they find errors or flaws, they should avoid them as they make further advances. That is how the Lord continues to bless his people through the generations.

PART 2

Metaphysics: What Is There?

4

Inadequate Philosophies

Now we turn specifically to the area of philosophy called metaphysics, which explores what is the nature of things. Answers here make a difference. We can illustrate by first considering a few non-Christian answers.

Materialism

We have already mentioned *materialism*. Materialism says that the world at its most basic level consists of matter and motion and energy. Any other layers consist of complex arrangements and interactions of matter.

This view has great difficulties. As we indicated earlier, it undermines the significance of persons. According to materialism, persons are merely complex interactions of material particles. This view tends to evaporate the significance of ethics. For example, let us suppose that Carol is a materialist. She may want to be kind to other people. But what does Carol say if she meets Joe, who tells her that he wants to dominate or crush other people in order to fulfill the evolutionary principle of survival of the fittest? Is morality just a matter of subjective preference, such that Carol prefers one kind of behavior and Joe another?

Modern materialism usually goes together with a materialistic version of biological evolution, which says that evolution is a purposeless process. There is no God to create human beings all at once, and neither is there a God who might work gradually to bring humans into existence from animal ancestors. The process of evolution has no human meaning to it unless we create one in our imaginations. Against this background, Joe may concede that evolution has produced feelings of kindness in Carol, but he may also argue that it has made him what he is. Evolution justifies his actions no more and no less than it justifies Carol's. So it is difficult to see how Carol can justify any real moral standards, as opposed to merely preferences that are actually morally neutral expressions of our hormones and our neurons.

Materialism has further difficulties with respect to understanding the ideas of mind and consciousness. Materialism says that neurons and chemical interactions in our bodies thoroughly control human behavior. Consciousness is either an illusion or an extra, unsought expression of what the underlying neurons are doing— what the matter is doing. Purposeless evolution cares only for survival and, therefore, for advantageous functioning of neurons. It cares nothing about consciousness as an extra layer.

We do find, however, that we can think about what we are going to do. And this element of thinking *about* is difficult to correlate with survival. Our neurons have to react to our situation in order for us to survive. But consciousness could be thinking about the moon or about mathematical abstractions at the same time that the neurons are reacting to a prowling lion. There is no guarantee that any causal correlation would exist between consciousness and the lion. In fact, there cannot be a causal correlation, because the causes all operate at the level of neurons. According to strict materialism, consciousness is either an outright illusion or an extra layer that causes nothing. Without a causal correlation, there is no reason to suspect that consciousness has any connection with truth. Consequently, we have no reason to suspect that materialism as a belief is true.[1]

---

[1] I have given a condensation of a much more elaborate and skillful argument by Alvin C. Plantinga, *Where the Real Conflict Lies: Science, Religion, and Naturalism* (Oxford: Oxford University Press, 2011).

The One and the Many

Materialism also has a difficulty with the classical problem of the one and the many. This problem besets many philosophies. What is the problem? The world contains both unity (the one) and diversity (the many). It contains many human beings and one humanity. It contains many dogs and one species, the dog species. Why? And what is the ultimate relation between the two, between unity and diversity? The problem of the one and the many raises the question, Which is prior, the one or the many, unity or diversity? At the most fundamental level, is the world one thing or many things? And how does the one relate to the many?

Modern materialism pictures the universe as composed of many bits of matter. So it appears at first that its fundamental starting point is with the many, that is, the many bits. At the same time, the many bits fall into regular classes. All electrons are alike, and all protons are alike. The likeness is an expression of unity. Where does the unity come from? Why are all electrons alike?

Modern materialism would at this point appeal to elementary particle physics. A physicist might say that all electrons are alike because they all obey the same physical laws. If so, it sounds as though the physical laws, which express unity, are prior to the diversity of distinct electrons. So how do the many electrons come into being through one set of physical laws? How do the many come from the one?

A physicist might say that the physical laws in their inner meaning already provide for the possibility of many electrons. But that is not a complete explanation. Mere possibility is not the same as actuality. Equations do not, in and of themselves, produce matter. So how do the many bits of matter come to exist?

If we can somehow overcome this problem, other forms of the problem of one and many still confront us. The physical laws depend for their expression on mathematics, which depends on the concept of *many* that is involved in numbers. Where do numbers come from? What is the relation of one and many in numbers? And why does the world of matter, which is conceptually distinct from the world of numbers, agree with the world of numbers? Here we have another kind of diversity—the diversity expressed in the distinction between two "worlds": the "world" of number and the "world" of matter. We also have unity, namely, the coherence between the two. Why?

A materialist could trace our knowledge of numbers back to our experience with distinct apples and oranges. But this distinctness in the apples is an instance of many, based on the many bits of matter in the apples. We are back to matter. The diversity in matter derives from the diversity in the laws, and the diversity in laws derives from the diversity in numbers, and the diversity in numbers derives from the diversity in matter. We are just going in a circle. At this level, materialism really offers no ultimate explanation of either unity or diversity, nor an explanation for why there is matter, with unity and diversity, and why there are laws, with their unity and diversity.

Thales

We can see the basic problems of philosophy in even simpler form if we consider an early case of Greek philosophy. The ancient Greek philosopher Thales is supposed to have said that "all is water." This proposal has difficulties similar to those we have already seen in modern materialism. (In fact, Thales offers us an ancient version of materialism.) Thales's view has difficulties both in accounting for persons and in accounting for one and many. The difficulty with persons is the usual one. How did persons arise, and how can they be significant if everything started with water? Without a personal God or gods to bring about the existence of human persons, how do we understand the uniqueness of persons? How can we have morality if we start with a materialist basis? And how can Thales *know* that all is water if he and everything else reduces to water?

The problem of the one and the many also besets Thales's thesis. The thesis sounds as if it starts from "water" as the one initial "thing." But how, if this thing is genuinely one, can it ever differentiate? How can we get many distinct things of many different types? If all is water, it seems we must conclude that all remains water, and then we are saying that "water is water." We have an "explanation" that does not explain.

Or suppose we start with many rather than with one. It is possible to interpret Thales's cryptic saying as meaning that we should start with thoughts about the diversity of "all" things. All things, as we observe them in their diversity, somehow have water as an underlying unity. But what is this unity that unites all the diversity? It must be a unity that is somehow already in each thing, so it is not "water" in the literal sense of the term. What we seem to be saying is that "all is all." Again, we have to ask whether we are really explaining anything.

Plato

According to Plato, another Greek philosopher, form and matter constitute the most basic structure of the world. The forms are eternal abstract objects of thought. The idea of the good is supposed to be the most fundamental, while other ideas include beauty, justice, piety, and virtue. These ideas or "forms" are imperfectly expressed in instances of beauty or justice on earth. For example, the eternal, abstract idea of a horse is expressed in particular horses that we observe. The expressions on earth are differentiated because they all have matter in them. The form, such as the form of a horse, provides for ultimate unity, while the matter, which is shaped by the form, results in the plurality of many horses.

Like the two philosophies that we have just considered, Plato's approach has trouble accounting for persons. The universe starts off purely with impersonal things—the forms are immaterial, abstracts, and therefore impersonal. In addition, matter is material and impersonal. So personal significance evaporates. Plato thought that every human soul had eternal preexistence. In some ways this is like making the soul itself divine or godlike. But each soul is supposed to find its meaning and satisfaction in knowledge and contemplation of the forms, which are impersonal. What is personal is really swallowed up in a impersonal world.

Plato also had a problem with one and many. Each form, like the form of a horse, is one in relation to its many material embodiments, the particular horses. But why do the many differ from one another if they are all the products of one form? Difference can only be construed as an imperfection. But where does imperfection come from? And how does the matter, which is conceived as eternally existing, relate to the forms?

Plato offered a mythological story about a demiurge, a godlike figure (a kind of finite god) who made individual things by copying the forms. But where did the demiurge come from, and why was his work imperfect? It is unclear whether Plato intended his story to be taken as an actual description or as a kind of myth to express something beyond expression. Taken either way, it leaves the question of one and many without an ultimate explanation, because the demiurge needs explaining: he is a being who apparently is distinct from both matter and the forms, and yet has significant relations to both. His existence and his relationships already presuppose unity and diversity, rather than explaining them.[2]

Polytheism

If we see the deficiencies of philosophies that take matter or form or some impersonal stuff (water?) as fundamental, we can consider whether personalist starting points do better. Greek polytheism is one such example. The ancient Greeks believed in many gods: Zeus, king of the gods and god of weather; Aphrodite, goddess of love; Ares, god of war; Poseidon, god of the sea; and others. According to this view, the gods are personal. That helps to impart some significance to human persons. But if there are many gods, human persons find themselves with divided allegiances, torn in several directions by conflicting agenda from the different gods. Moreover, none of the gods is ultimate, and they practice immoralities that make them unworthy of moral allegiance.

In addition, the problem of the one and the many is really not solved. The gods are many, but what unites them? Fate is an un-

---

[2] On Plato, see John M. Frame, "Greeks Bearing Gifts," in *Revolutions in Worldview: Understanding the Flow of Western Thought*, ed. W. Andrew Hoffecker (Phillipsburg, NJ: P&R, 2007), 18–23.

derlying impersonal force that outstrips them all. It brings in a certain unity. But what is the relation between fate and the gods? And since fate is impersonal, it undermines personal significance.

If non-Christian philosophies and worldviews do not have satisfying answers, what is the Christian way? We now turn to consider the positive instruction from the Bible about the nature of things.

5

Christian Metaphysics

We now consider metaphysics from a Christian point of view. Metaphysics studies what there is in its most basic or fundamental features. Some might say that it studies *being*.

So what is there? The Bible tells us in its opening verses. God always exists. In the beginning he created the world. The world exists because God brought it into existence. God is the Creator, while the world and everything in it are created. God is not to be confused with the world. He calls us to worship him and not any creature (Ex. 20:3–6). Theologians have accordingly spoken of the "Creator-creature distinction."

We can now proceed with more specifics. John Frame's book *The Doctrine of the Knowledge of God* focuses on epistemology, not metaphysics.[1] Yet the two are related. In part 1 his book discusses "The Objects of Knowledge." The objects of knowledge are the things that are. And Frame tells us what they are: God, the world, and ourselves. That is it.

Of course, we ourselves are creatures of God, and so if we treat the word *world* expansively, it includes us. Thus, we have God and the world. The world is everything that God created, including us. But because of the special role that each of us plays in his or her own knowledge, it is convenient for Frame to distinguish between the individual and the world around him. We can also distinguish

---

[1] Note also John M. Frame, *The Doctrine of God* (Phillipsburg, NJ: P&R, 2002), which has a chapter on metaphysics (chap. 12, pp. 214–37).

between human beings as a group and everything else in creation, because of the special role that human beings play (Gen. 1:26–30).

How does Frame know that these three things exist—God, the world, and ourselves? He does not say explicitly, but it is clear how he knows. The Bible mentions all three.[2]

So we have a beginning. But what more can we say?

More to Know

Human beings are finite. They do not know everything. And over time they can grow in knowledge. We can therefore fill in more and more details about God, the world, and ourselves as we go along in time. The process continues as long as we remain in this world.

The Bible has a fundamental role in the process, because it is God's communication to us. As we already observed, God never intended human beings to live merely by observing the world. Even before the fall into sin, he spoke to them. And the Bible constitutes a continuation of his speech, now available wherever it is translated.

The Bible has a role in the process in which God redeems us from sin, including intellectual sins. So, throughout our life on earth, we need to continue to use its guidance in every area of life. But it is also true that we can learn from observing the world and from communication with other human beings. Science, the humanities, and the arts can all bring us blessings. These contain many benefits of common grace. But since they are contaminated by sin, we need to test them using the Bible as our plumb line.

To put it another way, what the Bible says about the world offers a beginning rather than the end. The Bible itself gives mankind tasks: to "fill the earth and subdue it, and have dominion" (Gen. 1:28). Included in this program is a task of scientific explora-

---

[2] When we receive with humility God's speech to us in the Bible, we receive along with it an answer to the philosophical conundrums related to solipsism and "brain in the vat." We know that there is an external world because God tells us, and we can trust him. But how do we know that we are hearing God? When God speaks, he authenticates his own speech, through its wisdom, which reflects God the Son, and through the internal testimony of the Holy Spirit, whom God sends into our hearts. There could be much discussion here, but we must refer to other works—for example, John Murray, "The Attestation of Scripture," in *The Infallible Word*, ed. N. B. Stonehouse and Paul Woolley (Philadelphia: Presbyterian and Reformed, 1946), 1–54.

tion, which Adam commenced when he named the animals (Gen. 2:19–20).[3] Human beings are supposed to find out and learn much more about God and his world than they knew at the beginning. Ideally, they do this exploration in service to God, with love for God (Deut. 6:5) and in communion with God. This communion includes faithful reception and reliance on the verbal communication that God gives to human beings.

Types of Creatures

Genesis 1–2 provides foundational instruction to guide human learning about the world. As we have seen, we can start by saying that there exist God, the world, and ourselves. Genesis 1 then gives us further detail. It indicates that God created light (Gen. 1:3). He also made various distinct regions: the expanse above, called heaven (1:8); the dry land, called earth (1:10); and the gathered waters, called seas (1:10).[4] He also created specific kinds of creatures inhabiting these regions. He made various plants, which reproduce "according to their kinds" and grow on the dry land (1:11–13). On the fourth day he made the sun, the moon, and the stars in the heavens (1:14–19). The sea creatures fill the sea, and the birds fly across the heavens (1:20–23). The land animals roam the land (1:24–25). Finally, to crown it all, he made mankind in his image (1:26–30).

These creative acts of God made a wonderful beginning. And we have a wonderful beginning for our knowledge when we listen submissively to God's word. We know that God made all these kinds of things and that we can admire his wisdom, power, and goodness displayed in what he has made (Rom. 1:20).

Nowadays many people wonder about the relation of Genesis 1 and 2 to modern scientific description. They may be skeptical. They may think that Genesis 1 and 2 represent merely an outmoded, primitive account of origins. But Genesis 1 and 2 actually provide

---

[3] On how science fits into the overall biblical picture of the world and mankind, see Vern S. Poythress, *Redeeming Science: A God-Centered Approach* (Wheaton, IL: Crossway, 2006), especially chaps. 1–2 and 11.

[4] On heaven, see ibid., 94–96.

a foundation for science by indicating that (1) the world has order because of God's plan and power; (2) we as human beings have been commissioned to grow in understanding and dominion; and (3) because we are made in the image of God, we can have confidence that in a fundamental way our minds are in tune with God's mind. Of course we can make mistakes or have distorted views, but we may still have an underlying confidence that knowledge is possible, and by God's grace it may become accessible.

Thus, we have hope of understanding the world. Our minds are in tune with the character of the world because God made both the world and us. If interpreted correctly, science and the Bible fit together.[5] Working out the details takes patience, but we gain a better understanding than if we have a science with no deep foundation.

We can also see how the Bible affirms the significance of human beings as persons. We are made in the image of God and have the capability of hearing God and having fellowship with him because God is personal. The eternally personal character of God forms the ultimate foundation for the significance of finite persons whom he created.

Genesis 1 offers us a compact summary. It indicates that there are many kinds of plants and animals, but it does not give us all the detail. It is a sparse account.[6] We may note that it does not mention angels at all. Later passages in the Bible fill in detail by indicating that angels exist (Matt. 28:2). Evil spirits also exist; they were originally created as good angels but fell away (Jude 6). A fuller account could also have mentioned sea plants, like seaweed. Using microscopes, we have now added to our knowledge an awareness of microscopic animals and plants (e.g., single-celled algae). The expansion of human knowledge to include these new types of creatures is consistent with the role of Genesis 1–2 in giving us a beginning for human exploration.

Genesis 1–2 indicates that God created the world as an orderly whole, which displays his power. Given his power, we can see that

---

[5] See further ibid.

[6] On communication in language as sparse, see Vern S. Poythress, *Inerrancy and the Gospels: A God-Centered Approach to the Challenge of Harmonization* (Wheaton, IL: Crossway, 2012), chaps. 7–9.

it is possible that he created other worlds we know nothing about—other universes. It is possible because God is infinite in power. But we do not know of other worlds, and we do not need to know. The Bible instructs us on a more practical level. As a sparse account, it confines itself to what we need to know as we start interacting with *our* world.

It is also possible that God created living things elsewhere in the universe. Again, we do not know. Scientists wonder whether they might eventually find something living on Mars, or perhaps even on one of the moons of Jupiter or Saturn. Or might there be life in another planetary system around some distant star? That is up to God. He can create whatever kinds of life he wishes. Genesis 1–2 does not intend to be exhaustive, but is programmatic. It is a sparse summary, written to include simple readers and listeners in all cultures, as well as the learned.

Multiple Perspectives on the Created Order

Some people have looked askance at the organization in Genesis 1, complaining that some types of living things are omitted and others are allegedly "misclassified." We have already discussed the issue of omissions. Genesis 1 does not claim to be complete. What about alleged misclassification? Whales and dolphins get classified with other sea creatures in Genesis 1:20–23, and they apparently belong among "the fish of the sea" in Genesis 1:28. Yet they are not fish but mammals. There is no real difficulty here, since Genesis 1 is classifying animals according to location—sea, sky, or land—rather than developing a technical taxonomy such as what we meet in later scientific developments.

Moreover, the Hebrew word translated "fish" may be more flexible than our modern technical use of the word *fish*. It might also be used as a part for the whole in Genesis 1:28, which speaks of fish as representative for the larger group that includes all sea creatures. In keeping with its purpose of addressing many people in many cultures, the Bible appropriately uses words in an ordinary, flexible way.

The descriptions in Genesis 1 illustrate one use of *perspective*. Genesis 1 indicates that God created many distinct *kinds* of animals and plants. But it also groups together animals by their location, not by modern technical taxonomy, as we have noted. Human beings have a choice as to what *kind* of description and what kind of classification they may present. God, when speaking to human beings, has choices as well. Each choice of a kind of description presents one *perspective* on the world of animals.

We should note also that the Bible as a whole contains multiple passages that discuss creation. These passages give us multiple perspectives within the Bible itself.

For example, consider the relation of Genesis 1:1–2:3 to Genesis 2:4–25. Without going into a thorough analysis,[7] we may observe that Genesis 1 offers us a description that classifies the major kinds of creatures. It is chronological and taxonomic. Genesis 2:4–25, by contrast, after a short description of a relatively unformed situation in verses 4–6, starts with the creation of man. Everything else is explained in relation to man. God creates other things in answer to human needs. Thus Genesis 2:4–25 is oriented to the purposes of created things, especially in relation to man. It is *teleological*, or purpose-oriented, rather than more chronological and taxonomic.

Of course, a good deal of commonality exists between the two narratives, and some degree of common focus. In Genesis 2:4–25 some taxonomic interest crops up when Adam names the animals in 2:19–20, and chronological interest shows up when God responds to the lack of a helper for man by bringing a deep sleep on him and then creating the woman. Yet the dominant focus is on purpose, as the New Testament underlines when it comments on Genesis 2 by saying, "Neither was man created *for woman*, but woman *for man*" (1 Cor. 11:9). The word *for* indicates the presence of purpose.

The Bible also contains later passages about creation that build on Genesis 1. Among the principal passages are Job 38–41, Psalms 104 and 148, John 1:1–5, Romans 1:18–23, and Colossians 1:15–17.[8]

---

[7] For a more thorough analysis, we must refer to exegetical works. See especially C. John Collins, *Genesis 1–4: A Linguistic, Literary, and Theological Commentary* (Phillipsburg, NJ: P&R, 2006).
[8] We might also add Psalms 8, 19, and 147, though these psalms develop other themes as well.

All these passages have a unity. They all affirm the absoluteness of one God and his sovereignty over creation. They all presuppose a distinction between the Creator and the creatures he has made. But we can observe differences in texture, which arise from different interests and different foci.

PART 3

Perspectives

6

Introducing Perspectives

We may further explore the differences between the various passages by introducing three *perspectives* that help to highlight the differences. I have in mind John Frame's three perspectives on ethics, which need a brief explanation.

Three Perspectives on Ethics

In analyzing ethical issues, John Frame uses three complementary perspectives: the *normative* perspective, the *situational* perspective, and the *existential* perspective.[1] The normative perspective focuses on the *norms*, namely, God's commandments. It asks, What does God command me to do? The situational perspective focuses on the situation. It asks, Given my situation, what actions of mine can best promote the glory of God and blessing for my fellowman? The existential perspective looks at the person. What are my motives? What attitudes and actions are driven by love?

Within a biblically based approach, these three perspectives are perspectives on the same whole. Each leads to the others. Each implies the others and each presupposes the others. They intrinsically harmonize.

Let us see how. God speaks the norms; God created and rules over the situation; God created the people in the situation. God is

---

[1] John M. Frame, *Perspectives on the Word of God: An Introduction to Christian Ethics* (Eugene, OR: Wipf and Stock, 1999); Frame, *The Doctrine of the Christian Life* (Phillipsburg, NJ: P&R, 2008).

one God, and so there is harmony. Moreover, each of the perspectives when rightly understood leads to the others. God commands us to love our neighbor. His command is a norm for us. It is in focus when we use the normative perspective. The commandment to love our neighbor leads to inspecting our motives—the motive must be love. The concern for motives implies that we must engage the existential perspective. When God commands us to love our neighbor, it also implies that we must look at the situation of our neighbor. We must consider, given his circumstances, what he most needs and what would benefit him. God himself through his commandments thereby pushes us to engage in the situational perspective.

Conversely, if we start with the situational perspective, we must note that God is the most important person in our situation. We must find out what he desires and what pleases him. And so we are led into the normative perspective, where we consider his commandments as an expression of his desires. And we consider the rest of Scripture as well, because its instruction supplies a God-given context for understanding his commandments and his character more deeply. The situational perspective also leads to the existential perspective, because we ourselves as actors live within the situation, and ethically good action in our situation includes action that has the right motivations.

Using the Perspectives on Ethics

With this background, we can classify the passages about creation. The three perspectives interlock and interpenetrate, so that in the end all three concerns are present in all discourses. Yet, in terms of prominence, we may observe differences. We may say that Genesis 1:1–2:3 and Genesis 2:4–25 both display a *situational* perspective on creation. They set forth the kinds of creatures God made, and they do so in prose rather than poetry (though the prose is elevated in style).

Job 38–41, Psalm 104, and Psalm 148 are all poetic passages, and they all engage human attitudes more directly. By engaging human attitudes, they display an *existential* perspective on creation. Within this existential emphasis, we may see further variations. Job 38–41 is mostly a direct address from God, challenging presumption and laying out for our admiration the scope of God's wisdom, which surpasses our understanding. Psalm 104 is heartfelt praise. Psalm 148 calls for creation itself to engage in the praise. With some tentativeness, we may suggest that, within the broadly existential orientation of all three poems, Job 38–41 has a more intensive existential focus, asking human beings to wrestle with its revelation. Psalm 104 has a more situational focus, in that it runs through a good many details that have obvious correlations with the events of the six days of Genesis 1. Psalm 148 has a more normative focus, because it commands praise.

John 1:1–5 and Colossians 1:15–17 represent a situational perspective, in that they present prose exposition again. But rather than focusing on the world that God created, they both focus more on the God who created it. Both articulate how the second person of the Trinity has a distinctive role in creating the world.

Finally, Romans 1:18–23 represents a normative perspective. It focuses on the violation of norms—sin—in human response to the creational revelation of God.

When taken together, these passages underline the fact that God's work of creation, and the creatures that result from it, can be described from a number of complementary perspectives. These perspectives, when rightly understood, are not in tension with one another. The later passages build on Genesis 1–2, rather than putting forth contradictory alternatives to it. A unified picture of creation emerges when we consider all the passages together. There is unity. There is also diversity, because the significance of creation displays itself most fully to human understanding only when we visit all of the passages.

We also begin to understand how the passages not only reinforce one another but also deepen one another. Genesis 1 implicitly demands a human response of praising and worshiping God. But we can see more clearly and more deeply what this response ought to look like when we read Psalm 104. Genesis 1 implicitly implies that we should trust in the God who made us and the world, even when we cannot see why he is bringing some disaster. Job 38–41 makes the implication more explicit and deepens our appreciation of it. Genesis 1 already indicates that God created the world by speaking. John 1:1–5 and Colossians 1:15–17 indicate the Trinitarian depth behind what Genesis 1 describes.

The Significance of Perspectives

Since we have begun using multiple perspectives in an integral way in our reflections, it is worthwhile to say something more about perspectives.[2] Multiple perspectives inevitably arise because God has created multiple human beings. Human beings are all similar to one another because they are all made in the image of God. But they are also all different from one another. The Bible talks specifically about some of the differences when it discusses spiritual gifts in 1 Corinthians 12–14 (see also Rom. 12:3–8; Eph. 4:7–16). There are a variety of gifts within the body of Christ. First Corinthians 12 compares the variety of people to the variety of organs that make up a single physical body. Each organ has its own function, and all the organs work together within one unified body.

A Larger Diversity

This diversity within the body of Christ mirrors a larger diversity among human beings in general. We look different from one another. We are tall or short. We are of different ages. In subtle ways, we also have different interests and think differently.[3] One person identifies existentially more with Psalms 104 and 148, which praise God for creation. Another identifies existentially with Genesis 1, which classifies the creation. Still another identifies with John 1:1–5, because he loves to think about theological depth.

---

[2] For a fuller discussion, see Vern S. Poythress, *Symphonic Theology: The Validity of Multiple Perspectives in Theology* (Grand Rapids: Zondervan, 1987; repr., Phillipsburg, NJ: P&R, 2001); Poythress, "Multiperspectivalism and the Reformed Faith," in *Speaking the Truth in Love: The Theology of John M. Frame*, ed. John J. Hughes (Phillipsburg, NJ: P&R, 2009), 173–200, accessed January 26, 2012, http://www.frame-poythress.org/poythress_articles/AMultiperspectivalism.pdf, reproduced here in the next chapter; John M. Frame, "A Primer on Perspectivalism," May 14, 2008, accessed January 26, 2012, http://www.frame-poythress.org/frame_articles/2008Primer.htm.
[3] See Vern S. Poythress, *Redeeming Sociology: A God-Centered Approach* (Wheaton, IL: Crossway, 2011), chaps. 15, 17, and 26.

We can even see how God may raise up people with different gifts and different interests and use those people as his instruments to write his word, as we now find it in the various passages, Genesis 1, Job 38–41, Psalm 104, and so forth.

Roots in the Trinity

Human beings are both united and diversified. All human beings are united by being made in the image of God. They share a common humanity, and the common humanity includes many details: ability to worship, ability to use language, ability to think, common physical features, and so forth. Human beings also show diversity. Each individual is unique. We have unity in diversity, and diversity in the unity of one humanity. This unity in diversity is a creational imitation or reflection of the Trinity. The Bible teaches that there is one God. He has unity because he is one. The Bible also indicates that there are three persons in the Godhead: the Father, the Son, and the Holy Spirit. Each of the three persons is distinct from the other two. Thus there is diversity in God, the diversity of the three persons.

The unity and the diversity are equally ultimate. John 1:1–3 shows both that there is one God from the beginning and that God the Father and God the Son (the Word) are distinct from one another from the beginning ("the Word was *with* God"). The unity does not arise subsequent to the diversity, as if God started off as three independent persons who agreed at some point to combine their efforts and become one. Nor does the diversity arise subsequent to the unity, as if God started off as a purely undifferentiated unity and then split into three, or manifested himself in three ways (the error of *modalism*).

So God exists in unity and diversity. God created man in his image. So it is not surprising that human beings exist in unity and diversity. Yet we must also insist that God and man are not on the same level. God's unity and diversity are unique. The persons of the Trinity indwell one another in a unique way. The relation among the persons of the Trinity is ultimately mysterious to us,

because we are not God and we do not understand God comprehensively.

Human persons can have communion with one another. Husband and wife can be united and become "one flesh" (Gen. 2:24).
Husband and wife have reflected forms of unity in diversity. Ephesians 5:32 even says concerning the unity of husband and wife that
"this mystery is profound." But it is a mysterious unity among two
distinct creatures, each of whom is held morally accountable (Gen.
3:11–19). The mysterious indwelling of the persons of the Trinity is
more profound and deeper. It is not fully parallel to anything that
we see in the created world. God is Creator and is unique.

We can also observe a distinction of perspectives among the
persons of the Trinity. One of the important passages speaks of
the distinct persons as *knowing* each other: "All things have been
handed over to me by my Father, and no one *knows* the Son except the Father, and no one *knows* the Father except the Son and
anyone to whom the Son chooses to reveal him" (Matt. 11:27). The
Father knows the Son. Since the Son is God himself, in knowing
the Son the Father knows everything. He does so from the personal perspective of being the Father. Likewise, the Son knows the
Father. In so knowing, he knows everything. He does so from the
personal perspective of being the Son.

No exact parallel passage exists with respect to the Holy Spirit.
But one passage comes close: "For the Spirit *searches* everything,
even the depths of God. For who knows a person's thoughts except
the spirit of that person, which is in him? So also no one *comprehends* the thoughts of God except the Spirit of God" (1 Cor.
2:10–11). Here we can see that the Holy Spirit comprehends the
thoughts of God, and therefore comprehends God. He does so from
his personal perspective of being the Holy Spirit.

Thus, within God, there are three personal perspectives on
knowledge: the perspective of the Father, the perspective of the
Son, and the perspective of the Holy Spirit. These three belong
to one God. The Spirit knows God in knowing the thoughts of
God. The Father knows God in knowing the Son and the Holy
Spirit. The knowledge of all three persons agrees, since all three

know God and know all the thoughts of God. There is perfect harmony among the three persons, but also a distinction of persons. Therefore, there is also a distinction of personal perspectives on knowledge.

Perspectives among Human Beings

The character of God is unique. But human beings reflect in their knowledge the unity and diversity in God's knowledge. All human beings can share in knowledge. For example, they all know God, according to Romans 1:21. In addition, since each human being is distinct, each has his own personal perspective on knowledge. It is *he*—as distinct from anyone else—that knows God. Each person in his uniqueness knows God in a uniquely textured way, according to who he is as a person.

John Frame helpfully distinguishes two uses of the word *perspective*.[4] In a broad use, a *perspective* is the viewpoint of one human being in distinction from others. Each human being has a *perspective*, due to his or her individuality. Second, in a narrow sense, the word *perspective* refers to specific ways in which a single human being may choose temporarily to address a given issue. In the second sense, a single individual can use multiple perspectives.

Among human beings we see limitations in knowledge. Some people know truths that others do not know. So there is a distinction in the content of the knowledge.

We can also see distinctions in texture. Consider again our examples from Genesis 1, Job 38–41, Psalm 104, Psalm 148, and John 1:1–5. Some people have a deeper appreciation for poetry, such as we find in Job and in the Psalms. Their knowledge is in some ways poetically textured. Yet they can still talk to and share with people who have a deeper appreciation for the prose theology of John 1:1–5.[5]

---

[4] Frame, "Primer on Perspectivalism," where Frame speaks of "Perspectivalism in General" (the broader use) and "Triperspectivalism" (the narrower use).

[5] If we like, we can see in this threefold analysis of types of distinction in knowledge a manifestation of perspectives. Difference in the content of knowledge is a normative difference (because truth is normative; we are obliged to seek it). Difference in texture is a situational difference. The knowledge is differently "situated" in relation to other, neighboring expressions. Difference in the person who has the knowledge is an existential difference.

God planned and brought about the unity and diversity among human beings that we observe today. Diversity becomes painful and contentious when sin enters in, because sin produces strife, enmity, hate, selfishness, and dissension. But the unity and diversity within the redeemed body of Christ (1 Corinthians 12) show that some kinds of diversity are not *innately* sinful. In fact, they are good and delightful. God approves them. God approves the diversities in knowledge that we have just described, provided always that they are freed from the distortions of sin.

The Problem of the One and the Many

The character of God offers the ultimate explanation for the problem of the one and the many. In God himself, the oneness of God is not prior to the three persons, nor the three persons prior to the oneness of God. Since God is one in three and three in one, he is also capable of creating a world that has both unities and diversities in it, according to his will. His will has unity and diversity, according to the unity and diversity of God himself, and so the expression of his will within creation reflects the harmony of one and many in God.

Monolithic versus Trinitarian Unity

This interplay of unity and diversity suggests further implications for how we understand the goal of philosophy. Philosophy in the past has often aimed at a single, monolithic, final description of reality. In metaphysics, it has searched for a single, monolithic, final understanding of the nature of things. But the diversities among human beings, along with the diversity in the biblical passages about creation, radically undermine the plausibility of this goal. The Bible by its affirmation of the unity of God, and the unity of God's truth, encourages us to grow in knowledge and to learn from others. But the goal is not monolithic unity in which each person is exactly like all the others, with no diversity. The goal is increasing unity of the right kind through increasing diversity of the right kind.[6] All the biblical passages about creation give us metaphysics.

---

[6] John Frame hints at the value of diversity when, in a slightly different context, he criticizes the assumption that there must be only *one* proper organization of the fields of knowledge: "It seems to

In a sense they give us five or six or more different metaphysics, all in harmony with one another.

To put it another way, God is the Trinitarian God. By contrast, the religious view called *unitarianism* says that God is one but not three. According to unitarianism there is no differentiation of persons. Unitarianism is a false religion, because it contradicts God's statements about himself in the Bible. It is reflected at a creaturely level when we want a single, monolithic final description of reality, with no diversity left. That desire is *unitarian* in character, not biblically Trinitarian.

We can see a further example of unity in diversity in the Gospels. The four Gospels in the Bible—Matthew, Mark, Luke, and John—have four distinct human authors. They give us four perspectives on Christ and his life. The perspectives harmonize, but they differ in the selection of events that they narrate, and they differ in emphasis. Matthew emphasizes the Jewishness of Jesus— he is the king of the Jews. Luke emphasizes Jesus's ministry to the needy, the socially marginalized. John emphasizes Jesus as the revealer of the Father. All these are true. But they differ in texture. This unity and diversity are further explored elsewhere.[7]

Original and Derivative

The Trinity is the ultimate original for unity and diversity. Forms of unity and diversity within this world offer us created reflections of the original unity and diversity in the Trinity. This original character of God means that he is the *archetype*. An archetype is an original pattern that is reflected in something else for which it is a model. The reflection of the original is sometimes called an *ectype*. So God in his Trinitarian nature is the archetype for unity and diversity. Instances of unity and diversity within this world are ectypes.

---

me that there may be many legitimate ways to organize the subject matter of the universe for study, just as there are many ways of cutting a cake for purposes of eating and just as there are many ways of dividing up the color spectrum for purposes of description" (John M. Frame, *The Doctrine of the Knowledge of God* [Phillipsburg, NJ: P&R, 1987], 91).

[7] Poythress, *Symphonic Theology*; Poythress, *Inerrancy and the Gospels: A God-Centered Approach to the Challenge of Harmonization* (Wheaton, IL: Crossway, 2012); Frame, "Primer on Perspectivalism"; Poythress, "Multiperspectivalism and the Reformed Faith."

7

Multiperspectivalism

Since we are going to use perspectives in responding to the big questions, including especially the questions about the nature of things (metaphysics), I should say more about the significance of perspectives and how the use of them has developed historically into an approach called *multiperspectivalism*.

What is multiperspectivalism?[1] Multiperspectivalism appears as a characteristic aspect in virtually all the writings of John M. Frame. Recently, Frame himself has written a short piece, "A Primer on Perspectivalism," which summarizes its main features.[2] Let us focus on Frame's multiperspectivalism, but with a glance at the larger context.

Features of Multiperspectivalism

Human knowledge arises in the context of human finiteness. Any particular human being always knows and experiences truth from

[1] The rest of this chapter appeared initially as the essay Vern S. Poythress, "Multiperspectivalism and the Reformed Faith," in *Speaking the Truth in Love: The Theology of John M. Frame*, ed. John J. Hughes (Phillipsburg, NJ: P&R, 2009), 173–200; it is reprinted here, lightly edited, with permission from the publisher. Bibliographical information has been reformatted for the purpose of inclusion here, and some other minor changes have been made for clarity.

[2] John M. Frame, "A Primer on Perspectivalism," May 14, 2008, accessed November 12, 2008, http://www.frame-poythress.org/frame_articles/PrimerOnPerspectivalism.htm. A longer exposition, focusing specifically on ethics, is found in Frame, *Perspectives on the Word of God: An Introduction to Christian Ethics* (Eugene, OR: Wipf and Stock, 1999). See also Vern S. Poythress, *Symphonic Theology: The Validity of Multiple Perspectives in Theology* (Grand Rapids: Zondervan, 1987; repr., Phillipsburg, NJ: P&R, 2001). For the development of Frame's multiperspectivalism, see Frame, "Backgrounds to My Thought," in Hughes, *Speaking the Truth in Love*.

the standpoint of who he is.[3] He has a *perspective*. He can learn from others by listening sympathetically to what they understand from their differing backgrounds or perspectives. The diversity of human beings leads to a diversity in perspectives. Frame affirms both the limitations of any finite human perspective and the absoluteness of God's knowledge. "It [perspectivalism] presupposes absolutism [the absoluteness of God's viewpoint]."[4] The presence of God implies that truth is accessible to human beings and that there is a difference between truth and falsehood. In this way, Frame is an "absolutist" rather than a relativist. But he invites us to take seriously the insights and the differences in emphasis that arise from viewing a particular subject matter from more than one point of view.

Besides showing a wider interest in diverse human perspectives,[5] Frame introduces the use of perspectival triads and affirms their relation to the Trinitarian character of God.[6]

Frame uses primarily two triads. To discuss God's lordship, he uses the triad of authority, control, and presence. As Lord, God has authority over us, exerts control over us, and is present to us. Each of these three aspects of God's lordship can serve as a perspective on who God is and how he relates to us. These three perspectives are involved in one another, and each helps to define and deepen our understanding of the other two. All three aspects of lordship are involved in *all* of God's relations to his creatures.[7]

To discuss ethics, Frame uses another triad of perspectives, namely, the normative, situational, and existential perspectives.[8] Recall that the normative perspective focuses on the *norms*, God's

---

[3] "Because we are not God, because we are finite, not infinite, we cannot know everything at a glance, and therefore our knowledge is limited to one perspective or another" (Frame, "Primer on Perspectivalism").

[4] Ibid. See also Frame, "Backgrounds to My Thought," 6.

[5] In *The Doctrine of the Christian Life* (Phillipsburg, NJ: P&R, 2008), John Frame argues that each of the Ten Commandments has its own distinctive focus, but each can also be used as a perspective on the whole range of our ethical obligations. This argument illustrates that Frame is aware of the possibility of other perspectives beyond the perspectival triads that are most characteristic of his writings. See also Frame, "Primer on Perspectivalism."

[6] Frame, "Primer on Perspectivalism."

[7] See the extensive discussion of this triad in John M. Frame, *The Doctrine of the Knowledge of God* (Phillipsburg, NJ: P&R, 1987); and Frame, *The Doctrine of God* (Phillipsburg, NJ: P&R, 2002).

[8] The triad is introduced in Frame, *Perspectives on the Word of God*, and its use is developed extensively in Frame, *Doctrine of the Christian Life*. The triad for ethics is closely related to the triad for lordship (Frame, "Backgrounds to My Thought," 16).

law and his expressions of his ethical standards for human be-ings. The situational perspective focuses on the situation in which a human being must act, and endeavors to discern what actions promote the glory of God within that situation. The existential perspective focuses on persons and their motives, particularly the central motive of love.

Again, these three are involved in one another. God's norms tell us to pay attention to the situation—in particular, the needs of others around us. The norms also tell us to pay attention to our attitudes (existential). Similarly, the situation pushes us to pay attention to the norms, because God is the most important person in our situation, and what he desires matters supremely. The situation also pushes us to pay attention to the persons in the situation. Our own attitudes must be inspected for their potential to change the situation for good or ill.

Because God is Lord of all, these perspectives harmonize in principle. God promulgates the norms; God controls the situation; God created the human persons in his image. But in a fallen situation of sin, human beings have distortions in their ethical knowledge, and the use of one perspective can help in straightening out distortions that people have introduced in the context of another perspective.

The multiperspectivalism practiced by John Frame differs decisively from relativistic views that are sometimes called "perspectivism."[9] Frame does his work self-consciously within the framework of a Christian commitment. He is a follower of Christ and is committed to taking "every thought captive to obey Christ" (2 Cor. 10:5).[10] The Bible has a central role in his multiperspectivalism, because he believes that it is the infallible word of God,[11] and that God specifically designed it as a means to instruct us and free

---

[9] Friedrich Nietzsche emphasized the centrality of the variety of human perspectives in the process of attaining knowledge, and for that reason his epistemological approach has been called "perspectivism." Werner Krieglstein has built a viewpoint called "transcendental perspectivism," which endeavors to combine an acknowledgment of limited human perspectives with striving toward combining viewpoints in a search for higher truth. His approach is explicitly spiritualistic, in that it sees consciousness as universal. But his is a non-Christian form of spiritualism.

[10] Second Cor. 10:5 became an important principle in the apologetics of Cornelius Van Til, a tradition continued in Frame's apologetics.

[11] See the Westminster Confession of Faith, 1.4–5.

us from sin, including intellectual sin. The Bible is the infallible guide for sorting through ideas and separating truth from error in the process of using different perspectives.

Multiperspectivalism in Relation to the Reformed Faith

How does multiperspectivalism relate to the Reformed faith? Frame is Reformed in his theology and has spent his career teaching at Reformed seminaries.[12] How does his multiperspectivalism fit his commitment to the truths embodied in the Reformed confessions? In the early days, some people worried about whether multiperspectivalism would lead to relativism, and whether it was compatible with traditional Reformed theology. Over time, the growing body of Frame's writings has made it clear that he is building on Reformed orthodoxy and vigorously defending it, rather than flirting with the spirit of the age. Frame is indeed committed to the absolutism of God and not the relativism of non-Christian thinking.

But in theological style Frame's approach seems subtly different from some of the theological writing of past centuries. What is the relation? Do multiperspectivalism and the Reformed faith simply exist side by side, with no direct relationship? Is one dependent on the other? Do they aid one another?

We can try to answer these questions in two ways, either by looking at the origins of multiperspectivalism or by looking at its contemporary shape. Let us first look at the origins.

Origins of Multiperspectivalism

Frame's Multiperspectivalism

From an early point in his classroom teaching at Westminster Theological Seminary in Philadelphia, John Frame deployed his key perspectival triads. When I became a student at Westminster in 1971, Frame was already using as a major pedagogical tool both the triad for lordship (authority, control, and presence) and the

---

[12] Frame has taught at Westminster Theological Seminary in Philadelphia, Westminster Seminary California, and Reformed Theological Seminary in Orlando, Florida. See Frame, "Backgrounds to My Thought."

triad for ethics (normative, situational, and existential).[13] Both of these triads had obvious affinities with doctrines from classic Reformed theology.

The triad for lordship obviously linked itself to the long-standing Calvinist emphasis on the sovereignty of God. But the triad was also designed to express aspects of the way God related to human beings, both in his words and in his deeds. The classical Reformed tradition was accustomed to speaking about God's relation to humans as a covenant.[14] *Authority* comes into God's covenant with us because God is the authoritative covenant maker, and we are to submit to his authority. God *controls* the covenant relation both by protecting his people and by punishing and disciplining covenant violations. God is *present* via his covenant in inaugurating and sustaining a relation of personal intimacy between God and man. Thus, Frame's triad for lordship can be seen as reexpressing some of the classic themes in covenant theology in the Reformed tradition.[15]

The Influence of Cornelius Van Til

Frame's triad for ethics derives directly from Cornelius Van Til's work *Christian Theistic Ethics*.[16] In all his books Van Til made clear his own vigorous commitment to Reformed theology as the foundation for his whole enterprise. In his book on ethics, he emphasized the unique character of Christian ethics in contrast to all forms of non-Christian ethics. According to Van Til, Christians, with regenerate hearts and a commitment to follow Christ, have an approach innately *antithetical* to all kinds of autonomous thinking

---

[13] In 1971 Frame taught introduction to theology (including theology of the word of God), the doctrine of God, and ethics. His lectures have led to his books in the Theology of Lordship series: *Doctrine of the Knowledge of God*, *Doctrine of God*, *Doctrine of the Christian Life*, and *The Doctrine of the Word of God* (Phillipsburg, NJ: P&R, 2010). Frame also mentions the influence of G. Dennis O'Brien, a Catholic philosophy teacher at Princeton, who had some elements reminiscent of perspectival thinking, and George Lindbeck ("Backgrounds to My Thought," 4, 11).

[14] See the Westminster Confession of Faith, 7; Westminster Larger Catechism, 30–36.

[15] In "Backgrounds to My Thought," 6–7, Frame also indicates a connection between this triad and Van Til's treatment of the correlation of God, man, and nature in Cornelius Van Til, *An Introduction to Systematic Theology: Prolegomena and the Doctrines of Revelation, Scripture, and God*, 2nd ed., ed. William Edgar (Phillipsburg: P&R, 2007).

[16] Cornelius Van Til, *Christian Theistic Ethics*, In Defense of Biblical Christianity 3 (n.p.: den Dulk Christian Foundation, 1971). According to Frame, Van Til's triad can be traced back to the Westminster Confession of Faith, 16.7 (see Frame, "Backgrounds to My Thought," 14n12).

and autonomous ethics.[17] Autonomous thinking derives from an un-regenerate heart and is unwilling to submit to God's ways. In Van Til's view, Christian ethics is distinctive in its goal, its standard, and its motive. Van Til showed how these three—goal, standard, and motive—fit coherently together within a Christian approach.

This work by Van Til laid the foundation for Frame's perspectivalism. Van Til himself did not take the step of saying that the three aspects—goal, standard, and motive—could serve as perspectives on one another. But he came close to perspectivalism by stressing their coherence and mutual reinforcement. It remained for Frame, as a disciple of Van Til, to develop Van Til's insights into a fully articulate perspectivalism. The goal, when used as a perspective on the whole of ethics, became Frame's situational perspective. The standard became the normative perspective. And the motive became the existential perspective. The existential perspective has sometimes also been called the "personal" perspective to distinguish it pointedly from French existentialism. Frame's perspectivalism thus grew up within the soil of Reformed theology and the Reformed apologetics of Cornelius Van Til.

I would suggest that Van Til's apologetics contributed in another, less direct way. Van Til's emphasis on the antithesis between Christian and non-Christian thinking emboldened his followers to be willing to break fresh ground in their thinking. The antithesis implies that they should not merely adopt secondhand some non-Christian system of philosophical ethics and then make minor adjustments to try to use it within a Christian framework.

We can illustrate more specifically the distinctiveness of Christian thinking in the area of ethics. Frame has pointed out that non-Christian ethics has tended to take one of three major forms.[18] *Deontological* ethical systems start with absolute norms and base everything else on them. These systems owe their plausibility to

---

[17] See especially Cornelius Van Til, *The Defense of the Faith*, 4th ed., ed. K. Scott Oliphint (Phillipsburg, NJ: P&R, 2008); Van Til, *A Survey of Christian Epistemology*, In Defense of Biblical Christianity 2 (n.p.: den Dulk Christian Foundation, 1969); John M. Frame, *Apologetics to the Glory of God: An Introduction* (Phillipsburg, NJ: P&R, 1994); Frame, *Cornelius Van Til: An Analysis of His Thought* (Phillipsburg, NJ: P&R, 1995). Van Til built on earlier thinking, especially from Herman Bavinck, Abraham Kuyper, John Calvin, and St. Augustine, and of course from the Bible itself.
[18] See Frame, *Doctrine of the Christian Life*, part 2: "Non-Christian Ethics," 39–125.

prioritizing the normative perspective. *Existentialist* ethical systems start with the primacy of the individual, his will, and his personal decisions. These prioritize the existential perspective. Finally, *teleological* and *utilitarian* ethical systems start with the goal of maximizing human pleasure and well-being. These prioritize the situational perspective. All three kinds of approaches refuse to recognize the Christian God. So all three end up exalting one perspective as a kind of substitute for God and his authority. This one perspective is forced to become the monolithic source for everything else. By contrast, Christians can acknowledge the true God as the author of the norms (through his word), the Creator of the persons, and the governor over the situation.

Hence a Christian approach can affirm an intrinsic harmony among the three perspectives. It does not need artificially to create an autonomous, humanly generated source of ethics by making one perspective superior and giving it a godlike role. Instead, a Christian approach affirms that God alone is God. This affirmation, basic to the Christian faith, enables Christians to refuse to make God-substitutes in the form of favored philosophical sources for ethical thinking. And it enables believers to affirm that, because of God's sovereign authority and control, normative, existential, and situational perspectives cohere in harmony.

The Influence of Biblical Theology in the Tradition of Geerhardus Vos

John Frame also acknowledges the influence of biblical theology on the development of his theological thinking and his program: "Recall my emphasis in Part One [of *The Doctrine of the Knowledge of God*] on covenant lordship; that was biblical theology. The biblical theological method is prominent in my *Doctrine of the Word of God* and *Doctrine of God*."[19] That is to say, the whole structure of Frame's thinking about "covenant lordship," including his triad of perspectives involving God's authority, control, and presence, is "biblical theology." By "biblical theology" Frame means biblical

---

[19] Frame, *Doctrine of the Knowledge of God*, 209n35. Frame makes this remark in the context of a longer discussion of both the contributions of biblical theology and the dangers of prideful or immature use of it. See also his references in "Backgrounds to My Thought." *The Doctrine of God* and *The Doctrine of the Word of God* were subsequently published by P&R in 2002 and 2010.

theology in the tradition of Geerhardus Vos, the study of "the *history* of God's dealings with creation."[20] Frame cites both Vos and his successors, such as Edmund P. Clowney, Meredith G. Kline, and Richard B. Gaffin Jr., all of whom developed their thinking within the framework of Reformed theology.[21] Frame writes as a systematic theologian, but acknowledges the need for systematic theology to be sensitive to dimensions of Scripture highlighted in biblical theology.[22]

How does Frame's thinking about covenant lordship reflect biblical theology? In discussing covenant lordship, he intends to point to the rich material in the Bible itself concerning God's covenantal relations to mankind, to Israel, and to the church, both in the Old Testament and in the New Testament. Frame's categories of authority, control, and presence, as well as the master term *Lord*, are meant to evoke the richness of the history of special revelation. For example, authority, control, and presence are manifest in God's creation of the world in Genesis 1. God has the *authority* and right to bring forth creation. He perfectly *controls* what he brings forth through his various works during the days of creation. He is present through the Holy Spirit, who "was hovering over the face of the waters" (Gen. 1:2). In addition, God displays his authority, control, and presence in his interaction with Adam and Eve in Genesis 2–3, in his relations to Noah, Abraham, Moses, and so on. Frame's categories have a flexibility that allows us to see how they are at work in all manifestations of God's lordship, and in all the richness of covenantal relations through the Old Testament.

---

[20] Frame, *Doctrine of the Knowledge of God*, 207. See Geerhardus Vos, *Biblical Theology: Old and New Testaments* (Grand Rapids: Eerdmans, 1948; repr., Eugene, OR: Wipf and Stock, 2003), 13. Vos expresses a preference for the label "History of Special Revelation" (ibid., 23); Frame prefers "history of the covenant" (*Doctrine of the Knowledge of God*, 211). Both settle for "biblical theology" only because it is a more traditional expression.

[21] See Frame, *Doctrine of the Knowledge of God*, 207n33. Clowney, Kline, Gaffin, and Frame at an early period in their career were all students at Westminster Theological Seminary. And all later taught at Westminster for a time. Vos stayed at Princeton Theological Seminary after the founding of Westminster Theological Seminary as a split off of Princeton in 1929. But Vos's affinities with Westminster are still profound. So the developments of Frame's perspectivalism are closely tied to Westminster.

[22] Ibid., 212: "It is especially important for systematic theologians today to be aware of the developments in biblical theology, a discipline in which new discoveries are being made almost daily. Too frequently, systematic theologians (including this one!) lag far behind biblical theologians in the sophistication of their exegesis." Frame also notes that some advocates of biblical theology have gone to excess (ibid., 209–12; Frame, "Backgrounds to My Thought," 18). See also Vern S. Poythress, "Kinds of Biblical Theology," *Westminster Theological Journal* 70, no. 1 (2008): 129–42.

The flexibility of categories is next door to their ability to function as perspectives. A tightly circumscribed, technical category like "burnt offering" has great specificity in meaning and in use. If we use it outside its narrow sphere, we use it only playfully or metaphorically. By contrast, Frame's triad of lordship has the flexibility built in. Such flexibility in many cases is more characteristic of biblical theology than of traditional systematic theology. The built-in flexibility permits an easy extension of the categories into perspectives. For example, *everything* that God does, whether or not we explicitly label it as a display of his presence, inevitably involves his presence. Presence becomes a perspective in that it is characteristic of all passages in the Bible that involve God at all.

For example, God is present to reward the righteous and punish the wicked, as he promises in Psalm 1:5–6. God is present in listening to the pleas and groanings from those who speak the psalms of distress, such as Psalms 3, 4, 5, and 6. God is present in the life of David, to protect him from Saul's attempts to kill him. God is present with Jeremiah, to sustain him in the midst of the hostile reaction from his contemporaries. We could multiply cases.

Wider Uses of Multiple Perspectives

In sum, Reformed theology as a whole, the Reformed apologetics of Cornelius Van Til, and the biblical theology of Geerhardus Vos had important influence and offered important encouragement for the development of Frame's multiperspectivalism. But was the Reformed background *necessary* for the development? My account up to this point might suggest that it was. But within multiperspectivalism we find also a concern to listen sympathetically to other perspectives. Logically this concern embraces perspectives from people who occupy other streams of Christian tradition. Could other Christian traditions develop multiperspectivalism?[23]

Here also Van Til's apologetics has a positive contribution. Van Til has an emphasis not only on *antithesis* but also on *com-*

---

[23] More broadly still, could multiperspectivalism develop even outside of Christianity? Some forms of "perspectivism" crop up here and there (see note 9); but Frame's multiperspectivalism is grounded ultimately in the Trinity and is therefore possible only within the circle of Christian Trinitarian theology.

mon grace.[24] The doctrine of common grace says that God shows mercy and gives blessings even to rebels, and the blessings that God gives can include various human insights into truth. These insights come to non-Christians. How much more may we expect that God may give blessings and insights to Christians, including Christians outside the Reformed tradition. God bestows blessings not because our theology is already absolutely perfect, but out of his grace, which he gives on the basis of Christ's perfection.

Every genuine Christian has been regenerated through the work of the Holy Spirit and has become a "new creation" (2 Cor. 5:17; see John 3:1–8; Eph. 4:22–24). The Lord has renewed all believers' minds and set them on the path of righteousness, including righteous *thinking.* But all of us are inconsistent and still retain remnants of sinful ways of thinking. We need to help one another out of each other's sins. And God continues to bless us in ways that we do not deserve. Hence, in principle, if multiperspectivalism is indeed a valid approach, any Christian anywhere can receive insights from the Lord that lead him into a multiperspectival approach.

In fact the commandment to "love your neighbor as yourself" (Matt. 22:39) leads in this very direction. If you love your neighbor, you are willing to listen to him sympathetically. And if you listen, you begin to understand his perspective. Maybe you find some erroneous thinking. But you also find some positive insights. When you find insights, you incorporate your neighbor's perspective into your own thinking, and then you have two perspectives instead of one. At a basic level, people are doing sympathetic listening all the time, whether in marriage and family, at work, or in education. Multiperspectivalism can be seen as little more than a self-conscious description and codification of some of the processes that are innate in loving your neighbor.

In particular, Christian cross-cultural missions have always involved multiple perspectives. A Christian crossing from American to Chinese culture has an American perspective with which he

---

[24] See, for example, Cornelius Van Til, *Common Grace and the Gospel* (Nutley, NJ: Presbyterian and Reformed, 1973).

begins. As he learns more about Chinese culture, he learns about how things look from a Chinese as well as an American point of view. So he has two perspectives.

Similarly, biblically based Christian counseling involves multiple perspectives. The counselor has his perspective, which should be based on mature knowledge of Scripture. He listens to the counselee sympathetically and tries to understand the counselee's thinking and feeling and perspective. The counselor gradually develops an understanding of a second perspective, the perspective of the counselee, and then endeavors to bring God's truth in Scripture into the counselee's situation.

God is the ultimate source for whatever insights we receive concerning multiple perspectives. He can give us insight suddenly, in a moment, in a flash. But frequently God uses means. Scripture itself is, of course, a primary means. But God also uses the skills and insights of others within the body of Christ. For example, John Frame learned from Van Til, rather than developing his multiperspectivalism completely from scratch. The Christian counselor learns from the example of more mature counselors, as well as those who may undertake to instruct him in the art. The missionary intern learns from the missionary veteran. He sees how to move from one perspective to another both through instruction in general principles and through observing examples that embody the principles.

Thus, though it is possible in principle for people to develop a multiperspectival approach from scratch, it is certainly easier to do it when they build on the work of others.

My Own Growth in Multiperspectivalism

My own growth in multiperspectivalism is a further example of how one person learns from another. As a student at Westminster Theological Seminary, I was attracted to John Frame's teaching, including its multiperspectival dimensions, and adopted it as my own.

Frame's thinking was explicitly multiperspectival. But I also learned multiperspectival thinking from Edmund Clowney, who taught practical theology at Westminster. Clowney did not talk explicitly about perspectives. But his approach was nascently multiperspectival. How so?

Clowney's thinking used biblical theology. He followed the metaphorical and analogical aspects of Scripture as he showed how the Old Testament pointed forward to Christ. The Old Testament pointed forward partly through types and shadows that analogically pointed to Christ.[25] Thus Clowney helped me adjust to using some key categories like sacrifice, temple, and kingship in a flexible way as I saw relations between Old Testament institutions and Christ. This flexibility, as we have observed, is next door to perspectival practice.

Clowney also adopted a teaching found in Scripture and articulated in the Westminster Standards, the insight that Christ is our final prophet, king, and priest.[26] Christ's teaching ministry showed his work as a prophet. His working of miracles showed the exercise of power, and therefore his kingship. His sacrifice on the cross showed his work as priest.

But as I thought about these truths and combined them with Clowney's use of analogy and typology in the Old Testament, it seemed to me that the three kinds of work of Christ could not be neatly isolated. When Christ taught, he taught with *authority*. His teaching manifested a kingly claim. So his teaching was not only prophetic, but kingly as well.

When Christ cast out demons with miraculous power, that was a kingly work. But he characteristically drove out the demons using verbal commands, which were prophetic utterances (Luke 4:36). Moreover, the very character of his miracles revealed the

---

[25] This analogical connection was already propounded in the Westminster Standards: "This covenant [of grace] was differently administered in the time of the law, and in the time of the gospel: under the law it was administered by promises, prophecies, sacrifices, circumcision, the paschal lamb, and other types and ordinances delivered to the people of the Jews, all foresignifying Christ to come; which were, for that time, sufficient and efficacious, through the operation of the Spirit, to instruct and build up the elect in faith in the promised Messiah, by whom they had full remission of sins, and eternal salvation; and is called the old Testament" (Westminster Confession of Faith, 7.5; see also Westminster Larger Catechism, 34). Clowney developed these confessional themes further in books like *Preaching and Biblical Theology* (Grand Rapids: Eerdmans, 1961); and *Preaching Christ in All of Scripture* (Wheaton, IL: Crossway, 2003). See also Vern S. Poythress, *The Shadow of Christ in the Law of Moses* (1991; repr., Phillipsburg, NJ: P&R, 1995).

[26] Westminster Confession of Faith, 8.1: "It pleased God, in His eternal purpose, to choose and ordain the Lord Jesus, His only begotten Son, to be the Mediator between God and man, the Prophet, Priest, and King." See also Westminster Larger Catechism, 43–45. Frame also mentions the influence of Clowney's thinking on his triperspectivalism (Frame, "Backgrounds to My Thought," 15).

character of Christ. The miracles indirectly revealed something about who he was and the character of his kingdom. For example, his healing of the paralytic in Matthew 9:2–8 showed that Christ had power to forgive sins. The miracle taught something. And if it *taught*, it was indirectly *prophetic* as well as directly kingly.

We can also look at the promise to forgive sins. This promise by Jesus is a pronouncement involving the exercise of his prophetic function. But we can also observe that forgiveness comes on the basis of substitution and sacrifice—ultimately Christ's sacrifice. Forgiveness involves a priestly dimension. Forgiveness is a pronouncement of pardon from God the king. So forgiveness has a kingly dimension. A miracle that proclaims forgiveness has a prophetic dimension, because it *proclaims* forgiveness. It has a kingly dimension, because a miracle is an exercise of power. It also has a priestly dimension, because forgiveness involves reconciliation mediated by a priestly figure. Thus, the labels *prophet, king*, and *priest* can be used not merely in a more literal sense, but as *perspectives* on the whole of Christ's work. All of Christ's work is prophetic, in that it teaches things about him. All is kingly, because he is always acting with kingly authority. All is priestly, in that all his work is part of the total program for reconciling his people to God through his sacrifice.

So from Edmund Clowney I had a perspectival triad consisting of prophet, king, and priest. This triad came in addition to the triads that I was learning from Frame. Of course, Clowney's triad also belonged to the Westminster Standards before Clowney's time. But his use of biblical theology and its analogical structures encouraged me to employ these older categories in an extended, analogical way, and it was but a step to use them perspectivally.

When I had come this far, it was only a small step to consider the possibility of taking almost any category from biblical theology and expanding it into a perspective.[27] For example, start with the

---

[27] The idea of using biblical themes as perspectives is further developed in Poythress, *Symphonic Theology*. I intended the title to be another label for Frame's multiperspectivalism. My title was, I think, prettier and more colorful than *multiperspectivalism* and I hoped that it would stick. But the term *multiperspectivalism* is more precisely descriptive, and so it has remained the more conventional label.

theme of the temple. Stretch it out into a perspective. See it as a particular embodiment of the theme of "God with us," which is fulfilled in Christ (Matt. 1:23). In fact, John indicates that the temple theme is fulfilled in Christ, whose body is the temple (John 2:21). The temple is closely related to the theme of God's presence, one of the categories in Frame's triad of covenant lordship. If the idea of temple is stretched out in this way, it thus becomes a perspective on all of God's dealings with us.

When I came to Westminster in 1971, Frame was already doing things of a similar sort. In ethics, he argued that each of the Ten Commandments had its own distinctive focus, but that any one of the commandments could also be used as a perspective on the *whole* of our ethical responsibility.[28]

In his course on the doctrine of God, Frame argued that the great miracles in the Bible could be used to provide a perspective on God's providence and on God's character. Pedagogically, Frame could start his theological discussion with miracles and then go from there to look at providence, creation, and then the attributes of God.

This approach implies that miracles like the plagues in Egypt, the crossing of the Red Sea, the miracles of Elijah and Elisha, the miracles of Christ's earthly life, and the resurrection of Christ show in particularly intensive form God's authority, power, and presence. Miracles also provide pictures of redemptive power that can encourage us as we confront hardships in our own circumstances. Any one miracle can therefore become a perspective on the larger plan of God for our redemption.

Multiple Perspectives in the Work of Kenneth L. Pike

In many respects Frame's multiperspectivalism developed under the influence of the theology and teaching at Westminster Theological Seminary.[29] But in my life I received another influence. Beginning in the summer of 1971, I studied for several summers at the Summer Institute of Linguistics in Norman, Oklahoma, where

---

[28] See Frame, *Doctrine of the Christian Life.*
[29] See Frame, "Backgrounds to My Thought," 15–18.

Kenneth L. Pike taught tagmemics, a linguistic approach with multiperspectival characteristics. It is worthwhile for me to tell part of that story, because Pike developed his multiperspectivalism earlier than did Frame, and independently of the influence of Westminster Theological Seminary.[30] And yet, at bottom the two kinds of multiperspectivalism are virtually identical in spirit.

Pike was a Christian linguist who taught linguistics at the University of Michigan, but also spent a good deal of his career in the task of Bible translation with Wycliffe Bible Translators and its academic sister institution, the Summer Institute of Linguistics.[31] The challenge of translating a rich book like the Bible and the challenge of analyzing a spectrum of exotic languages with no discernible relation to Indo-European languages contributed to Pike's endeavor to build a linguistic approach that was both practical and rich. Over a period of decades, Pike developed an approach called tagmemic theory that explicitly incorporated multiple perspectives.[32]

In retrospect we can find tentative steps toward multiple perspectives as early as 1947, when Pike wrote a book codifying his work on sound systems of language ("phonemics").[33] To account robustly for the complexity of sound patterns over a multitude of languages of the world, Pike had to balance a number of dimensions in these patterns. In his analysis we can see the early stages of what later developed into a perspectival triad: contrast, variation, and distribution.[34] He also devoted attention to what later came to be known as particle, wave, and field phenomena. The

---

[30] Pike mentioned to me in personal conversation that he had read some of Cornelius Van Til's writing. But I am not aware of any direct connection between Westminster Seminary and Pike's perspectivalism.

[31] See the biographical information on Kenneth L. Pike at http://www.sil.org/klp/klp-bio.htm, accessed November 12, 2008.

[32] Pike tells the story himself in Kenneth L. Pike, "Toward the Development of Tagmemic Postulates," in *Tagmemics*, vol. 2, *Theoretical Discussion*, ed. Ruth M. Brend and Kenneth L. Pike (The Hague/Paris: Mouton, 1976), 91–127. Others also contributed to the development, including Robert E. Longacre, Kenneth Pike's wife Evelyn, and his sister Eunice. Pike's essay acknowledges contributions from many others.

[33] Kenneth L. Pike, *Phonemics: A Technique for Reducing Languages to Writing* (Ann Arbor: University of Michigan Press, 1947).

[34] Technically, "contrast" is more specifically "contrastive-identificational features" and includes features that help to establish the identity of a particular unit, as well as features that bring that unit into contrast with other, similar units. See the exposition in Kenneth L. Pike, *Linguistic Concepts: An Introduction to Tagmemics* (Lincoln: University of Nebraska Press, 1982), 42–51.

phenomena were there and were acknowledged, but Pike had not yet fully organized them by generalization beyond the area of phonemics (sound).

In 1949, after thirteen years of concentration on sound patterns, Pike began to concentrate on phenomena in the area of grammar.[35] Comparisons between patterns in sound and in grammar led him to summarize the patterns in terms of the three characteristic aspects of analysis of a linguistic unit mentioned above: contrast, variation, and distribution.[36] These formed a perspectival triad, the first that Pike developed. The three aspects are interdependent and interlocked with one another. In the actual phenomena of language use, they are not strictly isolatable, but are copresent dimensions in the total function of the language.

In 1959 Pike wrote an article entitled "Language as Particle, Wave, and Field."[37] Here for the first time he introduced three "views" of language. Pike explained that linguistics could look at language as consisting of particles (a static approach oriented to distinguishable pieces), waves (a dynamic approach, looking at flow and mutual influence), and fields (a relational approach, focusing on systematic patterning of relations in multiple dimensions). Each of these approaches can in principle be applied to the same piece of language, and people notice different patterns by using each approach. These views are three perspectives.[38]

By this time Pike was a self-conscious perspectivalist, but of what kind? His thinking continued to develop. By 1967 he was analyzing not only language but human behavior in general as "trimodal."[39] The three "modes" were the feature mode (identity and contrast), the manifestation mode (variation), and the distribution mode (distribution). He saw these three modes as interlock-

---

[35] Pike, "Tagmemic Postulates," 94.

[36] Ibid., 96. See the fully developed explanation of these concepts in Pike, *Linguistic Concepts*, 42–65.

[37] Kenneth L. Pike, "Language as Particle, Wave, and Field," *The Texas Quarterly* 2, no. 2 (1959): 37–54; reprinted in *Kenneth L. Pike: Selected Writings to Commemorate the 60th Birthday of Kenneth Lee Pike*, ed. Ruth M. Brend (The Hague/Paris: Mouton, 1972), 117–28. More mature explanation of the three perspectives can be found in Pike, *Linguistic Concepts*, 19–38.

[38] "His experience [the experience of an observer of language] of the factness around him is affected by his perspectives" (Pike, *Linguistic Concepts*, 12). On the relation of linguistic theories to human perspectives, see ibid., 5–13.

[39] Kenneth L. Pike, *Language in Relation to a Unified Theory of the Structure of Human Behavior*, 2nd ed. (The Hague/Paris: Mouton, 1967).

ing. His modal approach not only encompassed the earlier triads, but also uncovered further manifestations of them.[40]

In 1971, when I met him, Pike confided that he thought that the modes reflected within language the Trinitarian character of God. The triadic modes were three-in-one modes, each distinct, but each deeply interlocked with and presupposing the others, each also belonging to the unified whole, which was a linguistic unit. Each was a perspective on the whole.

Perspectives in Dorothy Sayers

Dorothy Sayers gives us an instance of perspectival thinking from a point even earlier in time than Pike or Frame. In 1941 Sayers published the book *The Mind of the Maker*.[41] There she starts with her own experience as a creative writer (she primarily wrote detective stories). Sayers finds in the process of artistic creation an analogy to the Trinitarian character of God. She observes that any act of human creation has three coinherent aspects, which she names "Idea," "Energy," and "Power." "The Creative Idea" is the idea of the creative work as a whole, even before it comes to expression. "This is the image of the Father."[42] "The Creative Energy" or "Activity" is the process of working out the idea, both mentally and on paper. Sayers describes it as "working in time from the beginning to the end, with sweat and passion. . . . This is the image of the Word."[43] Third is "the Creative Power," "the meaning of the work and its response in the lively soul: . . . this is the image of the indwelling Spirit."[44]

Sayers also observes that each of these three aspects—idea, activity, and power—is intelligible only in the context of the others. She affirms the coinherence or indwelling of each in the others.[45]

---

[40] The entire structure for a tagmemic framework for discourse can be derived analogically, starting with a single perspectival triad, namely particle, wave, and field. See Vern S. Poythress, "A Framework for Discourse Analysis: The Components of a Discourse, from a Tagmemic Viewpoint," *Semiotica* 38, no. 3/4 (1982): 277–98; Poythress, "Hierarchy in Discourse Analysis: A Revision of Tagmemics," *Semiotica* 40, no. 1/2 (1982): 107–37.

[41] Dorothy L. Sayers, *The Mind of the Maker* (New York: Harcourt, Brace, 1941). Sayers's thinking about the Trinity is visible even earlier in Sayers, *Zeal of Thy House* (New York: Harcourt, Brace, 1937).

[42] Sayers, *Mind of the Maker*, 37.

[43] Ibid.

[44] Ibid., 37–38.

[45] I have taken the liberty of reproducing here two paragraphs that are also appear in Vern S. Poythress, *In the Beginning Was the Word: Language—A God-Centered Approach* (Wheaton, IL: Crossway, 2009).

The Present Shape of Multiperspectivalism

Perspectivalism as an Implication of General Revelation

Now that we have looked briefly at some of the historical developments of perspectivalism, it is time to consider the character of the
product. What is the distinctive character of multiperspectivalism?

Our survey of the historical developments is still pertinent. A
form of perspectivalism related to the Trinitarian character of God
appeared independently in at least three different places: in the
work of John Frame, in the work of Kenneth Pike, and in the work
of Dorothy Sayers. The independence of these three works suggests
that God, as the archetype, has impressed ectypal images of his
Trinitarian nature on the order of the created world.[46]

Sayers and Pike derived much of their reflection from general
revelation in human artistic creativity and in language, respectively. At the same time, as Christians, Sayers and Pike had the
benefit of special revelation in the Bible, which articulated the
Trinitarian character of God. Sayers and Pike undoubtedly deep-
ened their reflections through the interaction that they discovered
between special revelational knowledge of the Trinity and patterns
of perspectival interlocking that they observed from general revelation.[47] At the same time, both authors direct their primary focus
toward subject matter coming from general revelation. Pike's published work in professional linguistics seldom mentions explicitly
his Christian commitment, let alone his Trinitarian thinking. Yet
his work shows clear triunal patterns in its use of perspectival
triads.

The Key Role of Persons

We may also note the important role played by the study of persons
and by the God-man relation in all of the historical instances of
Trinitarian perspectivalism.

Consider first Dorothy Sayers. At an early point she explicitly

---

[46] See the argument for the Trinitarian basis for scientific law in Vern S. Poythress, *Redeeming Science: A God-Centered Approach* (Wheaton, IL: Crossway, 2006), 24–26; and the Trinitarian basis for
language in Poythress, *In the Beginning Was the Word*.

[47] On the close correlation and interaction between general and special revelation, see Van Til,
Introduction to Systematic Theology, chaps. 6–11.

indicates that she is working with the concept of man as the image of God.[48] She undertakes to understand God's activity as Creator by analogy with human artistic creativity. In the process she uncovers a coinherent perspectival triad of idea, energy, and power. Creativity, as a characteristic of persons, becomes the key entry point for reflecting on the image of God, which has to do with man as personal. And man is in the image of God, who is personal and creative.

Next, consider Kenneth Pike. He is dealing with language, which is innately associated with persons. As a Bible translator, he is repeatedly confronted with the fact that God speaks in the Bible, and that God's speech is analogous to human speech. Thus, he has before him a natural bridge between the Trinitarian character of God and the nature of human language. Pike uncovered the key triad of particle, wave, and field by interacting with what was going on in elementary particle physics.[49] But at the same time, he was aware of the potential for persons, by choice, to take a stance in which they direct their awareness toward some one aspect of their situation. Personal choice introduces the possibility of multiple perspectives. Persons are central in his reckoning: "The observer standpoint is relevant to finding data: no 'thing-in-itself' (i.e. apart from an observer) is discussed in the theory [Pike's tagmemic theory]."[50]

John Frame obtained his fundamental triads in the context of persons. Frame's triad for covenant lordship comes, of course, in the context of covenant, which is a *personal* relation between God and man. The triad for ethics arises in the context of ethical responsibility, which must be fully *personal* responsibility. Edmund Clowney's triad of prophet, king, and priest comes in the context of considering the work of Christ, who is a divine person. Christ's work fulfills the pattern of the various persons in the Old Testament who served in the personal roles of prophet, king, and priest.

---

[48] Sayers, *Mind of the Maker*, chap. 2, pp. 19–31.
[49] Pike, "Tagmemic Postulates," 99.
[50] Ibid., 91. Pike's inclusion of the observer is all the more striking when it is contrasted with the tendency of much linguistic theory of the time to construct a formal system, dropping the persons out of the picture.

The Trinitarian Root of Perspectivalism

In retrospect, we may surmise that the role of persons in perspectivalism is no accident. Perspectivalism of a Trinitarian kind has its ultimate roots in the Trinitarian character of God. God is one God, and he is also three persons. The doctrine of the Trinity is itself fundamentally and deeply personal. We are confronted forcefully with the necessity for Trinitarian thinking especially when we see the personalism in the Gospel of John. The Son relates personally to the Father, and the Spirit is introduced as "another Helper," who will function toward the disciples like the Son (John 14:16; see also John 16).

The three persons are distinct from one another. The Bible describes their interactions. The Father sends the Son, and the Son obeys the Father (John 6:38–39; 12:49; 14:31). The Father glorifies the Son, and the Son glorifies the Father (John 13:31–32; 17:1–5). The Spirit speaks what he hears from the Father and the Son (John 16:13–14).

At the same time, all the persons of the Trinity are involved in all the acts of God. The Father created the world through the Word (that is, the Son) in the power of the Spirit (Gen. 1:2; Pss. 33:6; 104:30; John 1:1–3). So each person offers us a "perspective" on the acts of God. In fact, then, each person offers a "perspective" on God himself. Through the Son, that is, through the perspective that the Son gives us, we know the Father: "All things have been handed over to me by my Father, and no one knows the Son except the Father, and no one knows the Father except the Son and anyone to whom the Son chooses to reveal him" (Matt. 11:27).

The revelation of the Father through the Son is possible because the Father dwells in the Son to do his works:

> Whoever has seen me has seen the Father. How can you say, "Show us the Father"? Do you not believe that I am in the Father and the Father is in me? The words that I say to you I do not speak on my own authority, but the Father who dwells in me does his works. Believe me that I am in the Father and the Father is in me, or else believe on account of the works themselves. (John 14:9–11)

The mutual indwelling of persons in the Trinity, called *coinherence* or *perichoresis*, is the ultimate background for how we know the Father through the Son. This knowledge is *perspectival*. We know the Father *through* the perspective offered in the Son.

Human experience of perspectives derives from an ultimate archetype, that is, the plurality of persons in the Trinity and their coinherence. The plurality of persons implies a plurality of perspectives. The indwelling of persons in coinherence implies the harmony and compatibility of distinct perspectives, as well as the fact that one starting point in one person opens the door to all three persons. Each person offers us a perspective on the whole of God.

Hence, the archetype for perspectives is the Trinity. The persons of the Trinity know one another (Matt. 11:27). Such knowledge is personal. The Son knows the Father as a person, as well as knowing all facts about the person. The Son knows the Father as Father from his standpoint as the Son. Hence, there are three archetypal perspectives on knowledge, the perspectives of the Father, the Son, and the Holy Spirit. These three are one. There is only one God.

This unity in plurality and plurality in unity has implications for derivative knowledge, the knowledge by creatures. As creatures we have knowledge that is an ectype, a derivative knowledge, rather than the archetype, the original infinite knowledge of God. Ectypal knowledge must inevitably show the stamp of its Trinitarian archetype, because all knowledge, insofar as it is true knowledge at all, is knowledge of truth, and archetypal truth is God's truth, truth in his mind. His truth is manifest in the Word, who is the truth in the absolute sense (John 14:6). To know truth is to know truth from the One who is the truth, from the Son, and in knowing truth from the Son, we know the image of the truth in the mind of the Father.

In addition, it must be said, we know through the teaching of the Holy Spirit: "But it is the spirit in man, the *breath of the Almighty*, that makes him understand" (Job 32:8). A number of New Testament passages emphasize the role of the Holy Spirit in giving us saving knowledge of God in Christ: "When the Spirit of truth comes, he will guide you into all the truth" (John 16:13). This promise comes only to those who believe in the Son. The Spirit has a special redemptive role for believers.

At the same time, on the basis of broader statements like that in Job 32:8 (see also Ps. 94:10), we may infer that the special redemptive teaching by the Spirit has as its broader background a general creational activity of the Spirit in teaching human beings anything that they know at all. What the Spirit teaches in this creational activity derives from the source of knowledge in the Son, who is the Word, the wisdom of God (1 Cor. 1:30; Col. 2:3), and the truth of God (John 14:6). Hence all human knowledge has a Trinitarian structure in its source.

The Role of Man and the Centrality of Christ

Since human beings are made in the image of God, and they can enjoy personal fellowship with God, it should not be surprising that we find some of the most striking analogues to the Trinitarian mystery in human beings: their knowledge, their covenantal relation to God (covenant lordship), their ethical responsibility to God (triad of ethics), their language (Kenneth Pike), and their artistic creativity (Dorothy Sayers). At the heart of all these manifestations of God is the mediation of the Son of God. Consider first the theme of covenant lordship, as developed by John Frame. Isaiah predicts the coming of the messianic servant to bring final salvation, and identifies him both as the Lord of the covenant (Isa. 9:6–7) and as the covenant itself (Isa. 42:6; 49:8). Christ supremely and climactically manifests authority, control, and presence. He has the authority of God (Matt. 5:21–22; Luke 4:36; 5:21–24); he manifests the control of God in healing and in ruling the waters (Matthew 8); he is the presence of God, "God with us" (Matt. 1:23).

Christ also sums up in his person the various dimensions of our ethical responsibility. His righteousness is the ultimate norm, which is reflected in the particular normative pronouncements throughout the Bible. His person is the ultimate goal, because the goal of history is to display the glory of God in the glory of Christ (John 17:1–5; Rev. 21:22–24). His person is also the ultimate motive: Christlikeness is worked in us through the Spirit (2 Cor. 3:18).

Christ as the Word of God is the ultimate origin behind all manifestations of language (Pike). Christ the Creator is the ultimate origin behind all instances of human creativity (Sayers). Christ as prophet, king, and priest is the ultimate model for the Old Testament ectypal instances of prophets, kings, and priests (Clowney).

In affirming the centrality of Christ, we do not produce a Christomonism that collapses the full Trinitarian character of God into one person, or (worse) into the human nature of Christ. Rather, we retain the distinction of persons, and the distinction of the two natures of Christ; at the same time, we affirm the epistemological insight that any one of the themes concerning Christ can be a perspectival starting point for meditation on the whole.

Imaging

Man is made in the image of God, according to Genesis 1:26–28. But in the New Testament we discover something more: Christ is "the image of the invisible God" (Col. 1:15; see Heb. 1:3). The statement about Christ occurs in the context of Christ as Mediator of creation, rather than merely in the context of redemption. So we can infer that in the original act of creation, Adam was created not simply in the image of God, but after the pattern of the archetypal divine image, namely, the Son, the second person of the Trinity. Adam, be it noted, also fathers Seth "in his own likeness, after his image" (Gen. 5:3).

Meredith G. Kline has further reflected on this imaging structure, and extended the idea metaphorically, in the manner of the flexible terminology in biblical theology.[51] Theophanies in the Old Testament display or "image" God in visible manifestations. Kline sees a close relation between theophany, especially the cloud of glory, and the Holy Spirit. But theophanies include manifestations of God in human form, as in Ezekiel 1:26–28, and in some of the appearances to Abraham (Genesis 18) and others (Judg. 13:6,

---

[51] Meredith G. Kline, *Images of the Spirit* (Grand Rapids: Baker, 1980).

18, 22). These appearances in human form surely anticipate the incarnation of Christ, who is the final, permanent "theophany" in human form.[52] Hence, theophany is intrinsically Trinitarian. It is a revelation of the Father in the Son through the Spirit. How else could it be? If we as sinners stand before God in his holiness, we will die (Ex. 33:20–23; Isa. 6:5–7). We need mediation: specifically, we need the mediation of the Son, in whom dwells the Spirit, and who sends the Spirit to unite us to himself.

The central theophany is in the Son, in his incarnation. But Old Testament theophanies also include visible manifestations: in light, in cloud, in thunder, in fire, in a burning bush. These physical phenomena "image" God in a subordinate way, by displaying something of his character. The creation itself is described in a manner reminiscent of the language of theophany in Psalm 104:1–4. Hence, creation itself displays the character of God, which is exactly what the apostle Paul says in Romans:

> For what can be known about God is plain to them, because God has shown it to them. For his invisible attributes, namely, his eternal power and divine nature, have been clearly perceived, ever since the creation of the world, in the things that have been made. So they are without excuse. For although they knew God, they did not honor him as God or give thanks to him, but they became futile in their thinking, and their foolish hearts were darkened. (Rom. 1:19–21)

Theophany, as we have seen, is innately Trinitarian, and therefore perspectival. We see the Father in the Son. By implication, the creation itself displays the imprint of Trinitarian structure. Though man is the image of God in a unique sense, the created world "images" God in a great variety of ways. For example, the cloud that covered Mount Sinai and the cloud that filled the tabernacle (Ex. 40:34–38) uniquely manifested the presence of God. Ordinary clouds, by contrast, do not have this role. But they do reflect both the exaltedness and mystery of God. The fire in the burning bush and the fire on Mount Sinai and the tongues of fire

---

[52] See John 12:41, which alludes to Isaiah 6.

at Pentecost (Acts 2:3) were unique *theophanic* fire manifesting the presence of God. Ordinary fire is not, but it still reflects God in its power to consume and purify. Created things image God who is Trinitarian. The fire in Acts 2:3 stands for the Holy Spirit, whom the Father sends through the Son (Acts 2:33; see Rev. 4:5). Hence, creation is rich with the potential for perspectival investigation.[53] Yet the darkness of darkened hearts in idolatry throws up barriers to the clarity and depth of knowledge.

Reformed Theology as an Aid to Multiperspectivalism

The work of Dorothy Sayers and Kenneth Pike shows that a multiperspectival approach can develop directly from Trinitarian doctrine and general revelation. It need not have strong, direct dependence on the distinctives of Reformed theology. Nevertheless, multiperspectivalism enjoys affinities with some of the distinctives in Reformed theology. The affinities are most obvious with the particular form of Reformed theology that has taken root at Westminster Theological Seminary. We have already noted several.

1. Van Til's emphasis on antithesis emboldens students to think in a distinctively Christian manner and to be willing to break with the bulk of Western thought.

Antithesis, of course, is not uniquely a Reformed idea. Many people nowadays are waking up to the distinctions between a Christian worldview and various non-Christian worldviews. But Reformed theology emphasizes the radicality of the depravity in fallen human beings. Depravity extends to the mind (Eph. 4:17–19) and not merely to the will or the habits of the body. It affects the depths of the mind. And the effects can be subtle as well as overt. Hence, Reformed tradition offers fertile soil for taking seriously the distinctiveness of Christian thought.

Van Til also analyzes ways in which Christian thinkers of the past have fallen into compromises with unbelieving, non-Christian thinking. He thus emboldens Christians not to adopt uncritically

---

[53] Such investigation is part of the point of Poythress, *Redeeming Science*.

a metaphysical or epistemological framework that owes more to Kant or to Aristotle or to Plato than to Christ.

2. Van Til emphasizes the Creator-creature distinction. This distinction underlines the absoluteness and exclusiveness of the claims of God the Creator. Such an emphasis encourages Christians to make sure that God alone receives our allegiance. Monoperspectival reductions of the truth frequently make one perspective into a godlike origin for everything else.

On one level, knowledge of the Creator-creature distinction is common to all Christians, not merely Reformed Christians. But Reformed theology has made a point of dwelling on the absoluteness of God and trying to make sure that all theological reflection remains consistent with his absoluteness.

3. The Creator-creature distinction also reminds Christians that in the arena of knowledge they do not have to be God or to aspire to be divine in their knowledge. Christians can thus be free to admit that what they have is only finite knowledge, and that they have their knowledge only from the "perspective" of who they are with finite experience and a finite location. At the same time, because God reveals himself in general and special revelation, and supremely through Christ, Christians can be confident that they have genuine knowledge—knowledge of God, and knowledge concerning things around them.

Human perspectives are limited, but still valid (insofar as they are not distorted by sin). Any one Christian perspective coheres with the infinitude of divine knowledge, because the perspective comes as a gift from God. Multiple perspectives are intrinsically legitimate rather than an embarrassment or a frustration. Hence, admitting that you are a creature leads naturally to multiperspectivalism.

Suppose, by contrast, that you abolish the Creator-creature distinction in your own thinking. If you think God is on the same level with you, then your knowledge must be God's knowledge if it is to be true at all. You must be God. Or you must bring God down to your level in order to have assurance that your knowledge is valid. In that case, your perspective *is* God's perspective, pure and simple, and there is only one valid perspective—your own. That point of view is what Van Til and John Frame call "non-Christian rationalism." The human mind claims absolute autonomy and becomes the standard for truth. That approach has an intrinsic tendency toward monoperspectivalism. It exalts a single chosen perspective and ends up crushing out all diversity in human perspectives.

When such godlike claims become implausible, as they inevitably do, the non-Christian moves to the opposite pole, "non-Christian irrationalism." He admits that he is not God, that his knowledge is not infinite. But he does not give up his autonomy. He still clings to the ultimacy of his own perspective. So then he lapses into skepticism. He concludes that no one can know anything rightly because no one can attain infinity. Multiple perspectives then become relativistic, as is characteristic of much postmodernist thinking.

Christian thinking affirms the accessibility of God. Christian thinking is not postmodernist; it does not irrationalistically exalt diversity and give up unity. At the same time, Christian thinking rejects the modernist confidence in autonomous human rationality as an ultimate foundation for truth. Neither modernism nor postmodernism acknowledges the Creator-creature distinction. So neither agrees with the Christian answer, which is that we can remain creatures, in submission to the Creator. God gives us real but not exhaustive knowledge of the truth.

4. Reformed theology also emphasizes the comprehensive sovereignty of God. Comprehensive sovereignty encourages Christians to affirm the intrinsically harmonious relation between different perspectives, such as the normative, existential, and situational perspectives. God guarantees perfect harmony between the perspectives because he completely controls them all and all their manifestations. By contrast, if we are in doubt about the comprehensiveness of God's control, we in effect leave room for a final irrationalism. If we think that something may be even a little out of control, we have no guarantee that it will fit with complete harmony into other dimensions of truth and of patterning that we find throughout the world of thought.

Especially when we multiply the number of dimensions that

we inspect, the very multiplicity of insights can become threatening. If these are not united by the all-controlling God with an all-controlling, coherent plan, what will we do? The multiple insights need a single master perspective, a master key, if they are to be united at all. If we do not allow God to control every detail, we are likely to make for ourselves substitute gods. These gods can take the form of a master perspective that will bring us rationalistic harmony on our own autonomous terms. Or they can take the form of skepticism that gives up on harmony because there may be chaos and irrationalism at the foundation of what we investigate (this is the "polytheistic" solution).

5. Biblical theology in the tradition of Geerhardus Vos and his successors at Westminster Seminary introduced flexible categories and flexibility in thinking analogically. Such flexibility is next door to perspectivalism. At the same time, Vos affirmed the importance of believing in divine revelation and the harmonious character of God's plan for all of history. Hence, coherence among the perspectives is guaranteed beforehand.

This coherence in Vosian biblical theology contrasts with other, non-Vosian forms of "biblical theology": some deviant kinds of biblical theology may allow for contradictory points of view to crop up in different parts of Scripture. The contradictions are alleged to be there on account of the variety of human authors and circumstances. This kind of contradiction breaks up the unity of the perspectives and leads to denial of the accessibility of God's speech to us in the Bible (2 Tim. 3:16). God is seen as absent, or as hiding in obscurity somewhere behind the contradictions in the variety of human perspectives. Perspectives then lose their ultimate unity.

6. Van Til's teaching emphasizes the "equal ultimacy" of the one and the many in God. God is one God in three persons. In God, "the one"—that is, the oneness of God—is equally ultimate with "the many"—that is, the three persons. This equal ultimacy of the one and the many is the final foundation for the one and the many that occur at the level of the creature.[54]

---

[54] Van Til, *The Defense of the Faith*, 47–49; Van Til, *Survey of Christian Epistemology*, 96; Rousas J. Rushdoony, *The One and the Many: Studies in the Philosophy of Order and Ultimacy* (Nutley, NJ:

For example, there are many dogs, and there is one species, the species of dog. What is the relation between the two? Philosophers have found insuperable difficulties. If the one is prior, how did the many ever come about? Or if the many are prior, how did the many ever attain any subsequent unity? Van Til maintains that God's Trinitarian character is the final foundation answering this dilemma.

This picture of equal ultimacy is an encouragement for multiperspectival thinking on a human level. The diversity of human beings on earth is neither subordinate to nor prior to the unity of the one human race. (Adam was a single individual, but from the beginning God designed that he would bring into being a plurality of human beings.) The diversity in thinking among human beings, and the diversity in their perspectives, is neither prior to nor posterior to the unity in thinking that is common to all people made in the image of God. Thus, multiperspectivalism has a natural affinity to Van Til's thesis of equal ultimacy.

I have formulated the theme of the one and the many at a high level of generality. But it can be illustrated. The crossing of the Red Sea serves as one example of God's redemption. But it is a key example. God calls on Israel to look back on this example in order to take heart in the present (Ps. 78:2–4, 12–14). And he uses the exodus as an analogy for future redemption (Isa. 51:9–11). The one particular instance of redemption (one out of many) becomes a window or perspective through which we can view the general principle of redemption (the general pattern that unifies the instances). The instances are "the many." The general pattern is "the one." The general pattern is supremely manifested and embodied in the redemption accomplished by Christ. This one redemption leads to many "mini-redemptions" in the form of application of the benefits of redemption to each individual. The pattern of Christ's one redemption is also manifested typologically in the earlier "foreshadowing" of redemption in the exodus from Egypt.

7. The absoluteness of God, the finiteness of human knowledge, and the multiplicity of human viewpoints, when taken together,

Craig, 1971); Vern S. Poythress, "A Biblical View of Mathematics," in *Foundations for Christian Scholarship: Essays in the Van Til Perspective*, ed. Gary North (Vallecito, CA: Ross House, 1976), 161.

lead in a fairly obvious way to affirming multiple human perspectives, and to affirming an intrinsic harmonizability of human perspectives in God's absolute knowledge. But God's absoluteness leads us further. His absoluteness implies his ability to make himself accessible. As Frame observes, if God controls all things, and controls his relation to us, he can make himself present and available to us.[55] Within a Christian framework, transcendence (control) undergirds immanence (presence), rather than being in tension with it.

God's presence, his accessibility, together with his mercy displayed in Christ and the power of his Holy Spirit working in us, encourages us to seek him fervently. His absoluteness implies that we must conform our minds to him, rather than vice versa. This process of seeking him and conforming our minds to him leads naturally to appreciating the role of God in our epistemology. Our minds must be brought into conformity to him. We can never exhaustively understand the Trinity, but the Trinity is at the root of our epistemology. These thoughts together lead naturally to seeing the roots of multiple perspectives in the knowledge relations among the persons of the Trinity. These knowledge relations touch on the coinherence of the persons. The coinherence of the persons guarantees the coherence of perspectives at the deepest ontological level.[56]

There can be no other ultimate foundation for perspectives than in God himself. God alone is absolute. Thus absoluteness, a key concept in Reformed theology of God, serves naturally as a key incentive for moving toward multiperspectival thinking in human practice, a multiperspectivalism that imitates the coinherence of the persons in the Trinity.

Reformed Theology as Reforming

What does multiperspectivalism imply for the future? The finiteness of human knowledge, together with human access to God in Christ, provides the basis for progress. We can grow. We can know more of God in Christ (Rom. 11:33–36). Using a multiplicity of per-

---

[55] Frame, *Doctrine of the Knowledge of God*, 12–18.
[56] Thus multiperspectivalism has come to serve many areas: pedagogy, discovery (heuristic), ecclesiology (diversity of members in one body), analysis of conceptual terms (potential for varying use of a term), and ontology.

spectives aids growth. This growth includes the further refinement of human thinking, which in this world remains contaminated by sin and by the corruption of non-Christian influences.

Reformed theology itself, as a tradition, has not yet reached perfection.[57] Frame is thus not afraid to enrich that tradition, and even to challenge it, when he believes that he is following Scripture in so doing. Continuing to grow, which includes critically inspecting our heritage from past generations, is one implication of the depth of God's truth revealed in Scripture.

In fact, multiperspectivalism offers a radical challenge for growth. God in the absoluteness of his Trinitarian being is the final ontological foundation for the created order. And that has implications for language as a whole and for the category systems that have a role in human thinking, including theological thinking.[58]

In a postmodernist environment where the primary note is skepticism and antipathy to absolutist claims, we should be careful to strike a note in opposition to both modernism and postmodernism. Both commit themselves to human autonomy. The way of Christ is the way of discipleship, the way of firm reliance on his instruction, which is found in Scripture. That way does not despise the fruits of centuries of saints who have profited from Scripture. In particular, we profit from saints within the Reformed tradition, which has been a significant aid in the blossoming of multiperspectivalism.

Multiperspectivalism means appreciating all the perspectives offered by saints in past generations, and enriching them rather than discarding them for the sake of novelty or rebellion. It would be folly, as well as ingratitude, to cast off that tradition by accommodating modernity or postmodernity. In the process, we may also appropriate, in good multiperspectival fashion, insights that arise from common grace within both postmodernism and modernism. But we will do so in submission to Christ the Lord, who is the absolute God, in the unity with the Father and the Spirit.

---

[57] The reality of fallibility is affirmed explicitly in Reformed tradition in the Westminster Confession of Faith, 31.3: "All synods and councils, since the Apostles' times, whether general or particular, may err; and many have erred."

[58] See Vern S. Poythress, "Reforming Ontology and Logic in the Light of the Trinity: An Application of Van Til's Idea of Analogy," *Westminster Theological Journal* 57, no. 1 (1995): 187–219; Poythress, *In the Beginning Was the Word.*

8

Perspectives on God

We can now begin to employ perspectives on what exists. We begin with God, who is the Creator, the one whose existence is the foundation for everything else. John Frame's book *The Doctrine of God*[1] gives a massive exposition. So in this chapter we may confine ourselves to summarizing and supplementing some of what he says.

The Bible offers us many perspectives on God. God is Father, shepherd, king, husband (Hos. 2:16), fortress, light, and more. (For discussion of perspectives on God's Trinitarian character, see appendix B.) Let us consider one strand that will help us think about our relation to God: the passages that speak of God as king or Lord. As Lord, God has transcendent authority and power. He also exercises his authority and power in the world. In doing so, he shows himself to be *immanent*, or present, in the world.

Frame's Terms and Their Meanings

We are following John Frame at this point by using his triad of authority, control, and presence. This triad of perspectives expresses the meaning of God's *lordship*. His lordship comes to expression in the covenantal relationship between God and man (and subordinately in God's relation to other things that he has created). We then group together authority and control as aspects of transcendence, while presence is the expression of immanence. We may choose more

---

[1] John M. Frame, *The Doctrine of God* (Phillipsburg, NJ: P&R, 2002).

than one way of talking about such things. What matters is that we use terminology in the service of expressing faithfully the character of God, the God who reveals himself faithfully in Scripture.

Transcendence and Immanence

So God is both transcendent and immanent. Philosophical thinking about God has often seen transcendence and immanence in tension with each other. People may reason that if God is transcendent, he must be distant and inaccessible; he is not immanent. On the other hand, if he is immanent, if he is involved, then he is virtually a part of the world and is not transcendent.

But biblical teaching about God does not produce a tension. Precisely because God has authority and power, he has power to act in the world and to be present to his creatures. Conversely, his presence is always the presence of one who is Lord, who expresses his authority and requires our obedience. His presence brings to bear on us his authority and control.

John Frame expresses the compatibility of transcendence and immanence using a square diagram, which has come to be known as "Frame's square" (see fig. 1).[2]

The upper left corner (1) represents the biblical view or Christian view of God's transcendence. God has ultimate authority and exerts his control over all the world that he has made. The lower left corner (2) represents the Christian view of God's immanence. God is intimately present with all that he has made—especially with human beings, made in his image. His presence expresses his authority and control, so there is no tension between immanence and transcendence in this Christian view.

The right-hand side of the square represents the non-Christian position on transcendence and immanence. Of course, in a sense there are many non-Christian positions, but they show common features. They all try to evade the true nature of God by producing a substitute picture or counterfeit, which differs radically from the Christian position and yet shows enticing similarities to it.

---

[2] John M. Frame, *The Doctrine of the Knowledge of God* (Phillipsburg, NJ: P&R, 1987), 14; Frame, *Doctrine of God*, 113.

Figure 1

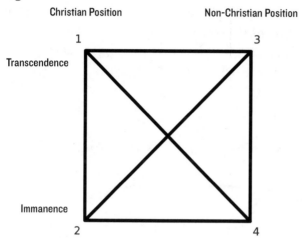

The upper right corner (3) represents the non-Christian view of transcendence. According to this view, God is inaccessible, distant, and uninvolved. The lower right corner (4) represents the non-Christian view of immanence. According to this view, if and when God becomes involved in the world, he is virtually identical to the world and is subject to the same limitations that characterize the world (see fig. 2 for the full picture).

Pantheism is one example of a non-Christian view. Pantheism says that God is identical with the world, thus expressing non-Christian immanence (corner 4). At the same time, pantheism implies that God is impersonal, so he (or rather it) ends up being distant and uninvolved in relation to the details of an individual's life. This feature of distance expresses non-Christian transcendence (corner 3).

Advocates of materialism do not believe in a personal God. But matter itself becomes the principal substitute for God. It imitates some of the features of God in being self-existent and virtually eternal. Matter is impersonal and thus uninvolved with persons. It thereby expresses non-Christian transcendence. It is also identical with the world, expressing non-Christian immanence.

In Frame's square, the diagonals of the square represent contradictions. The Christian view of transcendence in corner 1 contradicts the non-Christian view of immanence in corner 4. The Christian view of immanence in corner 2 contradicts the non-Christian view of transcendence in corner 3. These contradictions mean that non-Christians have a very different view of God, or of a God-substitute, than do Christians. They are trying to escape the claims of the true God.

Figure 2

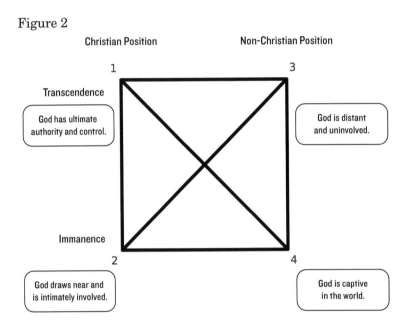

The horizontal lines in Frame's square represent similarities in language. A subtly crafted explanation of non-Christian transcendence in corner 3 can sound like the Christian view of transcendence in corner 1. Both can use the same words, such as *transcendence* or *exaltedness*. But the meanings differ. Similarly, an explanation of non-Christian immanence in corner 4 can sound like Christian immanence in corner 2. But the meanings differ.

What difference does it make? The Bible teaches that God is radically distinct from what he creates. He is eternal, while his creatures are not. He is all-powerful, while his creatures are not. The distinction between God the Creator and his creatures is a most basic metaphysical distinction. But Frame's square shows that non-Christians can misconstrue the distinction. They make plausible claims, and the claims can creep into the minds of Christians as well. Frame's square makes it plain that we must have the right *kind* of distinction between God and his creatures. The distinction affirms his authority and control; it does not imply that he is distant and uninvolved.

Epistemological Implications

As usual, metaphysics and epistemology (the nature of knowledge) go together. The metaphysical distinction between God and creation carries with it implications for how we think about knowledge, both knowledge of God and knowledge of the world.

A Christian naturally has a distinctive approach to knowledge because God is the primary knower. God knows himself completely: "All things have been handed over to me by my Father, and no one *knows* the Son except the Father, and no one *knows* the Father except the Son and anyone to whom the Son chooses to reveal him" (Matt. 11:27).

What about *human* knowledge? Human beings are created in the image of God:

> Then God said, "Let us make man *in our image, after our likeness.*" (Gen. 1:26)

> So God created man *in his own image,*
>   *in the image of God* he created him;
>   male and female he created them. (Gen. 1:27)

Human beings are intelligent, thinking creatures because God made them that way. Their thinking imitates God's thinking. But there is a difference. God is the original. His knowledge is infinite and unsearchable (Ps. 147:5; Isa. 40:28). Human knowledge is derivative and limited.

Human beings at their best imitate God by thinking God's thoughts after him. Any truth that we know, God knows first. Truth resides first of all in God's mind. He is the ultimate authority for knowledge because he is transcendent. And then, as a human being comes to know, what he knows reflects the truth of God. But that does not mean that the finite human mind becomes identical with God's infinity. People think God's thoughts after him *analogically*. Their thinking is analogous to God's because they are made in the image of God. But the analogy does not amount to identity.

Thus we have two levels of knowledge: God's knowledge and human knowledge.[3] Most philosophy has tackled the question of knowledge as if there were only one level. That disturbs the whole project and sets it off in a wrong direction.

Transcendence and Immanence in Knowledge

We may summarize the difference between Christian and non-Christian thinking about knowledge by using Frame's square again. This time, we ask what transcendence and immanence look like when we consider the issue of knowledge (see fig. 3).

The upper left-hand corner (1) summarizes the Christian view of God's transcendence. God's transcendence implies that he knows everything and that his knowledge is the standard for all knowledge. The lower left-hand corner (2) summarizes the Christian view of God's immanence. God through his presence, through the Holy Spirit, gives knowledge to people. This knowledge includes knowledge of God himself and of truths about the world, truths that God has established. Our knowledge can be true, even though it is derivative.

Now let us consider the right-hand side of the square. The upper right-hand corner (3) symbolizes the non-Christian view of God's transcendence. This view says that God is unknowable. The non-Christian view of God's immanence, in corner 4, says that we as human beings can serve as the ultimate standard for what can and cannot be the case, and for what counts as knowledge. God, if he exists and if we talk about him, must conform to our knowledge. Our knowledge is treated as if it were ultimate rather than derivative.

---

[3] Technically, we know that there is at least one other kind of knowledge—knowledge by angels and demons. We do not know much about this kind of knowledge—no more than what the Bible tells us. Since angels and demons are created by God, their knowledge is creaturely knowledge. As such, it is fundamentally like human knowledge, rather than like God's unique, original knowledge.

Figure 3

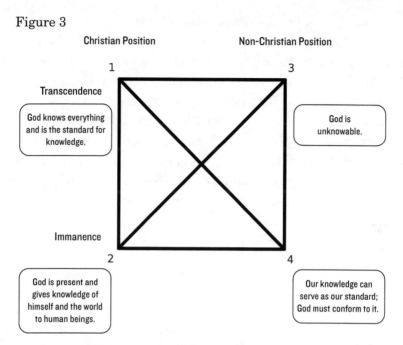

Christian Position

Non-Christian Position

1

Transcendence

God knows everything and is the standard for knowledge.

3

God is unknowable.

Immanence

2

God is present and gives knowledge of himself and the world to human beings.

4

Our knowledge can serve as our standard; God must conform to it.

As usual, the diagonals of the square indicate contradictions. The non-Christian view of immanence (corner 4) contradicts the Christian view of transcendence (corner 1). If we are the standard, that contradicts the idea that God is the standard. Similarly, the non-Christian view of transcendence (corner 3) contradicts the Christian view of immanence (corner 2). If God is unknowable (corner 3), that contradicts the Christian claim that he has actually made himself known to us (corner 2).

The horizontal sides of the square represent similarities. The non-Christian view of transcendence in corner 3 can *sound like* the Christian view of transcendence in corner 1. It can use the same word *transcendence*. Or it can say that God is *mysterious* and beyond comprehension. A Christian view can say the same thing. But the meanings are different on the two sides of the square. For a Christian view, not to *comprehend* God means that we do not understand him completely or understand him in the same way that he understands himself. But in a non-Christian view the ideas of incomprehensibility and mystery can be changed to imply that God is unknowable.

Similarly, the non-Christian view of immanence in corner 4 is similar to the Christian view of immanence in corner 2. Both sides would say that we have knowledge on which we rely. But in a non-Christian view this truth is distorted in order to infer that it is possible for us to function as our own ultimate standard.

Much grief in the history of philosophy could be avoided by keeping clear the distinction between these two ways of thinking. The distinction has relevance not only when we think about knowing God, but also when we think about knowing truths about the world. In both cases, our thinking and our knowledge should imitate God, but on a creaturely level, in which we acknowledge God's ultimacy (corner 1).

God Himself

Some people have worried about whether Frame's triad of lordship, by focusing on God's relation to man in covenant, does justice to God as he exists prior to human existence and prior to creation. When we discuss transcendence and immanence, the same question can arise. After all, the ideas of transcendence and immanence represent a way of condensing the meaning of God's lordship, and God's lordship comes to expression in covenantal relations between God and man.

When we focus on a covenant, we are focusing on *relations* between God and creatures, not simply God by himself. For example, transcendence occurs in the relationship between God and his creatures. God transcends creation. God exercises authority *over* creatures, so that his authority comes to expression in a relationship. Similarly, God exercises control over creatures, and his control over the world is also a form of relationship between him and creatures. Finally, God is immanent in creation, so immanence also expresses a relation between God and creation.

But God existed prior to creation. He did not have to create a world. God does not *need* a relationship to a created world in order to be God and to be complete. The reality of God's eternal existence leads us to ask what we can say about God in distinction from what we say about his relationships to us and to the world. In talking about God's relationship to us, have we really said anything about God as he really is? Or are we speaking *only* about God in his relations to us, which are clearly less ultimate than God himself?

In my opinion, this worry does not take into account the way perspectivalism works or the way that our knowledge of God works. The triad for lordship offers a perspective, or rather three interlocking perspectives, on who God is, as well as on his relations to us. Frame's triad for lordship reflects within divine-human relations the triunity of God. Or, to put it another way, through God's relationships to us we come to know him. How else would we know him, after all? A divinely given perspective on God gives us God, just as Christ's revelation of the Father gives us knowledge of the Father.

God is eternally triune. Having created the world and human beings in it, God now relates to mankind in accord with who God always was and is. For example, God's authority over us expresses in relation to us and the world the fact of God's absoluteness as moral standard, which is associated with the role of God the Father as source. God the Father is the authority to whom God the Son responds in love. God's authority has eternal reality and does not spring into being only at the point at which God creates the world.

Next, God's control over us expresses his omnipotence, which is a manifestation of the innate power of the eternal Word and the Holy Spirit. God's power exists eternally, not only in relation to us. By his power the Father eternally begets the Son.

God's presence with us expresses God's omnipresence, which has an eternal manifestation in the presence of the persons of the Trinity to one another (John 1:1), and this eternal presence among the persons of the Trinity is associated with the Holy Spirit. God the Father has always been authoritative, God the Son has always been all-powerful, and God has always been present to himself in the fellowship of the persons of the Trinity through the Holy Spirit.

In contemplating the aspects of lordship, we are therefore talking about God, and not merely a shadow of God suitable for creatures. In God's lordship we come to know him in his eternal

Trinitarian nature, which is authoritative, all-powerful, and all-present.

Suppose, on the contrary, someone theorizes that we know a shadow of God only, and not God himself. We know "God-in-his-condescension-to-us," which our theorist says is only a shadow of the real thing, the true God. If this theory were right, we would be idolaters, because we would be worshiping only a shadow. That consequence destroys the whole purpose of the Bible, which is to lead to us to know and worship the true God, not a substitute. The theory about a shadow of God represents a form of non-Christian transcendence.

On the other hand, another theorist may say that since we know God and our knowledge is genuine and is knowledge of who God really is, our knowledge of God is the same as God's knowledge of himself. Such a theory would then imply that our knowledge could serve for practical purposes as an ultimate standard. We would have fallen into a non-Christian concept of immanence.

Or a theorist could go in another direction and say that, since all we have as knowledge is knowledge of "God-in-his-condescension-to-us," we must use that knowledge *as if* it were ultimate. Once again the theorist gives us a non-Christian concept of immanence in which our knowledge for practical purposes functions as an ultimate standard. By suggesting that "all we have" is a fixed body of "knowledge" of "God-in-his-condescension-to-us," the theory may also covertly suggest that we do not have personal communion with God, but have only communion with this alleged body of "knowledge." The disappearance of communion with God represents a form of non-Christian transcendence, where God (that is, the God who actually exists, in distinction from the body of "knowledge") is distant.

We must avoid both traps, the trap of non-Christian transcendence and the trap of non-Christian immanence. Covenantal communion with God, in Christ through the Spirit, gives us knowledge that is in accord with our capacity. Our knowledge is not the final standard (Christian transcendence). But our knowledge of God is real (Christian immanence).

We know that God has authority, control, and presence, all of which reveal who he really is. We know because he has told us, and his communication, which the Holy Spirit empowers us to receive, *really tells the truth*, not merely a shadow of the truth. That truth telling is rooted in Christ, the eternal truth of God.[4]

According to the principle of divine transcendence, God calls us as creatures to submit to the truths that he has revealed. If we go beyond those truths by picturing for ourselves a god who is *other than* the kind of God that he himself has revealed, a god who is always hidden *behind* biblical revelation, or a god who is ultimately unknown, we are acting in rebellion against God. We are acting according to a non-Christian principle of immanence, in which we go our own way, however much we may try to persuade ourselves that we are honoring God's transcendence.

We can also fall into traps if we try to prioritize a few pieces of biblical revelation. A theorist could say, for example, that almost all the Bible is presenting God in his relationships to us, but that a few verses, perhaps John 1:1 and Exodus 3:14, or perhaps 1 Timothy 1:17, present us with God as he eternally exists. In reply, we may observe, first of all, that John 1:1 and Exodus 3:14 and any other "special" verses that a theory singles out are, like all the rest of Scripture, covenantal communication adapted to us, suited to our capacity as creatures. All of Scripture is suitable for us. The fact of being suitable reveals God's eternal wisdom. Suitability itself reveals God! We run the temptation of trying to pry behind that universal suitability when we single out a few verses. The singling out of these verses may suggest that those verses, and they alone, get us beyond the level of suitability.

This theory also tempts us to fall into non-Christian immanence with respect to the few verses, because the theory proposes that in the few verses we obtain a more exalted knowledge that functions to control the rest of Scripture. The theory also falls into non-Christian transcendence with respect to all the other verses, because it implies that the other verses are "merely" suitable and do not give us the ultimate form of knowledge, "real" knowledge.

---

[4] See Frame, *Doctrine of the Knowledge of God*, 32–33.

God allegedly remains "hidden," "distant," behind the texts because of their being merely "suitable."

Second, when we single out a few verses, we run the temptation of depreciating the knowledge that God gives us through many other verses. (We thereby fall into non-Christian transcendence, where we undermine confidence in knowledge of God.) We may overlook or depreciate the fact that God's relationship to us through any verse that he speaks to us gives us knowledge of God, not merely knowledge of our relationship or knowledge of a "god-in-relationship." "And this is eternal life, that they *know* you the only true God, and Jesus Christ whom you have sent" (John 17:3). We know God through Christ. Christ incarnate is the ultimate "perspective" through whom we know God. Through covenant and through a relationship to God in Christ, we know him.

Mystery

Before leaving the subject of epistemology, we should underline one further difference between a Christian approach and a secular philosophical approach. According to a Christian viewpoint, our knowledge always involves personal interaction with God. We are never masters of the process. Because God plays a leading role in our knowledge, and because our knowledge of God involves mystery, *all* our knowledge includes mystery at every point. Only God's knowledge of himself is nonmysterious. Historically, Western philosophy has striven for complete transparency, complete mastery, and absence of mystery. Underneath the surface, it has desired godlike knowledge—virtually to be God. That is one echo of the fall of man, in that he desired to "be like God, knowing good and evil" (Gen. 3:5).

9

Perspectives on the World

We may now turn to consider perspectives on the world. As we have observed, every human being brings to bear one or more perspectives on the world. There are multiple perspectives because there are multiple human beings. And, apart from sin, this multiplicity reflects God's original design. God endorses it.

God's Ruling by Speaking

We may refine our ideas by thinking about what the Bible says about God's creating the world and governing it providentially. We will again build on work already done, this time in my book *Redeeming Science*. As indicated there, creation and providence take place by God's speaking. For example, "God said, 'Let there be light,' and there was light" (Gen. 1:3). God's speech specifies everything. He specifies that certain things will exist: light, the expanse of heaven, the sea, the dry land, the plants, and so on. He also specifies *how* they will exist. The plants will grow on the land. They will reproduce "according to their own kinds" (Gen. 1:12). Providentially, he specifies the coming of snow and ice and their melting:

> He sends out *his command* to the earth;
>   *his word* runs swiftly.
> He gives snow like wool;
>   he scatters frost like ashes.

He hurls down his crystals of ice like crumbs;
  who can stand before his cold?
He sends out *his word*, and melts them;
  he makes his wind blow and the waters flow.
    (Ps. 147:15–18)

God specifies everything: "he upholds the universe by the *word* of his power" (Heb. 1:3).

We do not directly hear the words that God sends out to command the world of nature. *Some* of his words are recorded in Genesis 1, but this is only a sample and a summary. Clearly there is much more than what the Bible records.

The Bible also indicates that God has words to say to us as human beings. The Bible presents his words in written form.[1] God had them written down with the purpose that he would still speak to us as we read Scripture today: "For whatever was written in former days was written for *our* instruction, that through endurance and through the encouragement of the Scriptures *we* might have hope" (Rom. 15:4). All of what the Bible says informs us about the world. What it says is true, because God is truthful. But that is not all. The Bible's speech is *definitive* for the world, because God's speech is original and superior to the world that he created.

Multiperspectival Metaphysical Reality

The entire Bible, then, is God's communication to us concerning what the world is and how it is. It is God's own metaphysical statement. We ought not to equate God's word to us in the Bible with God's words of command that control the entire universe. But the one is akin to the other. Both are authoritative. The multidimensional character of what the Bible says suggests that God's word governing the universe is also multidimensional. It specifies and defines many dimensions to reality, not just one.

If we are not convinced by this comparison between the Bible and God's words of command to creation, we can consider another route to the same conclusion. We can know God; we can understand

---

[1] See especially John M. Frame, *The Doctrine of the Word of* God (Phillipsburg, NJ: P&R, 2010).

him. But we cannot *comprehend* him in this full sense of the word *comprehend* (see chap. 8). Our inability to comprehend God suggests also our inability to comprehend God's word governing the universe. If we are not going to comprehend it, how may we nevertheless get a reasonable understanding of it, short of comprehension? How would we understand without knowing God?

We cannot; we must know God. And how may we best know God, if not through the way of Christ, as Christ speaks to us in the Scripture? Scripture is our natural instructor as to the metaphysics of the world, since the metaphysics of the world is completely determined and specified by God's speech governing the world, and his speech takes place in Christ the Word (John 1:1).

We may proceed still another way. The archetype for truth is in the mind of God. God knows all truth. In addition, Christ is the truth (John 14:6). When Christ says that he is the truth, the immediate context has a focus on redemptive truth. Christ is "the way, and the truth, and the life" (John 14:6), where the terms *way* and *life* deal with the way to redemption and fellowship with God. And in this verse the life of which Christ speaks is the eternal life in communion with God.

But truth in redemptive focus has a close relationship to all truth whatsoever. Christ and the Spirit mediate the truth. Christ as Creator of the world, in fellowship with the Father, is the source of all truth whatsoever. We know Christ through multiple perspectives, as is illustrated by the four Gospels and by the multiple analogies instructing us about God and about the Trinitarian character of God. Hence we always receive the truth multiperspectivally. God expresses the truth multiperspectivally, because he has one complete, unified body of knowledge as known by the Father, the Son, and the Holy Spirit.

We conclude, therefore, that the metaphysics of the world is just what the Bible says, in all its multiple genres, multiple subject matters, multiple discussions of these multiple subject matters, and multiple paragraphs, which interlock with multiple human beings, whom the Bible presents with multiple opinions and multiple points of view (not all of which, of course, are approved by God!).

The world is incredibly rich! Enjoy it! Praise God for everything! Praise him for what you see and hear and experience, not only as you read or listen to the Bible, but in all your experience. God makes your experience just what it is in all its richness and in all its uniqueness as *your* experience. At the same time, you can appreciate other people's experiences as you interact with them and to a degree share experiences because they have resonances and similarities with your own.

We are all made in the image of God. Enjoy it! Bask in it! The experience is going to be so much more enjoyable, of course, the richer your fellowship is with God himself, who is the archetype, the source of all wisdom, joy, richness, and beauty that we experience. God is also the providential sustainer, who gives us our own life, each one of us, day by day.

When we describe this experience of interaction with the world, we presuppose that we have first of all experienced redemption through Christ. "You must be born again" (John 3:7). Unbelievers, as we have said, experience many blessings through common grace. But they are missing the heart of it all. God designed us for fellowship with him. "Our hearts are restless till they find their rest in You."[2]

We find rest in a life renewed by the Spirit, forgiven of sin, and restored to fellowship with God. Then we can look at the world with clear eyes. It is wonderful in the richness of its structure. God displays his wisdom again and again in this richness. He made a rich world, a multidimensional world, reflecting the archetypal richness that is himself. The world is beautiful because God is beautiful.

Science as Ultimate?

What about science? Does science give us a more ultimate view of the world? Hundreds of years ago, people may have felt a fascination for philosophies that claimed to get down to the bottom of the world. Now, in the mainstream of modern culture, our fascination

---

[2] St. Augustine, *The Confessions of St. Augustine*, 1.1.1, in *A Select Library of the Nicene and Post-Nicene Fathers of the Christian Church*, ed. Philip Schaff (Grand Rapids: Eerdmans, 1979), 1:45.

is with science. Science, it is thought, digs down to the inner structure of the world. It gets us to the bottom of things, or at least close
to the bottom.

For example, some people confidently tell us that the table in
front of us is not *really* solid, but mostly empty space, with nuclei
and electrons flitting around. The sun does not really move in the
sky, but the earth spins and goes round the sun. The rainbow is
not really the colors we see, but physical phenomena involving
the refraction of electromagnetic radiation of different frequen-
cies through liquid drops of dihydrogen oxide (commonly known
as water).

In reply, we can observe that sciences give us perspectives. Often
science supplies multiple perspectives even within a single field. As-
tronomers, for instance, can make calculations about relative positions of planets starting either from the earth or from the sun as an
origin for their mathematical calculations. Or they may start from
the moon or from Mars. Anyone who knows how the mathematics
works knows that it will come out with the same results from each
of these starting points, because they are related to one another by
transformations of coordinates.[3] The calculations may sometimes
be easier with one choice or another as a starting point, depending
on the type of calculation. One may choose one's perspective.

God's coherence, along with the derivative coherence that he
specifies by his word of command, guarantees the coherence of the
perspectivally related points of view. The coherence is beautiful,
and any one perspective offered in science is beautiful in reflecting
the wisdom of God. Together, the different perspectives are like different facets in a jewel. People rightly have a fascination with and
admiration for science, because at its best it reflects and displays
God's wisdom and magnificence.

Science at its best means thinking God's thoughts after him,
particularly those thoughts of his that lead to his words governing
aspects of the created world. In this process, it is *we* who are doing

---

[3] To obtain the full power of the system of transformations, one must make the transition to Ein-
stein's general theory of relativity, which allows systems of coordinates accelerated with respect to
one another. See Vern S. Poythress, *Redeeming Science: A God-Centered Approach* (Wheaton, IL:
Crossway, 2006), 218.

the thinking. Science supplements rather than undermines the ordinary world of experience, because God has given us the ordinary world *as well as* the technical details and technical expositions of science. The technical explanation supplies us with additional layers of rich wonders, about which we did not know just from ordinary casual observation with our own eyes. They are indeed wonderful, marvelous, and beautiful, displaying the wonders of the wisdom and power and beauty of God.

But in idolatry we may find ourselves carried away in the wrong direction by the wonder and amazement of it all. And so we give praise to science and scientific explanations, as if these were themselves the gods who made the world. They are not. The real God who made it, designed it so that we could see rainbows and see the sun move in the sky. He also gave us the pleasures of exploration and discovery of more dimensions, such as when we mathematically view the earth from the standpoint of the sun as center. These matters are discussed more thoroughly elsewhere.[4]

Previous generations may have been more likely to think that some philosopher or philosophy has gotten to the bottom of the world. A particular philosophy provided an attractive, plausible explanation that seemed to be more ultimate and more "solid" than the changing and sometimes confusing world of ordinary experience. The plausibility and attractiveness come from a perspective. For example, some philosophers have compared the world to a living organism. And the Bible itself, using the poetry of personification, indicates that there are some analogies here. But the analogies with life and with organisms are only one dimension. They go back to an origin in God, who is the living God, and whose life is reflected in the changes he brings about in the world, including the processes in living things.

Empiricist philosophy says that the "bottom" of the world is sense experience. Is that right? It is a perspective. We receive our daily experience in the context of sounds and sights and tastes and touches. Those are some of the dimensions of the world, and the Bible talks about them. But when the Bible speaks of them, it tells

---

[4] Ibid., chaps. 15–16.

of their connections with many other dimensions as well. We do not merely hear a sound; we hear a person telling us something. We do not merely see a red blotch; we see a rose. The person's words and the red rose are real. God governs them, and he gives us just the experience that we are having, day by day.

But what about dreams and optical illusions? Are they an exception? God who rules everything is also the one who gives people whatever dreams and optical illusions they experience. Their experience is "real" experience. But of course it has a different relation to other people than does normal waking experience. God has made dreams to *be* dreams, in distinction from waking experience, and gives us the wisdom to understand the difference. And there are all kinds of dreams, only some of which we remember when we wake. Extraordinary experiences, along with "normal" experiences, are all part of the richness of a world that reflects God's wisdom and glory.

Reductionism

Both modern science and ancient philosophy, when taken as ultimate descriptions, give us forms of reductionism. They *reduce* the world to sense experience, or to matter and motion, or to some other dimension out of the world in its totality. When people use modern science this way, it becomes *scientism*, a total worldview. It becomes like a religion, because people have faith in it and give their ultimate commitment to an idea. They think that scientific explanations offer not only one dimension but an ultimate description, "the bottom" layer of the world.

Both scientism and most kinds of secular philosophy *reduce* the world to one dimension of the whole. They treat all the other aspects as either unreal or derivative. But reductionism is poverty stricken, not only in its threadbare endpoint consisting of one dimension, but also in its explanatory power. Where do the other dimensions come from, if we assume that they are ultimately unreal? The explanations always end up presupposing that we know about these other dimensions.

As an example, consider how people attempt to reduce life to matter and motion. Living things consist of cells, and cells consist of molecules, and molecules consist of atoms, and atoms consist of protons, neutrons, and electrons (and in the latest theory, protons and neutrons consist of quarks). So it all "reduces" to matter and the laws of motion. Or does it? God does govern the electrons and the atoms and the molecules. That is wonderful, and we may use that level as a perspective. But when we use it as a perspective on life, we already know intuitively how to distinguish life from nonlife. And we do not make the distinction merely by inspecting the atoms!

We understand life partly with reference to purposes and functions that keep cells and organisms alive—metabolism, cell division, information processing (in DNA and protein manufacture), signaling between cells, signaling within one cell. Decades ago Michael Polanyi pointed out that we cannot understand a machine or a living thing only by chemical and physical analysis, because such analysis, though wonderful on its own level, never includes insights as to whether the machine is broken or intact, functioning or nonfunctioning.[5] Often without consciously realizing it, biologists are constantly using ideas about purpose and function that in fact cannot be "reduced" to chemistry. God by his wisdom has specified coherence between the chemistry and the distinctly biological functions in cells.

In reductionistic explanations one dimension has become a substitute god. It, rather than God, explains the richness of the world. But that is fanciful. If we deduce richness from one dimension, it is because secretly our knowledge of other dimensions has already seen traces of them reflected in the one with which we started. We are using one dimension *as a perspective*. It is insightful; but it is not "ultimate," as if it disqualifies all other perspectives.

---

[5] Michael Polanyi, *Personal Knowledge: Towards a Post-Critical Philosophy* (Chicago: University of Chicago Press, 1958), 328–31. What is true of machines is true also of living things, in that they contain molecular machines within their cells. But living things show organic development, unlike mechanical machines. So it is even harder to explain living things on the basis of chemistry alone than to explain mechanical machines on the basis of chemistry.

Flight from God

Scientism and secular philosophy nevertheless attract people. Why? They seem to give explanations, as we have said. One substitute or another offers the only plausible way of doing an ultimate explanation without appealing to a personal God. And in sin we do not want a personal God, the God of the Bible, because he holds us morally responsible and we are guilty before him.

Secret Knowledge

Scientism and secular philosophy can also be attractive because they allegedly offer forms of *secret* knowledge. When scientists and philosophers write books, their knowledge is no longer completely secret. But it is still inaccessible except to the initiate. Advanced science requires prolonged study and training and considerable intellectual skill. Study of philosophy also requires intellectual interest and aptitude. A person's feeling that he understands what a philosopher says gives him a sense of superiority to most of the world.

Pride is a widespread human sin. In one sense, we can view it as the root of all sins: Adam and Eve showed pride in their own judgment when they preferred to eat the fruit of the forbidden tree rather than trust what God said. Pride is close to self-centeredness, in which each of us becomes his own ultimate god. Intellectual pride is one form of pride, tempting particularly to intellectuals and those with intellectual gifts. The smart person finds that he is able to understand sciences or philosophy, and such understanding gives him a position superior to everyone else—the rabble who live in the gutters of life by not lifting up their faces to see the profound truths that he has seen. Ah, the glory of it.

But of course it is a false glory. If the smart person sees a truth that others do not, it is because God has gifted him with being smart, and with being in circumstances that give him access to the truth. In addition, God in common grace has sent his Holy Spirit actually to give the truth (Job 32:8). There is nothing for anyone to boast of (1 Cor. 4:7; Eph. 2:9). Yet we do it. Sin is rooted in us. And

so are pride, and selfishness, and uglier things still. No one wants
to think about such unpleasantness if he can avoid it.

Secret knowledge, then, has a terrible attraction. And what
about the Bible? The Bible is not secret. God had it written for ordinary people, not just for the learned. Ordinary people, including
weak, poor, and thoroughly unintelligent people, have believed it
and placed their faith in Christ. The well-bred person might think,
What a lot of despicable ignoramuses and weaklings these Christians are! But God hates human pride, and he bars the door to the
proud. He saves the weak and the ignoble, partly to bring disgrace
to those who think they are too good for this "ignorant" religion:

> For since, in the wisdom of God, the world did not know God
> through wisdom, it pleased God through the folly of what we
> preach to save those who believe. For Jews demand signs and
> Greeks seek wisdom, but we preach Christ crucified, a stum-
> bling block to Jews and folly to Gentiles, but to those who are
> called, both Jews and Greeks, Christ the power of God and the
> wisdom of God. For the foolishness of God is wiser than men,
> and the weakness of God is stronger than men.
>
> For consider your calling, brothers: not many of you were
> wise according to worldly standards, not many were powerful,
> not many were of noble birth. But God chose what is foolish in
> the world to shame the wise; God chose what is weak in the
> world to shame the strong; God chose what is low and despised
> in the world, even things that are not, to bring to nothing things
> that are, so that no human being might boast in the presence of
> God. And because of him you are in Christ Jesus, who became
> to us wisdom from God, righteousness and sanctification and
> redemption, so that, as it is written, "Let the one who boasts,
> boast in the Lord." (1 Cor. 1:21–31)

Open Truth

Would it not be interesting if God gave us the Bible so that weak
and ignorant people, by reading it and trusting in him through
Christ, could know the deepest nature of the world? They could
know that the world is a multidimensional creation of God. What

if, contrary to human expectations, God left behind in the darkness those who in their pride cannot bring themselves to believe that the truth about the world could be so open?

"Would it not be interesting?" I ask. But it is not only "interesting." In fact, God has brought it to pass in one fundamental sense. Philosophy, we have said, seeks wisdom. God has made Christ our wisdom (1 Cor. 1:30). Do you want to know the secret of the universe? Come to Christ "to reach all the riches of full assurance of understanding and the knowledge of God's mystery, which is Christ, in whom are hidden *all the treasures* of wisdom and knowledge" (Col. 2:2–3).

"It cannot possibly be that easy," people may say. In fact, it is not easy for any of us to come to Christ and give up our pride. It is "impossible with man," as Jesus says (Luke 18:27), because human pride gets in the way. "Truly, I say to you, the tax collectors and the prostitutes go into the kingdom of God before you" (Matt. 21:31).

10

Perspectives through Language

Philosophy, we have said, explores "big" questions. One direction in which exploration can take place is through the attempt to produce very general statements about the nature of the world. Philosophy becomes a generalizing operation. We can see this tendency in the metaphysical work of Aristotle, who considered the question of "being as such." What is "being as such"? It could mean that we try to find the most general characteristics or deepest characteristics that are common to everything that exists. That search leads easily to attempts to make very general statements.

The One and the Many in Categories

Several difficulties surround these attempts. One of the most basic difficulties about generalizing arises from the equal ultimacy of the one and the many. The theme of one and many is closely related to unity and diversity, which we discussed earlier (chap. 4). (We build here on Cornelius Van Til, who drew attention to the problem, and later works in the Van Tilian tradition.) Any general category, such as the category of horses, involves an interlocking of one and many. The one is the general category, namely, all horses together, or the species of horse. The many are the many horses that exist, whether now or in the past or the future. God ordains both the one and the many and their relation to one another in this world.[1] So the decision to give priority to the one—the generalization—already distorts the character of the world that God created.

The difficulty also has a practical side. In practice, we learn about what a horse is by discussions that may refer to particular examples of horse, and we learn about particular horses partly by classifying the individual examples as belonging to the category *horse*. To confine ourselves just to general statements makes things pedagogically difficult. And we may not really be sure what we mean, because a general category without ties to examples is not stable. We may try to evade the difficulty by defining our new general category using other generalizing words. But then these other words are either tied to examples or defined in terms of still other words, and so on. We cannot permanently escape the need for particulars—that is, for examples.

The history of metaphysics has included many cases where part of the key to the project is the use of specially selected general categories. These general categories, it is hoped, offer an insight into the "deep" structure of the world. They claim to offer a kind of ultimate, foundational analysis of what things are like. Aristotle offered one such analysis in his book *The Categories*. According to Aristotle, everything not composite (decomposable into separate parts) is (1) substance or (2) quantity or (3) quality or (4) a relation or (5) where or (6) when or (7) posture or (8) state or (9) action or (10) being affected.[2]

Aristotle works out his analysis as a prelude to fitting the categories into propositions. Propositions are simple assertions consisting of subject plus predicate, like "Socrates is a man," or "All

---

[1] See Vern S. Poythress, *Logic: A God-Centered Approach to the Foundation of Western Thought* (Wheaton, IL: Crossway, 2013), chap. 16.

[2] "Each uncombined word or expression means one of the followings things:—what (or Substance), how large (that is, Quantity), what sort of thing (that is, Quality), related to what (or Relation), where (that is, Place), when (or Time), in what attitude (Posture, Position), how circumstanced (State or Condition), how active, what doing (or Action), how passive, what suffering (Affection). Examples, to speak but in outline, of Substance are 'man' and 'a horse,' of Quantity 'two cubits long,' 'three cubits in length' and the like, of Quality 'white' and 'grammatical.' Terms such as 'half,' 'double,' 'greater' are held to denote a Relation. 'In the market-place,' 'in the Lyceum' and similar phrases mean Place, while Time is intended by phrases like 'yesterday,' 'last year' and so on. 'Is lying' or 'sitting' means Posture, 'is shod' or 'is armed' means a State. 'Cuts' or 'burns,' again, indicates Action, 'is cut' or 'is burnt' an Affection" (Aristotle, *The Categories: On Interpretation*, trans. Harold P. Cooke, [Cambridge: Harvard University Press, 1962], 1b25–2a4).

dogs are animals." These propositions in turn form the building blocks for syllogistic reasoning. Aristotle's version of logic heavily influences what he thinks is most basic about the world.

Simplifications in Aristotle

Aristotle's logic and his categories constitute a reduction. The complexities of communication in language have to be pruned down. This pruning is evident in the focus on one type of sentence form, namely, a simple clause consisting of a subject, a linking verb (*is*), and a predicate expression. What about whole paragraphs and discourses, where people develop their thinking in richer ways? What about complex sentences? What about single-clause sentences that have several pieces (for example, bitransitive clauses such as "Sue gave the gift to Cheryl")? If we follow Aristotle, we are leaving these complexities aside. The simple clauses are supposed to have the form "A is B," or maybe "All A's are B's." In addition, to function within a syllogism, the terms, such as *man*, *dog*, and *animal*, have to have stable single meanings. They must be used *univocally*. When we add this requirement, the difficulties multiply, because natural languages have flexible vocabulary.

Here again we can build on work already in place. The difficulties with postulating perfectly univocal meaning are discussed in my book *Logic*.[3] These difficulties are related to the attempt to reduce language down to a skeletal structure. Such a reduction offers a kind of perspective on language.

The Word *Horse* as a Perspective

We can illustrate the perspectival character of the process by using the example of the word *horse*. This word can be used in a loose sense by ordinary people. It can also be used in a more technical sense, as a synonym for the more precise biological designation of a particular subspecies of animal, namely, *Equus ferus caballus*, the domestic horse. Thus we have at least two distinct uses of the

---

[3] Poythress, *Logic*, especially chaps. 15–23.

word *horse*. It is up to us which we choose to use at a particular time. Each offers a perspective.

Some people might think that they can avoid perspectives and reach pure objectivity through science, which develops the technical meaning of the word *horse* as a species. The species *Equus ferus* includes wild horses, since these can interbreed with domestic horses. Thus, we already confront complexity. Because of the possibility of interbreeding, the differentiation between domestic horses and wild horses is not perfectly stable. We can also wonder what to do about horses with physical defects, or horse embryos, or defective embryos that miscarry, or genetically engineered horses whose DNA may have special elements not found elsewhere in the natural breeding-horse population. The boundaries of what counts as a *horse* are still not perfectly precise. But, ignoring these difficulties, we can claim to have a precisely defined word *horse*.

How did we achieve this precision? We achieved it using lots of words. The precisely defined version of the word *horse* functions not in pristine isolation, but as a kind of condensed, one-word symbol that tells us through a contextual specification that it is equivalent in meaning to *Equus ferus caballus*. This longer Latin expression is in turn not self-sufficient in pure isolation from the rest of language. It tells us to go look at a paragraph-long definition, or a book-long discussion of *Equus ferus caballus*. The precision and stability of the word *horse* have been produced by using a lot of words, and a lot of multidimensional communication among horse specialists, and communication among scientists studying biological taxonomy, physiology, DNA sequencing, and so on.

The word *horse* functions like a perspective on this larger body of knowledge. This larger body of knowledge can also be viewed as offering a kind of perspective on horses. When we learn this body of knowledge, we have resources for seeing horses in new ways.

Now suppose that we use the word *horse* not in a technically precise way, but in a more ordinary way. The word can be considered to offer a trail of meaning leading out into practical experiences with horses, horse trainers, horse veterinarians, horse breeders, and language-using discussions of breeds of horses, caring for horses, raising horses, and so on.

Meanings are complicated. The idea of having a pure, isolated meaning that is perfectly stable is an ideal. We can receive perspectival insight by starting with a single word. But if we look carefully at what we are doing, we use relationships between meanings. The ideal of an isolated meaning, if taken to be a deep clue to the nature of the world, is an illusion. Philosophers and philosophical discussions can easily fall victim to this illusion, because they want deep truth that can be perfectly mastered in isolation. From the standpoint of such philosophical desire for mastery, the real world and ordinary language about the world are incredibly "messy" and impossibly complex.

I am saying that the world is complex, and language is complex, because God made it so. If we try to simplify, we are leaving something out. If we admit to ourselves that we are leaving a lot out, we may still achieve something by using a perspective. But desire for mastery of knowledge easily seduces us into thinking that our perspective or our insight is uniquely deep.

We can put it another way. God gave us language, and language is complex. God himself speaks to himself in language in John 17, where the Son speaks to the Father. So, in the context of God's speaking, language is in fact infinitely rich in meaning. This infinite richness has its origin in God's speaking. We as human beings reflect the richness on a finite level when we communicate because God created us in his image.

Here we can build on work already done on language.[4] Language reflects the character of God and Trinitarian structure *all the way down*. Both the complexities of human communication, complexities of long discourses, and the seeming simplicity of a single word reflect Trinitarian mystery. The persons of the Trinity indwell one another in what is called *coinherence*. Ectypal images of coinherence occur throughout language. One piece does not exist in perfect isolation from the rest.

---

[4] Vern S. Poythress, *In the Beginning Was the Word: Language—A God-Centered Approach* (Wheaton, IL: Crossway, 2009).

In the reality of God's purposes, words and categories have richness to them. A philosopher may desire to have a perfect, self-sufficient philosophical category that penetrates to the deep structure of being. That very desire cuts against the grain of what the world in fact is. From such desire arise some of the failures and reductionistic moves in the process of trying to have perfectly stable categories.

Categories in natural language will disappoint philosophical desire in several ways: (1) In their meanings they have attachments to analogies, rather than being purely univocal. (2) The unity of one category interlocks with the diversity of examples and instances illustrating the category. (3) Meaning is stable, but not perfectly stable, because there are fuzzy edges and vaguenesses. (4) Form (including sound, written form, and grammatical form) and meaning interlock. (5) Meaning is colored by the context of a larger discourse, and by the larger human context of human actions and their environment. (6) Meaning is colored by the persons who are involved in communication. (7) Meaning is colored by religious commitment—whether a person is regenerate or unregenerate.[5]

The Precision in Technical Terms in Science

People might wonder whether the development of technically precise terms in science represents an exception to the principles I have just enumerated. The expression *Equus ferus caballus* represents one such technical term. The term *oxygen* as a name for a chemical element is another, as are terms like *force* and *acceleration* in physics. In responding to such developments, we may note several points, corresponding to the complexities enumerated in the previous paragraph.

First, scientists still use analogies. Scientific models are a form of analogy. And when difficulties or anomalies appear, the flexibility that remains in the analogies can help progress.

Second, the one and the many go together. Scientists intend

---

[5] Poythress, *Logic*, chaps. 15–21.

their generalizations to apply to specific cases. Apart from specific cases, whether specific experiments or specific evidence from the past or hypothetical cases that can at least be pictured in thought experiments, the generalizations are empty.

Third, even with the added precision of technical scientific terms, a careful inspection shows vaguenesses in meaning. For example, the technical label *Equus ferus caballus* for the subspecies of domestic horse leaves vague the boundary between a domestic horse and a wild horse, and between a normal horse and a defective horse. We can imagine a horse-like creature that becomes so defective in so many respects that we hesitate about whether it is still unambiguously a horse.

Fourth, without form, we have no words. Not only ordinary words but technical words and technical expressions depend on unity of form and meaning for their recognition and their use. What use is it to have a technical term *force* unless it has a spelling and a sound so that we can use it in a sentence?

Fifth, meaning is colored by a larger context of discourses. Once we think about it, this truth is particularly prominent in the case of technical scientific terms. Scientists develop technically precise terms in interaction with extended experiments and theoretical reflections. The terms owe their precision to extended human work, involving lots of thinking and lots of words. The terms are in a sense isolated from everyday use. But this very position of isolation is produced by means of a lot of words and a lot of thinking and a lot of experimental interaction. And the meanings cannot really be learned and understood adequately by apprentices apart from more words and more human conversation and more thinking and more interaction with the world. Thus the words function *within* a larger scientific context that sustains their precision and "isolation." Paradoxically, the so-called isolation of these meanings is isolation by means of a rich context of meaning.

Sixth, the personal purposes of the scientists are always involved. It takes persons to teach the next generation of scientists. Michael Polanyi was particularly effective in drawing attention to the personal dimension of scientific knowledge and scientific practice.[6]

Seventh, religious commitment colors scientific knowledge. Non-Christians often regard scientific laws as impersonal mechanisms. A Christian knows that scientific research involves thinking God's thoughts after him analogically, and that our human formulations approximate the word of God controlling the world.[7]

The process of forming technical terms, as mentioned in the fifth point, is particularly important. It takes time, effort, and significant interaction with details about the world to develop workable technical terms that have practical value in science. Up until the twentieth century, philosophers too often felt that they could achieve their goal if they just thought hard enough and clearly enough. In reply, we may observe that God was not compelled to create the world in just the way that we find it. He exercised creativity. And that creativity implies that we must go out and look at the world, and dig about, rather than just relying on reasoning out what *must* be the case. The world has plenty of surprises.

Among the surprises, for example, has been the rise of the theory of relativity and quantum theory in twentieth-century physics. Both theories had the effect of overthrowing what many physicists and metaphysicians thought must be the "ultimate" structure of the world. By and large, nineteenth-century physicists construed the world in terms of an ultimate structure of absolute time, absolute space, and absolute particles with absolutely fixed motions and energies. None of those aspects of their vision have matched the twentieth-century developments.

Some twentieth- and twenty-first-century philosophers have tried to learn a lesson from this. They have interacted with scientific developments. This is good, but science is a vast enterprise. It involves vast institutions, vast amounts of human interaction, vast amounts of assumptions and rules of thumb and techniques and personal motivations passed on from generation to generation. At

---

[6] Michael Polanyi, *Personal Knowledge: Towards a Post-Critical Philosophy* (Chicago: University of Chicago Press, 1958).
[7] Vern S. Poythress, *Redeeming Science: A God-Centered Approach* (Wheaton, IL: Crossway, 2006), chap. 1.

its best, it is rich. And the construal of its meanings is rich. Scientists themselves, as well as philosophers of science, can easily be reductionistic when they reflect on this richness. Philosophers who try to get to the "bottom" of the nature of the world inevitably bring personal perspectives to bear. And multiple philosophers generate multiple perspectives. The same holds true when scientists philosophize about the meaning of their discipline and its insights.

Perspectives on Grammar

The Trinitarian substructure of language extends not only to the meaning of individual words, but to grammar as well.[8] Grammar has contrast, variation, and distribution, in imitation of the Trinitarian character of God.

Aristotelian logic presupposed that a clause structure of the form "A is B" (as exemplified by "dogs are mammals") was the simplest, and treated it as the "bottom." We can observe that at this level of clause, the clause types can function as perspectives on one another. "The Father loves the Son," from John 3:35, is an instance of a transitive clause. Transitive clauses have their archetype in Trinitarian love. But we can also turn the expressions around. "The Father is a person who loves the Son." That new expression has the grammatical form "A is B." Or we can consider the expression "Let us think about the Father's love for the Son." The expression "The Father's love for the Son" is a phrase rather than a clause. Or consider the statement, "God is loving." That general statement is climactically embodied in the fact that the Father loves the Son. Or consider the statement "God is love" (1 John 4:8, 16). That statement too needs to be interpreted in the context of our knowledge that the Father loves the Son (see also 1 John 4:9–21).

As I will show later in a discussion of the "theophanic analogy" for the Trinity (see appendix B), the Holy Spirit can be closely associated with one or another distinct attribute of God. This principle includes the attribute of love. The Holy Spirit is the Spirit of love:

---

[8] Poythress, *In the Beginning Was the Word*, chap. 31.

God's *love* has been poured into our hearts through the Holy Spirit who has been given to us. (Rom. 5:5)

For you did not receive the spirit of slavery to fall back into fear, but you have received the Spirit of adoption as sons, by whom we cry, "Abba! Father!" (Rom. 8:15)

Since God adopts us as sons through the Spirit, he includes us by grace as objects of love, in analogy with the love that the Father has for his Son.

Moreover, since in John 3:34–35 the gift of the Spirit from the Father to the Son is *the* focal manifestation of the Father's love, we may virtually say that the Spirit is the love of the Father.

By taking all these expressions together, we may see first that love is rooted in the Trinitarian character of God. Second, God's expression of love to us, our reception of his love, and our experience of his love in our lives take place in a manner consistent with and structured by his Trinitarian character, as well as in harmony with the accomplishment of redemption in time and space through the work of Christ. Third, the various grammatical expressions used to express the meaning of God's love interlock with one another. All the grammatical forms have Trinitarian roots. All exist in relation to one another. We may conclude that Aristotle's preference for the form "A is B" gives us only one perspective out of many.

We may remember also the principle that the one and the many interlock and come together in all our knowledge. That is, we know each individual horse (the many) against the background of some knowledge of the general category "horse" (the one), and vice versa. Likewise, we know the meaning of the general clause structure "A is B" (the one) against the background of numerous instances (the many) where we meet that same grammatical structure. Among these instances, the truths about God have the primacy, because he is the original. A truth like "God is love" thus offers a foundation for all the particular truths of the form "A is B" that speak about the created world.

"A is B" is not transparent to human understanding. Rather, it manifests both the character of God, who gave us language, and the character of the Trinity, which is the archetype on which language as we experience it is based. More specifically, it reflects the pattern that finds its origination in God, in truths such as "God is love."

In a similar manner, God's own nature in the Trinity offers the final foundation for language and grammatical forms of other kinds, not just "A is B."

"In the beginning was the *Word*, and the Word was with God, and the Word was God" (John 1:1). This mystery is profound. We will never comprehend God. Derivatively, the mystery of language is profound, and we will never comprehend it.

Conclusion about Metaphysics

We should not be seduced by reductionistic explanations, whether they come from the lips of scientists or from philosophers. In Christ lie "hidden all the treasures of wisdom and knowledge" (Col. 2:3). True human wisdom exults in enjoying him and enjoying a world rich in reflections of divine wisdom and divine mystery. Christ the Logos, the Word of God, expresses himself in the divine words specifying fully the very nature of the world. That specification has a richness that surpasses what we understand as we look at the richness of natural language. The Bible, by giving us the very language of God, gives us the true metaphysics.

If we consider philosophy and metaphysics to be related primarily to later human reflections, we may say that philosophy is theology (as John Frame has indicated). Theology, as the application of the Bible's teaching, supplies what we need to know about the big questions.

Implications for Theology

Our view of metaphysics has implications for how we do theology. Theology through the ages has often appropriated material from philosophy. Does this appropriation create difficulties?

Philosophical Baggage

Because of God's gift of common grace, unbelieving philosophers may still give us valuable insights. But they may also give us baggage bound up with a philosophical system constructed in rebellion against God. Their system may involve reductionisms or implicit claims for the ultimacy of a single perspective. Theologians have often appropriated key general terms whose meaning was first developed in the context of philosophy. And this prior philosophical development may include the desire for perfect categories and a desire for a single set of terms that give us the metaphysical "bottom" of the world.

In particular, theology in the ancient church shows influences from Platonism. Traditional theology since Thomas Aquinas often uses pieces of a fundamental system of categories borrowed from Aristotelian philosophy. People who have read widely in traditional theology can see terms like *essence* and *accidents*, *actual* and *potential*, *substance* and *qualities*, and types of cause—*formal*, *material*, *efficient*, and *final* cause. These terms go back to Aristotle. Such terms can offer some insights if we think of them as perspectives.

But they do not give us the foundation of the world. Other, cross-cutting perspectives are possible.

Essentials and Accidents

We may take as an example the use of the terms *essence* and *accidents*. In Aristotle's view, a property is *essential* to something if its presence is necessary to have that something be what it is. A property is *accidental* if its presence is not necessary, but may be there is some cases and not be there in others. For example, we may reason that for something to be a horse, it needs to be organic and living and mammalian. These three properties are therefore *essential* properties of a horse. It is not necessary that it be black. So being black is an accidental property.

Though we used the particular example of a horse, the aim of philosophical discussion is very general. The terms *essential* and *accidental* are very general terms. The philosopher hopes to use these terms in discussions across the board, concerning virtually anything that exists. That very generality can create difficulties, because there is a philosophical desire to have the generality without entanglement—entanglement in the particularity. We confront here the difficulty of the one and the many, and their coinherent entanglement.

We may also observe that the analysis of things in terms of properties follows the lead of Aristotle. His approach to logic treated the form "A is B" as most ultimate, as a kind of "bottom" to language and to the world. Within this form "A is B," A is typically a thing, and B is a property. This treatment leads to philosophical approaches in which the bottom of the world consists in things or substances (A's) with properties (B's). Such an approach amounts only to one perspective. If it is viewed as ultimate, it is reductionistic. It does not do justice to the ultimacy of divine speech and its richness.

Setting aside the difficulties coming from this reduction, let us go on to consider what it means to distinguish between essential and accidental properties. What we call "necessary" depends on context.[1] A rocking horse or a statue of a horse does not need to be either organic or living. So being alive is not "necessary" in this context. Aristotle would object that such use of the word *horse* is equivocal. But behind this objection we may meet the desire for univocal terms, with no analogy built in.

Even if we restrict ourselves to flesh and blood horses, we may still have difficulties. What about a horse that has just died? Is it still a horse? Or is it only the corpse left over from a horse? It is certainly not a dog or a sheep or a cat. Suppose we say that it is still a horse, albeit a dead horse. How long does it remain a horse after it is dead? A corpse gradually decays and, if left long enough, is no longer easily recognizable. When does it stop being a horse? We may sense that there is really no exact boundary. It depends on how we want to use the word *horse*, whether in a narrower or a broader way.

Even if we restrict ourselves to horses that are living animals, we may discover difficulties in distinguishing the essential from the accidental. Suppose we have a breed of horses all of which are black. Does that imply that being black is necessary for the breed? Or does it only happen to be the case that all are black? Suppose that we could check the genetics of this breed and establish that the DNA common to this breed pretty much guarantees that inbreeding will continue to produce black-colored offspring. So, then, is being black essential? Maybe. Suppose by genetic engineering we could switch off or change just one gene in such a way that some of the offspring might be other colors. Do we still have the same breed? Who says?

If we try to determine exact boundaries using the commonalities in the DNA, we still confront the difficulty that different horses within the same breed will show small variations at some points in their DNA. We can choose to define the breed narrowly as including only horses that have matching DNA at *every* point where the DNA of the currently living horses of the breed shows exact matching. Or we may allow some further variation. Because of mutations, some of the next generation may show variations that do not match any of the current living generation.

---

[1] Vern S. Poythress, *Logic: A God-Centered Approach to the Foundation of Western Thought* (Wheaton, IL: Crossway, 2013), chap. 64.

Suppose that a mutation at one point naturally produces an offspring that is not black. Then is this offspring the beginning of another breed? It depends on how narrowly we want to define the breed. And as finite human beings, we are not going to be able to anticipate beforehand all possible situations that might represent variations on the breed. It looks as though our personal perspective has a role in the decision about how narrow we want to consider the breed to be.

The example with horses is actually fairly easy, because biological classifications are typically very stable in this world. But not all classifications are equally stable. What about the dialogues of Plato discussing what is good, what is justice, what is piety, what is bravery, what is love? Within each of these discussions we might introduce the distinction between the essential and the accidental. What is essential to justice, and what is accidental in the sense of being present in some examples of justice but not in others? Can we tell?

An issue like this one is particularly challenging because justice goes back to God, who is the God of justice. God's character is the origin and archetype for justice. The justice of God coheres with his goodness, his truthfulness, his holiness, his mercy, and his faithfulness. His faithfulness is a *just* faithfulness. So how do we separate what is joined together in God? How do we *master* justice? To master justice, we have to know God. And if we know God, we know him in all his attributes. So justice is not perfectly separable. Everything we know about God is potentially relevant, since his justice is an all-knowing, faithful justice.

If God specifies what constitutes justice in weights and measures, is not that specification *necessary* to weights and measures, and if necessary then essential? Would it be so even though not every feature of the specification would be pertinent to justice in matters of personal injury? Does the word *essential* have a perfectly clear meaning?

Essentials and Accidentals with an Individual

Consider now Sally the horse, a black mare. Might we say that she is necessarily black if we know that producing black skin comes from her DNA make-up? But perhaps the blackness is epigenetic rather than gene-based. So is it still necessary? We can also consider the matter of time. Maybe her skin blackened only after she was born, even though it was genetically "programmed" that way from the beginning. It was a "necessary" development, we might say, given her DNA. But what if some processes went wrong somewhere in the development, and the development did not take its normal course with respect to skin color?

Over time, Sally grows older. Aristotelians would be inclined to say that only what is the same over all her life is "essential." But in God's plan, was it not essential that she be a newborn and then a young colt before she matured? So these stages are "essential" in some sense. And, given the details of God's plan, should not we say that it was necessary that she develop a lame foot on February 27, 2011, because that is what God had planned? So in this sense everything that happens to Sally is "essential"—essential from the standpoint of the necessity of the fact that God's plan will be executed in time.

In his logical analysis Aristotle focused on general truths, not on particular truths about Sally. But the two interlock, because of the interlocking of the one and the many. Some philosophers have claimed that human knowledge is only of universals. According to this conception, a person cannot "know" Sally, because she is unique. But such claims are ridiculous when viewed in the light of biblical revelation. If the one and the many interlock, knowledge about general categories (the one) is available only in connection with knowledge of the many. And, of course, we can know God, who is one and who is unique.

What about environmental context? Is it not necessary to the life of a horse that the horse have an environment, including ground under foot, and things to eat? So are these relationships "essential"? And are they "properties"? The word *property* suggests adjectival features that are semi-independent of the environment. But a pure separation from the environment, from context, is a reductionistic move—ultimately an illusion. We cannot perfectly separate properties from relations, any more than we can separate God the Father's having love from his having love for his Son.

The Aristotelian distinction between essence and accidentals builds by common grace on the idea of necessity and contingency, both of which are rooted in God's character and his plan for the world. We may therefore sense that we can use these categories by virtue of common grace. Yet a more thorough inspection shows that the categories are contaminated by Aristotle's overall system and his desire for autonomous understanding.

We may suggest that the categories run aground because they have been introduced reductionistically, without reckoning with several realities:

1. *The presence of analogy.* In producing the category *horse* it is presupposed that we have a perfectly stable idea of horse, with no sense of using analogies with the particular horses that we have seen.
2. *The interlocking of one and many.* Sally the horse belongs among all the other horses. She is one among many. The judgment about necessity is affected by whether we are focusing on her or on all the horses together. The different stages in Sally's life are also, in a sense, many forms of Sally, all of which are one Sally. So the entanglement of one and many occurs over time as well.
3. *The question of stability of meaning.* We too easily presuppose that we know exactly what necessity and essence are, independent of context, and what it means to be a horse, independent of context.
4. *The interlocking of form and meaning.* The word *horse* has a history to it, and is not merely a disembodied idea, free of all history and all relationships to human beings and their environments.
5. *The interlocking of meaning and context.* What is "necessary" depends on the context of discussion.
6. *The reality of time.* What changes in this world is as significant in the plan of God for the world as what remains the same.[2]

---

[2] Aristotelian philosophy attempts to do some justice to time by using the categories *potential* and *actual.* But then these categories are beset with complexities, much like the categories *essential* and

In a word, ectypal coinherence of aspects and perspectives on Sally kills the hope for gaining a precise, controlled, masterful distinction between essence and accidents.

Conclusion

We may generalize from this one example. We do not know with perfection precision what a term like *horse* means. Nor do we know exactly what the terms *essential* and *accidental* mean. We can extend the principle to all the words in natural languages. They do have some meaning: the word *horse* does not mean the same as the word *mouse*. We can communicate meaningfully because of the stabilities that belong to words. But terms have vaguenesses, contextual relationships, and one-and-many relationships built into them—none of which Aristotle wanted to acknowledge. The multidimensional character of our words, our concepts, and our language reflects the mystery of the Trinitarian character of God. We do ourselves a disservice if we act as if we could perfectly master meanings and master the language that we use. Since language and thought cohere, the same holds for our theological *thinking*. Let us be circumspect. Let us understand the Trinitarian origins of language before we proceed with confidence.[3]

As an aside, this multiperspectival understanding of language suggests one way in which the writings of John Frame and me differ in *texture* (not necessarily in practical conclusions) from some theology of a more technical kind that writers have produced both in the past and in the present. Frame and I prefer not to rely very much on technical terminology (though we acknowledge its useful-

---

accidental. We may mention only one difficulty: the word *potential* can suggest *innate* potential, as if development of a certain kind were deterministically programmed into a creature in such a way that the development toward a final goal of being "actual" is inevitable if only there is no interference. In the end, this is an impersonalist picture—as it must be in Aristotle, because he has removed God from his worldview. The whole picture is a picture of autonomous development, not development in communion with God. Development is pictured as independent of the presence of God and of the possibility of surprises in the way in which God causes one particular horse or one particular tree or one particular human being to grow to maturity.

[3] Vern S. Poythress, *Symphonic Theology: The Validity of Multiple Perspectives in Theology* (Grand Rapids: Zondervan, 1987; repr., Phillipsburg, NJ: P&R, 2001); Poythress, *In the Beginning Was the Word: Language—A God-Centered Approach* (Wheaton, IL: Crossway, 2009); and Poythress, *God-Centered Biblical Interpretation* (Phillipsburg, NJ: P&R, 1999); are all written in order to help in developing our understanding of the Bible without overlaying it with contaminated philosophical baggage.

ness, and we use it when convenient). When theological discussion endeavors to attain special precision and multiplies technical terminology, it runs the danger of overestimating its precision and making mistakes parallel to those of Plato and Aristotle. It also runs the danger of presuming that its terminology and the theses expressed using the terminology reveal in a unique, monoperspectival way the ultimate structures of God and the world.

Some strands of postmodern thought criticize philosophy and theology on grounds akin to mine. They see lack of perfect stability in meaning. They see analogy where technical practitioners see absolutely stable, literalistic use of technical terms. They see the interlock of form and meaning. They see the possibility of other viewpoints from other languages and cultures in cases where technical practitioners presume the ultimacy of their own monoperspectival approach.

Postmodern thought can show common-grace insights in such criticisms. Yet it does not lead to spiritual health; its critical stance remains captive to the ideal of autonomous reason, now utilized for the critique of reason. Postmodernism tends toward skepticism or relativism about language and culture, because it does not acknowledge how both language and culture give clear testimonies to the presence of God. God gives us stability and ability to understand and effectively communicate through the languages and cultures that he has established and that he provides for us as gifts. Though we must contend with sinful corruptions since Adam's fall into sin, languages and cultures remain gifts that provide channels for knowledge rather than barriers that make knowledge impossible.

We must leave to other books a full discussion of God's presence in language and culture, and how he provides stability and genuine knowledge in the midst of language and culture.[4] If we trust God, we have good grounds for confidence in communication and in understanding culture.

---

[4] Poythress, *In the Beginning Was the Word*; Poythress, *Redeeming Sociology: A God-Centered Approach* (Wheaton, IL: Crossway, 2011).

PART 4

Examples of
Metaphysical Analysis

12

Metaphysics of an Apple

We will now consider some examples to illustrate how a multiperspectival metaphysics works. Through specific examples, we want to underline the true nature of metaphysics. The ultimate metaphysics of the world is to be found in God himself. God through his word of command and through his comprehensive rule over the universe specifies every dimension of the world that we enjoy. We should rejoice in his bounty and recognize all the dimensions. We need to avoid imagining that some one dimension, rather than God himself in his majesty and wisdom, is a kind of ultimate foundation that is most basic and somehow explains all the rest.

In a way, this approach is like saying that there is *no* metaphysics of the kind that most philosophers have sought—there is nothing within creation that serves as a final foundation. No "ultimate" system of abstract categories reaches down and makes transparent to human reason the foundations of existence. That is because creation as a whole and every individual creature have their foundation in God's plan, his commands, his governance, and his presence. We can know God, but we cannot comprehend him.

Personal Choice

A bag of Granny Smith apples sits on our kitchen table. I pick one to analyze.

Let me analyze the apple from a particular perspective. Which perspective? It is up to me to choose. I am a human being whose viewpoint is textured not only by my spatial position but by my entire previous experience and the individuality of my mind. Out of a multiplicity of alternatives with which I am familiar, I choose as my first perspective one with which I am particularly comfortable: the triad of contrast, variation, and distribution.[1] This triad constitutes three perspectives in one. As usual, the three interlock. There is a personal, social, and theological history behind my use of this triad, into which we need not enter.[2]

God in his wisdom and majesty ordains all perspectives by all human beings, though of course he does not morally *endorse* sinful biases in those who have the perspectives. God knows the perspectives beforehand. His plan for my apple includes the reality that he has ordained all perspectives on the apple. The metaphysics of the apple, as expression of his wisdom, includes in principle all perspectives.

A Triad of Contrast, Variation, and Distribution

First, think about the perspective that focuses on contrastive-identificational features. My apple is distinct from the others in the bag. It *contrasts* with them. I measured it, and it is about 2.5 inches or 6.5 centimeters in diameter. It has a dimple at the stem end and a more complicated dimple at the other end. It is about the same shape and size and color as the other apples in the bag. I can still distinguish it from the others because it has a distinct spatial location in relation to them and in relation to the table. It also contrasts more notably with some red apples that my wife bought, because it is green. It belongs to the Granny Smith variety of apples. It also contrasts with oranges, pears, bananas, and other fruits by shape, texture, taste, and inner structure (if we cut

---

[1] Vern S. Poythress, *In the Beginning Was the Word: Language—A God-Centered Approach* (Wheaton, IL: Crossway, 2009), chap. 19; Kenneth L. Pike, *Linguistic Concepts: An Introduction to Tagmemics* (Lincoln: University of Nebraska Press, 1982), 41–65. See also the feature mode, manifestation mode, and distribution mode in Pike, *Language in Relation to a Unified Theory of the Structure of Human Behavior*, 2nd ed. (The Hague/Paris: Mouton, 1967), 84–97.
[2] Vern S. Poythress, "Multiperspectivalism and the Reformed Faith," in *Speaking the Truth in Love: The Theology of John M. Frame*, ed. John J. Hughes (Phillipsburg, NJ: P&R, 2009), 185–87, reproduced in chap. 7.

into it or bite into it). It contrasts also with food items that are not fruit—meat, milk, fruit juice, vegetables, and so on. It contrasts with household items that are not food.

Second, my apple displays *variation*. In principle, the kinds of variation include variation in the single apple I have chosen, variation among all the apples in the bag, variation among all Granny Smith apples, and variation among all apples of all varieties. Let us focus on my apple in its individuality. It looks different when viewed from different angles. I can look directly down on the stem end, or view it from one side with the stem pointing upward, or from the side with the stem pointing downward, or pointing downward and to one side, or pointing downward and slightly forward, and so on. There are a great variety of rotational positions. Roughly speaking, the apple looks about the same from various angles if I rotate it around the axis passing through its stem and its core. But there are slight variations in shape, texture, and color. All these spatial perspectives belong to one distinguishable, "contrastive" apple.

We can also consider variation in time. The apple over a period of days gradually ripens. If we wait long enough, it will start rotting or molding. The details vary over time. I also experience variation depending on whether the kitchen in which it sits is lighted by overhead ceiling lights, by sunlight alone, by sunlight plus ceiling lights, by no spatially confined light source (as at twilight), or by almost no light at all (at nighttime, when I would have to feel for the apple to find it). The temperature of the apple varies, depending on how hot the kitchen is or whether I put the apple in the refrigerator.

I can also experience the same apple in another way by peeling it, cutting it up, examining its core and seeds, or eating it. Or I could feed it to an animal. We can still identify it as the *same* apple. We use primarily contrastive features for such identification. But we also use our knowledge concerning typical variations in apples. We are not surprised if we see some ripening or the beginning of overripeness. We are confident that we still have the same apple, even though its looks have changed.

Third, consider *distribution*. Distribution is a more precise designation for structural contexts that are most relevant for interpretation. My apple sits near the top of a bag of Granny Smith apples. Its belonging to the bag is its immediate spatial "distribution." The bag in turn is "distributed" among other items on the kitchen table. The table is "distributed" within the kitchen. The kitchen is "distributed" among the rooms of the house. This kind of distribution is spatial, one form of what Kenneth Pike calls *distribution as part of a structural sequence*.[3]

There are two other kinds of distribution. My apple is *distributed* in the class of Granny Smith apples in the bag, which belongs in turn to the class of all Granny Smith apples, which belongs in turn to the class of all apples of all varieties. This kind of distribution is called *distribution as a member of a substitution class*.[4] Finally, my apple can be classified by a multiplicity of characteristics: size, color, spatial location, apple variety to which it belongs, degree of ripeness, and peeled or unpeeled. Each of these characteristics can be viewed as one dimension out of the total description of my apple. The many dimensions together form a *system* of description and classification. My apple is then *distributed* in this system. This kind of distribution is called *distribution as a point in a system*.[5]

All of these descriptions from all three perspectives—contrast, variation, and distribution—have been ordained and specified by God from the foundation of the world. Everything about my apple is so specified. If another human being comes and does his or her own analysis of the apple using the same perspectives, the analysis may come out slightly different. God specifies all these differences as well. He specifies all the details of all the perspectives, because his plan for the world and for its history is comprehensive. Nothing takes him by surprise.[6] My apple is what it is within the context of God's plan. To understand my apple is to understand it in relation

---

[3] Pike, *Linguistic Concepts*, 62–64. The term *sequence* is apt for describing the linearity of speech and writing, but not so apt in the case of three-dimensional spatial embedding. An easy adjustment in conceptuality is all that is necessary.

[4] Ibid., 62.

[5] Ibid., 65.

[6] On universal sovereignty, see, for example, John M. Frame, *The Doctrine of God* (Phillipsburg, NJ: P&R, 2002); Vern S. Poythress, *Chance and the Sovereignty of God: A God-Centered Approach to Probability and Random Events* (Wheaton, IL: Crossway, 2014).

to God's plan. God's plan in a sense *is* the ultimate "metaphysics" of the apple. It includes not only what the apple shares in common with all other apples or all other fruits, but also everything that is unique to it as a single apple, distinct from all others.

We can see interlocking of the one and the many. There is one apple with many facts about it and many perspectives that describe it. There is one class consisting of all apples, and each apple within the class is one of many belonging to the one class ("distribution as a member of a substitution class").

We can also appreciate interlocking among the three perspectives, namely, contrast, variation, and distribution. The contrastive features are possible only by means of variation within each of them. For example, the diameter that I measured, 2.5 inches, is a contrastive feature that distinguishes my apple from bigger or smaller apples. But my contrastive feature is only approximate. It is "about" 2.5 inches. There is possible variation if we try to make a more exact measurement. I said that my apple was green. But there are different shades of green, even among Granny Smith apples, and even at different locations on the skin of the same apple. The different shades constitute variation.

The contrastive feature of diameter exists also in a distributional context, a context in which we define diameter as one measurement in a whole system of possible quantitative measurements. The contrastive feature "2.5 inches in diameter" thus exists only by virtue of the use of variation and distribution. It also invokes other contrasts, for example, the contrast of that one feature with other features of the same apple (such as greenness or relative ripeness). One contrastive feature, namely diameter, *contrasts* with other possible features that focus on other matters.

In short, a deeper attention to a contrastive feature shows that this feature is intelligible because of a triadic presence of contrast, variation, and distribution *in* this one feature. Contrast presupposes variation and distribution for its own intelligibility.

Similar observations hold for variation. As we have noted, the apple varies in appearance depending on whether we look down on its stem end or look sideways with the stem facing up, and so on. Each variant contrasts with the other variants. Each variant is defined using contrast, variation, and distribution in its definition. For example, the variant in which we look at the apple from above the stem end has allowable variation in the exact position above the stem that we choose to take. This position *contrasts* with other possible positions for viewing. The shape and texture of the apple, viewed from above, *contrast* with the shape and texture, viewed from one side. All the viewpoints constitute a system of distribution parallel to the systems for viewing other three-dimensional objects from different directions. The view from above the stem is part of a distribution class consisting of views from various distances above the apple.

Thus, contrast, variation, and distribution interlock. Each depends on the others. Each leads to the others. For example, observation focusing on the contrastive perspective, when performed in detail, includes within it information about contrastive, variational, and distributional perspectives on the contrastive perspective with which we started.

God's Presence

This interlocking is an ectypal form of coinherence. The persons in the Trinity indwell one another in a unique, archetypal way. This mutual indwelling is the archetypal coinherence. Ectypal coinherence is specified by the word of God, which is the word of the Father spoken through the Son in the Holy Spirit.

We can see a more directly analogical representation of Trinitarian coinherence if we observe that the triad consisting in contrast, variation, and distribution has a close relation to the fundamental triad of classification, instantiation, and association, introduced as a reflection of the distinctive archetypal roles of God the Father, God the Son, and God the Holy Spirit, respectively.[7]

God is distinct from my apple and from everything else that he has made. But he also manifests his presence in the apple. He manifests "his invisible attributes, namely, his eternal power and

---

[7] Vern S. Poythress, "Reforming Ontology and Logic in the Light of the Trinity: An Application of Van Til's Idea of Analogy," *Westminster Theological Journal* 57, no. 1 (1995): 187–219.

divine nature," "in the things that have been made" (Rom. 1:20). The apple manifests who God is. What we are now discussing can be considered another perspective: the relation of the apple to God.

The apple is a wise construction, apt for human nourishment. It therefore manifests the wisdom of God and his goodness ("he did good . . . with food and gladness"—Acts 14:17). God's word is divine, and therefore reflects the coinherence of divine persons. Contrast, variation, and distribution in divine utterance specify contrast, variation, and distribution in the apple. Thus it should not be too surprising that the contrast, variation, and distribution we see in the analysis of the apple reflect the archetypal unity and coinherence in the Trinity.

What is the "being" of an apple? The apple derives from divine speaking. Divine speaking specifies not only that the apple will exist, but also that it will be what it is in relation to other apples and in relation to human beings. The divine word is foundational for the entire structure. Thus, the "metaphysics" of the apple includes all the dimensions of divine specification. It therefore includes derivative, ectypal coinherence of contrast, variation, and distribution. It also includes many other aspects (as we will see below).

My apple is beautiful. It reflects the beauty of God. It reflects his beauty when I just enjoy how it looks. It reflects his beauty in the ectypal coinherence of contrast, variation, and distribution and the way in which such coinherence reflects God's original harmonious beauty. It is different from any other apples, and in its differences also it reflects the differential beauty in God (which is related to variation).

The Triad of Particle, Wave, and Field Perspectives

Let us now consider a second perspective on the apple, namely, the triad of particle, wave, and field perspectives.[8] The three perspectives once again interlock. The particle perspective is the static or stationary perspective: we consider an apple as a stable, integral

---

[8] Poythress, *In the Beginning Was the Word*, 52–57; Pike, *Linguistic Concepts*, chaps. 3–5.

whole, as a unit. It is an apple. It is identifiable as a piece of fruit. In the wave perspective, we consider the apple as experiencing *dynamicity*; it develops and changes in time. It grows on a tree; it is picked; it is sorted and packed. It is delivered to a grocery store. It is purchased and brought home. It is eaten. We can also consider the apple as having a dynamicity in space. It may be jostled about with the other apples in the bag. The exact boundary between it and neighboring apples may not be clear, particularly if the skin is broken open and the flesh of two apples comes together.

The field perspective focuses on *relations*. The apple is identifiable in relation to the tree that produced it and the biological classification to which it belongs, in relation to the house in which it sits, and in relation to the people who may at any moment decide to consume it.

This triad of perspectives goes back to God who ordained it. He ordained the capabilities that we human beings have of using multiple foci in analyses. He ordained that apples have static stability, dynamic change, and relational multiplicities that correspond to these human perspectives. This multiperspectival character of an apple is an aspect of its "metaphysics," since it is an aspect of the divine specification, which is the ultimate foundation for this apple.[9]

Stability and Time

The particle perspective on the apple focuses on what is the same. It is a kind of "static" perspective. The wave perspective focuses on what changes. It is dynamic. What is the same about the apple does not undermine or compete with what changes. The two are equally ultimate.

We can draw broader philosophical lessons from this example, lessons about the relation of stability to change. For Plato, knowledge was knowledge of the *forms*, which were unchanging. He prioritized stability over change. Aristotle tried to deal with development in time, partly through his idea of potential and ac-

---

[9] Kenneth Pike's creativity with perspectives extends even further, in his development of a variety of human foci of attention (Pike, *A Unified Theory*, 37–72, 78–81, 98–119).

tual. But the slant of his perspective still privileged constancy over change. Such a view is one-sided. In God's world, both constancy and change are specified by God's speech. Each presupposes the other.

We cannot appreciate change except by identifying it as movement *away from* an earlier state. When we think about change, we tacitly rely on the constancy of our memory and our ideas. For example, when we observe that the apple ripens, it is still the "same" apple. We presuppose the constancy when we describe something as ripening, because the "something" is what we perceive as constant. If we cannot identify an apple as in some sense "the same" apple that we observed earlier, we cannot talk about change in the apple. Conversely, whenever we identify constancy, we presuppose that constancy shows itself by interaction with us and the world. We have to see that we are looking at an apple, and our seeing is a process in which the apple is interacting with the world, through light or touch. The interaction is a kind of change.

The third perspective, the field perspective, focuses on relationships. Relationships interlock with stability and with change. Each must be present for the others to make sense.

Plato's and Aristotle's philosophies prioritized essence and the static. Other philosophies sometimes privilege change (process philosophy; contemporary emphasis on narrative) or relationships (structuralism). Such moves are reductionistic. In fact, they are illusory, because they hide from themselves their tacit dependence on all three perspectives in their interlocking character.

Frame's Triad for Ethics

We have only begun. We can choose another perspective on the apple, distinct from everything that we have used so far. We choose Frame's triad for ethics: normative, situational, and existential perspectives on ethics.

First, consider the normative perspective on the apple. What does God command concerning the apple? His word in the Bible nowhere mentions this specific apple. But his word does specify that we are to live by his word in every area of our lives. My life includes this apple. So I apply what God's word says to this new situation—the situation with this apple in it. The normative perspective has led naturally to the situational perspective, where I consider the apple as part of my environment. The normative perspective, by focusing on God's word in Scripture, leads to a knowledge that this apple has providentially been created by God. It is a product of an apple tree, which is part of the order of living things that God first set up in Genesis 1:11–13. "And God said, 'Let the earth sprout vegetation, plants yielding seed, and *fruit trees* bearing *fruit* in which is *their seed*, each according to its kind, on the earth.' And it was so" (1:11).

This initial word from God establishes a permanent pattern, which we see continuing to this day. The seeds in apples, when planted, yield apple trees, and apple trees grow apples (Ps. 104:30). This normative insight leads to the conclusion that my apple, lying on the kitchen table, has come about through the word of God, which establishes both the general pattern and the subsequent detailed executions and embodiments of the pattern in each particular tree and each particular apple (Gen. 1:11).

The normative perspective also leads to the conclusion that we should praise God for his bounty, which includes the bounty of apples:

> May the glory of the LORD endure forever;
>> may the LORD rejoice in his works,
> who looks on the earth and it trembles,
>> who touches the mountains and they smoke!
> I will sing to the LORD as long as I live;
>> I will sing praise to my God while I have being.
> May my meditation be pleasing to him,
>> for I rejoice in the LORD.
> Let sinners be consumed from the earth,
>> and let the wicked be no more!
> Bless the LORD, O my soul!
> Praise the LORD! (Ps. 104:31–35)

> Praise the LORD from the earth. . . .

Mountains and all hills,
  fruit trees and all cedars! (Ps. 148:7, 9).

The normative perspective thus has led us to the existential perspective, where we focus on our attitude toward the apple. Praise God for apples! Praise God for this apple! Praise God for his wisdom in the details! Praise God for the beauty of this apple!

Frame's triad for ethics also leads to a related triad for objects of knowledge. As we have indicated in chapter 5, there are three objects of knowledge: God, the world, and ourselves, corresponding to the normative, situational, and existential perspectives, respectively. My apple, as a created object, is an object belonging to the world, which is the second of these three objects of knowledge. And so it is natural to use the situational perspective in considering the apple.

But knowledge of the apple comes together with knowledge of God. Any truth about the apple is a truth that resides first of all in the mind of God. When we know truth, we know it in connection with knowing God, who is truth. Truth comes from God, so we also should acknowledge God as source. As we have seen, the apple manifests God's invisible attributes, so that we know God right along with knowing about the apple.

Finally, we know ourselves in connection with knowing about the apple. Self-consciousness is always in the background. We are aware of the apple from various perspectives, which are ours to choose.

God has made a world in which knowledge of God, the world, and self are correlated and interlocked. The apple exists by ordination of God in relation to God, the world, and self. This relatedness is one aspect of the "metaphysics" of the apple, that is, God's specification of it.

The Poetry of Apples

We can also ask what more metaphorical or poetic associations are evoked by apples. The exact associations vary with culture and with the individual. For example, in the Western world we have a long-standing tradition that Adam and Eve ate an *apple* from the forbidden tree, the tree of the knowledge of good and evil. Genesis 3 talks about the "fruit" of the tree. It never specifies what *kind* of fruit it was. Of course it is possible that it was an apple. But maybe it was a pear, or a peach. We do not know. The rest of the Bible never fills in this detail. The detail that says it was an apple arises only from later tradition, which is fallible. Perhaps the tradition merely goes back to someone's guess, a guess that grew and grew until it became a fixed part of Western literature.

Western literature is not the word of God. It does not have any special authority from God. But neither is it a mere "accident"—it is not outside God's control. God rules over all of history, including the history of Western literature. But that does not mean that he morally endorses everything in literature. God is in control of what happens both in the case of the Bible and in the case of all other documents. We say that he *ordains* or *governs* the results, including each document that anyone has ever written. But the Bible is unique because it is the word of God. God speaks it, and that implies that it is authoritative and that God's goodness and holiness back up what he says in it.

With this understanding, we can consider the significance of Western literature and its traditions. God ordained the Western tradition about the apple as a part of our history. He also ordains that not all cultures have the *same* exact literary history. So there may be cultures that have received the Bible and therefore know about the forbidden tree, but have not received the Western tradition that suggests that the fruit was an apple.

Thus, the association with apples with the forbidden tree is but one possibility. In a sense, we should associate the forbidden fruit with all the fruits that we know. None of these fruits is forbidden to *us*, of course, because the original restriction was with respect to one special tree. God did not forbid eating the same kind of fruit from a different tree.

Many questions about the details of the forbidden fruit cannot be answered. Their unanswerability is one more reminder of our

finiteness and the distinction between us and God. Even this limi-
tation has a positive function for us.

We can also have confidence that God ordains all of the kinds
of thoughts that belong to the immediately preceding paragraphs.
God ordains that my encounter with my particular apple can lead
to all these thoughts. If the apple does lead to such thoughts, it is
because God planned from the beginning that this particular apple,
in distinction from any other, should be the occasion for me, as distinct from any other human beings, to develop the thoughts that
I have just developed. And apples from previous generations have
in a sense been the occasion for developing the Western tradition
that identifies the forbidden fruit as an apple.

Thus, this, my apple, and some other apples from the past,
have particular roles in relation to the forbidden fruit. God has
so planned it. Consequently, these roles for the apple, as part of
God's comprehensive plan, are part of the "metaphysics" of my
apple.

To put it another way, poetry is not nonsense. Poetry makes
more indirect associations. It "creates" associations imaginatively,
we might say, because of human creativity. This creativity reflects
the archetypal creativity of God. No human being is "creative" in
an absolute sense. Every creative thought he or she receives is a
gift from God (1 Cor. 4:7). God's creativity is thus manifested in the
poetry of Western tradition about an apple.

Biblical Poetry about Apples

The Song of Solomon talks about apple trees and apples:

> As an *apple* tree among the trees of the forest,
>   so is my beloved among the young men.
> With great delight I sat in his shadow,
>   and his *fruit* was sweet to my taste. (Song 2:3)

> Sustain me with raisins;
>   refresh me with *apples*,
>   for I am sick with love. (Song 2:5)

Oh may your breasts be like clusters of the vine,
    and the scent of your breath like *apples*,
and your mouth like the best wine. (Song 7:8–9)

Who is that coming up from the wilderness,
    leaning on her beloved?

Under the *apple* tree I awakened you.
There your mother was in labor with you;
    there she who bore you was in labor. (Song 8:5)

We do not know for sure whether apples had some poetic association with love and love making in ancient Israel. If they did not,
the Song of Solomon has the effect of *creating* a new association of
just this kind. The sweetness of apples stands for the sweetness
of love. The satisfaction of eating stands for the satisfaction of the
pleasure of love (Song 5:1). The smell of apples, either by its own
pleasantness or by association with eating apples, may suggest an
association with the desire for love (Song 7:8). Other associations
may be awakened as well. The association of apples with eating
may lead to thinking about the role of the mouth in eating, and
from there to the role of the mouth in kissing ("Let him kiss me
with the kisses of his mouth!"—Song 1:2). Poetry is often not about
evoking just one narrow association in the form "This stands for
that." Could the ripening of apples evoke the thought of the ripening of love?

The associations evoked by an apple are not merely *intellectual*
associations, as if we were asking ourselves mentally, Now what
associations can I create by deliberately forcing them? The associations may not even be articulable. Like a moving piece of music, the
apple moves us without our specifying some particular "thought"
or some particular mood that a poet tried to create. Man is more
than intellect, particularly in poetic interaction.

A multiperspectival approach can underline the individuality of
poetic response from a single reader or a single person responding
in appreciation to poetry. What do apples evoke for you? For me?
As before, God does not endorse all responses—he does not endorse
the sin that is in us. But he ordains the creativity of individual

human minds and hearts and feelings in which associations arise. The associations vary from one individual to another; they are not always the same. My apple, the apple in my kitchen, has a never-to-be-repeated role in the plan of God—that it would evoke some associations as I think about it and smell it.

I am not poetically inclined; I am not gifted in that way. But others are. Let them more fully enjoy the apple with their more abundant creativity of association. For this too the apple is ordained. Poetry, in other words, is part of the metaphysics of apples. The Song of Solomon is an illustration of the larger principle. It teaches us about the nature of the world.

Among the things it teaches are the importance and centrality of love. When we come to grips with the deficiencies in our own attempts at romantic love, it does not take much time to ask how the deficiency is to be remedied. And then we awake to another association—that the Song of Solomon is, at least in part, about the marriage of King Solomon (Song 3:11). Marriage in the Old Testament becomes a metaphor for the love of God for Israel. And Solomon is a type of Christ, the final Bridegroom (Eph. 5:22–33). We have plenty of associations, if we want to follow them.

In the Song of Solomon, apples become an emblem for love. They "become," I say, but God ordained this "becoming." So the meaning of apples, even from the creation of the world, is bound up with this becoming. If apples are an emblem for love, they are, by further moves of association that God has planned, an emblem for God's love for us: he gives us food. The sweetness of my apple communicates the sweetness of God. And apples are therefore also an emblem of Christ's love for his church. This emblematic character is one aspect of the metaphysics of apples. And it is one aspect of the metaphysics of my apple, the one at home in the kitchen.

An Apple's Function in Personal Relationships

Particular objects like apples exist within a web of ecological relationships, as the ecologists will tell us. When an apple enters into relation to human beings, it also exists within a web of personal relationships among human beings. These relationships arise and dynamically change in accordance with God's design. Let us illustrate the principle with my particular apple, the one on the kitchen table.

My wife bought the bag of apples at the grocery store. The process of buying is one aspect of the inferred knowledge that I have about the apple. The process itself can be analyzed for its relationships.[10] My wife expresses her love for me and our family when she goes to the grocery store and when she prepares meals. She is serving us, not merely herself.

The case with my apple is particularly striking, because Granny Smith apples are one of my favorites, but she does not like them. They are too tart. She prefers the sweeter varieties. I am glad to see her bring home some red variety for herself. I like almost any variety of apple, but she knows that I particularly like the Granny Smiths. The fact that these Granny Smiths are in the house *in addition to* another kind that we could both eat is a particularly striking expression of love, in my eyes.

So the Granny Smiths symbolize my wife's love for me. They do so against the background of some rather complex circumstances, which are special to my household. But there it is: they symbolize love. And that fact brings us round again to the apples in the Song of Solomon. I see an association between my apple and the Song of Solomon that no one else in the world appreciates in the way that I do. It is *my* wife and *my* apple. Other people may have wives who bring them home their favorite apples, but my relationship to my apple is still distinct. It is distinct because I am who I am, and my wife is who she is, and this apple is what it is at this time and this place in the whole history of the world. Ordaining it all is God, who is who he is (Ex. 3:14).

This apple, and not another, is a more intensive emblem of my wife's love. According to Ephesians 5:22–33, my wife in her relationship to me reflects and expresses the relationship of the church to Christ, which is a relationship of love. And the church's love not

---

[10] Vern S. Poythress, *Redeeming Sociology: A God-Centered Approach* (Wheaton, IL: Crossway, 2011), chap. 7, and elsewhere.

only reflects God's love, but is an expression of it, since that love arises through the power of the Holy Spirit, as the Spirit of Christ, who brings love into the church and its life. It is through the Holy Spirit that God enables my wife and me to love one another. If we are experiencing love in the Holy Spirit, we are also experiencing the love of the Holy Spirit, which is the love of God, right in the midst of our loving one another. God is present.

God made it so. God in his wisdom ordains the relationships. He ordains the personal relationships between me and God and the Song of Solomon as the word of God and Christ's love as husband to his bride, the church. God ordains the love relationship between me and my wife. God also ordains particular ways love is expressed at particular times. Apples, raisins, pomegranates, frankincense, aloes, and all the other cornucopia of created things mentioned in the Song of Solomon can serve in poetic ways to express the personal love that God has for his people. The metaphysics of my apple includes its role in a cornucopia.

Frame's Triad of Lordship

Because of the influential role played by John Frame's triad of perspectives on lordship, it is fitting that we use this triad in analyzing my apple. The triad consists in three perspectives: authority, control, and presence. These perspectives focus on the nature of God's covenantal relations to human beings—and more broadly to the whole created world. The three perspectives interlock, as usual, and each is a perspective on the others. They express and reflect Trinitarian coinherence.

Consider first the perspective of *authority*. God has authority over those to whom he relates in covenant. His authority is shown particularly in commandments, like the Ten Commandments. God exercises authority not only over human beings, but over the world as a whole. He has authority to command what happens. "God said, 'Let there be light,' and there was light" (Gen. 1:3).

We have used something close to this perspective in viewing God's relation to the world through speaking. God speaks commands and specifications. His speech has the authority to determine the character of the world. His authority is complete. And so we may infer that God specifies the many details about apples that are not mentioned explicitly in the Bible.

The second perspective is *control*. God not only has the *right* to rule, as expressed by his authority. He *does actually* rule, as expressed by his control. The state of my apple in all its details conforms completely to the specifications laid down by his speech. His control has brought about the growth of the apple on its tree, its ripening, its transport to the grocery store, the transactions in the grocery store, and the stable position of the apple in the bag on the table.

The third perspective is *presence*. God is actively involved in the world as a whole and in what happens to my apple. People can distort this idea of presence into *pantheism*, the belief that God is identical to the world. Pantheism is a non-Christian distortion of the doctrine of God's immanence. The Bible indicates that God is completely distinct from the world. He is not caught in its movements and development. At the same time, he is present as the Lord of the world. He is present in the apple, and in the apple's changes, and in the apple's relations to what is around it. We meet God and know God in the presence of the apple. His eternal power and divine nature are revealed.

Scientific Perspectives

In my description and analysis of the apple, I have used what might be labeled perspectives from ordinary life. Human beings can make the observations I have made without having special scientific training. By elaborating on these perspectives, I want to emphasize that God's rule specifies them all. In so doing, his sovereign rule produces *reality*. The textures of these perspectives all give us reality, rather than an illusion thrown up by an unknown reality.

As we might expect from a multiperspectival approach, the affirmation of the reality of these perspectives does not depreciate the reality of technical scientific investigation. Various sciences and various subdivisions within the sciences give us what we might call *technical perspectives*. These perspectives can be very useful in carrying out God's program for human beings exercising dominion. We discover layers of meaning not immediately visible to casual human inspection. And these layers of meaning may enable us to construct new tools that increase our dominion. We grow both in knowledge (science) and in power (technology, used for dominion). Both science and technology grow in a situation where human beings are sinful. So both are subject to distortion and abuse. But the distortion is a distortion of that which was good in the original design of God in an unfallen world.

We should not despise science and technology as God intended them to be. We should, however, critically inspect existing human science and technology because of the influence of sin. So, given the present state of science, let us use some scientific or technical perspectives on my apple. Science has enjoyed extensive development in the last few centuries, so we can only touch the surface of what is possible.

First, consider quantitative and spatial perspectives. We count one apple. We measure its diameter in inches or in centimeters. We consider its spatial shape, as well as the shape of seeds and core within it. We can undertake a quite precise three-dimensional description of its internal parts as well as the shape of its surface.

Second, consider a physical perspective. My apple is a solid object, which can be approximately described by the mechanics of rigid objects. We can describe mass, center of gravity, moment of inertia, compressibility, and elasticity. We can, with Newton's laws of motion, describe its trajectory when thrown in a vacuum. If we bring in aerodynamics, we can describe what happens with its motion through a fluid, whether air or water or oil. We can describe the apple's colors in terms of reflections of light in certain frequency bands in the electromagnetic spectrum.

Third, consider a perspective on composition. We can describe its material composition at the level of elementary particles (electrons and quarks), or the level of more ordinary particles (protons, neutrons, and electrons).

Making a transition to chemistry, we can describe individual atoms, molecules, and biochemical reactions within the apple. We are then making the transition to biochemistry and molecular biology.

We may study the apple as a fruit at the level of its tissues and its physiology. We may also study the organisms that have made their home in the apple—bacteria and fungi. My apple shows no signs of having been bothered by insects or worms, but its history includes the possibility that a farmer took measures to protect it from pests.

We may also study the apple from the perspective of geology. The apple came from a tree that grew in soil in a certain location on the earth. The trace minerals in the apple may reveal something about the composition of the soil. Commercial information may also give us hints as to where apples of the Granny Smith variety are raised, and from where the grocery store most likely stocked its bags of Granny Smiths.

We may also venture into the study of agriculture. What goes into the growing of Granny Smith apples?

We may venture into both specialized areas and general areas related to human beings and their interaction with apples. We are then making a transition more into areas associated with social science. We consider the vehicles used to transport apples; the transportation system; the economic system; the network of businesses and business agreements linking the farm to the grocery store; the legal system, which supports businesses' confidence of receiving a reward for their efforts; the political system supporting the legal system; a supply system furnishing material to support these other networks; and so on. Understanding the history of my apple in detail and in context leads us into interacting with all these areas.

We may also move forward toward the time when the apple will be eaten. We may study human physiology of the digestive system and the neurology of taste and smell, which contribute to the appreciation of my apple.

The Power of General Laws

Scientific and technical analyses focus on general patterns of events rather than on my particular apple. They lay out general principles or laws or regularities for apples, apple growing, and commercial treatment of apples on the way to consumers. The general principles have practical power. They enable farmers, businessmen, grocers, and plant physiologists to make coherent plans for the future. They construct networks of human activity and purposes and supplies of various kinds in supporting structures to facilitate the smooth functioning of farming and an economic system that supplies apples in a dependable way at a reasonable price. The knowledge of the generalities has greater leverage for these purposes than knowledge of my apple in all its specificity.

It is tempting, because of our admiration for the general principles, to think that my apple has no importance. It is *merely* one of a kind. But we have a principle of equal ultimacy of the one and the many. This equal ultimacy holds for God, who is both one God and three persons. Derivatively, it holds for apples. We do not come to know generalities about apples without some observations and experiments with particular apples and particular soils and particular apple trees. We use those particulars, of course, to arrive at the generalities. But the generalities make sense only when we understand that they apply to particulars. The two are inextricably related.

For commercial purposes and for scientific understanding we *choose* to value the generalities. The fact of choice is significant. We make a decision to have a certain kind of generalizing focus because of what we value at the time. But we can choose other things: perhaps to do a still life of my apple, or to savor it as it is eaten. We cannot eat a generality.

If, then, we are thinking about a desire for "ultimate" metaphysics, it is wise to be aware of our choices. Metaphysically, the one and the many are equally ultimate. When we choose a perspective, we may temporarily and for our purposes prioritize the one—the generality. Or, conversely, we may prioritize the many, which we inevitably do when we eat an apple.

Thus, sciences give us perspectives. They do not give us metaphysical ultimates. This conclusion is obviously true when we consider the multiplicity of sciences, and the multiplicity of perspectives within any one science. Yet it tends to be forgotten. Philosophical materialism says that the world is "ultimately" matter and motion and energy. Such an assertion is indeed a philosophy. It is not merely "read off" the obvious and indubitable "results" of science. It is first read in, and then read out. Instead of going this way, we affirm the reality of all valid perspectives, not only multiple perspectives from various sciences, but also multiple perspectives from ordinary life. If we believe, on the basis of Scripture, that God has designed all the perspectives, multiperspectival metaphysics describes from a human point of view what God has done and is doing.

13

Metaphysics of Walking

As a second example, we consider the process of human walking. What is walking? (Readers who are content with having the example of an apple may wish to skip to chap. 15 or 16.)

The One and the Many

We can consider many instances of walking. Who is doing the walking? We can distinguish the walking of any one human being from the walking of every other. We enjoy multiple instances of this one kind of activity. Thus the category "walking" has many instances: Albert's walking, Barbara's walking, Cindy's walking, and so on. The relation of the general category to the many instances is a relation of one to many. As usual, it reflects the archetypal relation of one and many in the Trinity.

We can also distinguish walking at different times. Let us suppose that Sue takes a regular walk every morning. We can distinguish her walk today from her walk yesterday. Maybe she goes further today than she did yesterday. Maybe she strained a muscle yesterday evening, so that her gait in her walk this morning shows the effects of the strain. We can focus on the unity of one person, Sue, doing a regular walk. We can focus on one particular walk, the walk that she does today. Or we can focus on the diversity of the distinct walks that she accomplishes day by day. The diversity interlocks with the unity. As usual, we have the one and the many. Each presupposes the other.

Hypothetically, even if Sue took a walk only once in her life, we could view her walk either in its singularity or as one instance of many *possible* walks that she could have taken at other times. And, of course, her one walk would belong as one instance to the total class of walks by all other human beings at all times.

Contrast, Variation, and Distribution

Let us apply the categories of contrast, variation, and distribution as a triad of perspectives. Walking *contrasts* with other activities: running, jogging, crawling, sliding, swimming, rowing, reading while sitting, watching TV while lying down, and of course sleeping.

Consider variation. We can walk quickly or slowly, in cold weather or warm, uphill or downhill, in a circle or in a line. We can wobble or stagger or limp or go smoothly. All these possibilities, in their diversity, belong to the one unified kind of activity known as walking. We can see the one and the many. The one is the unified category of walking, while the many are the variations in style. Each case represents a *variant* form of walking.

Consider distribution. Walking as a human activity takes place in contexts. One kind of context is the context of before and after. If we walk from point A to point B, we have a sequence consisting of start (A), process (walking), and goal (B). Sue may have an activity at point A (eating breakfast), a second activity in the process (listening to an iPod or talking on a cell phone while walking), and a third activity at the destination (meeting someone for lunch). Sue's purpose in walking has ties with what happens at point A or B. Or perhaps Sue's walk is for exercise. With that purpose, it still has to fit into a certain temporal sequence of activities during the day. Sue may follow a fixed order. She walks every morning after getting up and before having a shower. The walking, we say, is "distributed" in the sequence of events. Kenneth Pike calls this *distribution as part of a structural sequence.*

An activity of walking can belong to two distinct larger classes, depending on its purpose. Walking for exercise belongs to a larger class of exercise activities: jogging, swimming, stretching exercises, doing sit-ups, doing knee bends, and so on. Walking to go somewhere belongs to a larger class of activities for getting somewhere—running and jogging might do, but also bicycling, driving, or going on a bus. Some walks may have both purposes simultaneously, in which case they belong to both of the larger classes, but in different ways. Any particular walk is *distributed* in the class of exercise activities or travel activities or both. Pike calls this *distribution as a member of a substitution class.*

Finally, we can classify walks by multiple kinds of classifications: speed, length, style of gait, type of person walking, purpose for walking, weather while walking, and so on. Any walk is *distributed* in a multidimensional network that classifies it by multiple criteria. Pike calls this *distribution as a point in a system.*

Interlocking

As usual, contrast, variation, and distribution each presupposes the others. The contrast between walking and hopping, for example, presupposes that we have a distinction between using the same foot or alternating which foot touches the ground. This distinction in turn presupposes that we have at least two feet that contrast with one another. The continuity of the same foot between different times involves variation, and each foot has a distribution in space, in time, and in multiple dimensions of classification. In running, there are times when both feet have simultaneously left the ground, whereas in walking at least one foot is always touching the ground. Here we have a contrastive feature dealing with touching the ground. This contrastive feature includes variation, since the amount of time during which both feet touch the ground together may vary. And the distinction between the two forms of locomotion depends on an understanding of how various events are distributed in time: first one foot on the ground, then the other foot, then the first foot leaving the ground, and so on.

Contrast, variation, and distribution interlock, manifesting an ectypal coinherence, and thereby reflecting the presence of the Trinitarian God, who governs walking. Since God governs the whole world by his word of power (Heb. 1:3), we can infer that he governs walking by his word. By speaking in the Son through the Spirit, God specifies how human beings walk, in unity and diversity. It is wonderful.

Hierarchy

Pike's linguistic analysis introduces the term *hierarchy* to describe a multiple-level structure of embedding.[1] Pike uses the concept primarily in the context of analysis of language, but we can apply it to an analysis of walking.[2]

The process of walking is spread out in time. It may also be spread out in space, if several people are walking together. But let us suppose that we are focusing on one individual walker, Sue. Her walk is preceded by other activities, and succeeded by still others. It fits into a time slot between other activities during the day. Perhaps her walk belongs to a larger time unit devoted to exercises of more than one kind. The unit of action that we call "her walk" is a recognizable unit, embedded in a larger unit of time, "Sue's exercise unit." We can also mention that we can view such units of cultural action from either an insider's perspective or an outsider's perspective. Sue herself has the view of an insider. But some non-Western cultures may not have "exercise units." They get quite enough physical activity during the day without setting aside extra time just for exercise. So these cultures would view Sue's exercise unit from an outsider's perspective.[3]

We will now focus on an insider's perspective. Sue has a unified period of activity with common, unifying features: she has several *physical* activities, and these activities together have the purpose of a physical workout. We have called her physical workout her "exercise unit." This exercise unit, let us say, fits into a larger complex of activities in the morning. So we have a larger unit, Sue's "weekday morning activity time." This unit in turn is embedded

---

[1] Kenneth L. Pike, *Linguistic Concepts: An Introduction to Tagmemics* (Lincoln: University of Nebraska Press, 1982), 67–106; Pike, *Language in Relation to a Unified Theory of the Structure of Human Behavior*, 2nd ed. (The Hague/Paris: Mouton, 1967), 565–97.

[2] Pike, *Unified Theory*, 101, uses hierarchy in analyzing a football game.

[3] On insider and outsider viewpoints, see Vern S. Poythress, *In the Beginning Was the Word: Language—A God-Centered Approach* (Wheaton, IL: Crossway, 2009), chap. 19; Poythress, *Redeeming Sociology: A God-Centered Approach* (Wheaton, IL: Crossway, 2011), chap. 18.

within the full day's activities: Sue's "daily schedule." And the daily schedule fits into a weekly schedule, and so on.

Each of these embeddings involves a part fitting into a whole. The parts fit into wholes *hierarchically*. We can discern larger and larger wholes, and, metaphorically speaking, we can picture these wholes as "above" the parts of which they are composed. The hierarchy is the rising structure of larger units above the smaller ones.

Several parts make up a whole, but on occasion the composition of the whole from the parts may display variation. For example, on one day Sue spends the whole morning on a special trip with the children, and she has no time for exercising. In this case, the whole is made up of only one main part.

We also find structure in the way that the parts fit into the whole. Sue may have designed her exercise unit so that through a number of activities she exercises most of the muscles of her body.

We can also analyze Sue's walk in terms of its smaller parts. Perhaps she walks toward a fixed point and then returns, so that her walk has two parts. But there are also smaller parts. Each step is a part. And the steps alternate between right foot and left.[4] They move her body progressively forward.

We can also look at simultaneous movements that go into walking. While the right foot and the left foot perform alternating motions, so do the right arm and the left arm. There may be some rotation of the hips. Once we have learned to walk, we largely take these motions for granted. But people recovering from physical impairments may find them no longer easy. Walking may also be destabilized by malfunction of the balance system in the inner ear and the cerebellum. So we could consider how our sense of balance functions in walking.

Particle, Wave, and Field

We next apply the particle, wave, and field perspectives to walking.

First, consider the particle perspective. Sue's walk on a particular day is a unified act, which we can consider and discuss as

---

[4] Poythress, *Redeeming Sociology*, chap. 30.

a stable whole. It is distinct from the activities preceding it and following it.

Second, consider the wave perspective. Sue's walk is spread out in time, and in the course of the walk she moves from one location to another in succession. The walk develops. If it is a long walk, she may tire. Her leg muscles gradually warm up. Her breathing gradually speeds up. If she is feeling stress from a previous concern, the stress may gradually melt away in the course of the physical activity. The wave perspective views the walk as a process.

Moreover, we can look at the beginning and the end of the walk each as a process rather than as a sudden shift. Sue's change into and out of an exercise outfit may be a regular part of her walk, so that if we wish, we can consider these actions as part of the overall process of "doing a walk." Does her walk start when she goes out the front door of her house, or when she starts walking to the door? Or does it start, in a more serious mode perhaps, when she reaches the street?

If we say that it starts when she goes out the door, we can still consider that going out the door is a process. Her body gradually moves through the doorway. Does "going out the door" start when she touches the door handle to open it, when it is fully open, when her body begins to go through the doorway, or when her body is midway through the doorway? When does this process of "going out the door" end? Using the wave perspective, we can draw attention to the fuzzy boundary between doing her walk and the activities preceding (or following) it.

Third, consider the field perspective, which focuses on relations. We can consider the relation of Sue's location to her surroundings at various points in the walk. We can consider the relation of the entire path of the walk to the layout of the neighborhood. We can consider the physiological relationship between muscle activity, muscle warmth, breathing, and tiredness. We can characterize her walk in comparison to other people's walks, and in comparison to her own walking at other times, which may be faster or slower, longer or shorter.

As usual, these three perspectives interlock. A wave of motion presupposes two stable points or particles between which the motion takes place. We recognize a particle in relation to comparisons with other distinct particles, thus using relationships and evoking the field perspective. The field perspective in considering relationships presupposes particles between which the relationships exist. Relationships can undergo change, and the idea of change presupposes the wave perspective.

All these complexities in walking display the wisdom of God, by which he creates complexity that fits harmoniously into unities.

Frame's Triad for Ethics

Next, we can apply Frame's triad of ethics to walking. First, we use the normative perspective. The ability to walk is a gift from God, for which we *ought* to praise him. The word *ought* here indicates a normative evaluation. If we have made a commitment to meet someone, we have an obligation to be there, and walking may be one way that we fulfill that obligation. We have an obligation to care for our bodies (inferred from 1 Cor. 6:19; Eph. 5:29; 1 Tim. 5:23), and walking as an exercise may be one way that we fulfill the obligation.

Using the situational perspective, we focus on the situation of walking. We may have to consider whether the neighborhood is safe before we start a walk. Does the weather allow a walk? Should we dress warmly or lightly, depending on the temperature and the wind?

The existential perspective focuses on motives. We may walk because we are fanatical about physical fitness, and fitness has taken on idolatrous proportions in our life. Conversely, we may decline to walk even if we need exercise, because we are too lazy or too preoccupied with other things. We may walk because we love the outdoors and praise God for it. We may walk and praise God because of the feeling of relaxation or well-being that we gain as we walk. We may walk because we love the outdoors and praise what we regard to be an impersonal nature, or "Mother Nature." Maybe we walk in order to serve the idol of self, because we want to have an attractive body in order to receive admiration. We can have good or bad motives underneath what looks like the same kind of activity.

The Poetry of Walking

The word *walk* can be used metaphorically. In the English Standard Version the word occurs twenty-six times within the New Testament letters, and in almost every one of those occurrences it functions as a metaphor for Christian living. For example:

> We were buried therefore with him by baptism into death, in order that, just as Christ was raised from the dead by the glory of the Father, we too might *walk* in newness of life. (Rom. 6:4)

> . . . in order that the righteous requirement of the law might be fulfilled in us, who *walk* not according to the flesh but according to the Spirit. (Rom. 8:4)

> But I say, *walk* by the Spirit, and you will not gratify the desires of the flesh. (Gal. 5:16)

We can find similar ideas in the book of Proverbs, sometimes with the word *way* or *path*:

> My son, do not *walk* in the *way* with them [evildoers];
>   hold back your *foot* from their *paths*. (Prov. 1:15)

Psalm 1 begins with the blessing,

> Blessed is the man
>   who *walks* not in the counsel of the wicked. (Ps. 1:1)

In the book of Acts, Christianity is described as "the Way":

> But when some became stubborn and continued in unbelief, speaking evil of *the Way* before the congregation . . . (Acts 19:9)

> About that time there arose no little disturbance concerning *the Way*. (Acts 19:23)

But this I confess to you, that according to *the Way*, which they call a sect, I worship the God of our fathers. (Acts 24:14)

But Felix, having a rather accurate knowledge of *the Way*, put them off. (Acts 24:22)

Christian living is like walking. It has a regular pattern. Metaphorically, it follows a "way" or a "path," the path of righteousness. It takes place by energy, the energy of the Holy Spirit (*"walk* by the Spirit"—Gal. 5:16). We who belong to Christ are supposed to pay attention to how we act, to make sure that we continue in the right direction, following Christ. On the other hand, the metaphor of walking suggests that we are not self-consciously attentive at every moment. After we have been Christians for a while, we continue according to patterns and habits that have already grown into us in earlier practices of righteousness. We may pray and read our Bibles and serve others and go to church at regular times. The walk continues over time—in fact, all of our life on earth, subsequent to our initial coming to the Way.

Thus, physical movement with attention and exertion, in the form of walking, becomes a metaphor for spiritual movement, spiritual activity. In addition, for a Christian, physical walking becomes in itself also spiritual walking! Every activity, including every physical activity, should have as its deepest motive following Christ.

When we move ourselves through spatial locations, we perform one of the most basic and elementary things that human beings do. It is fitting that this basic action should express our loyalty to Christ and should then become a picture for all actions. We said that Christian "walking" is a metaphor, but we can also view it as a synecdoche, that is, a part for the whole. Physical walking is one activity among many. It is a part of living. It stands for all of living. Even when we are physically walking for exercise, we can use the time in praying or in praising God, or in making godly plans, or just enjoying the sense of movement and rhythm that God gives us in the experience.

We can see still more connections between walking and the

central realities of Christian faith. First Peter 2:21 tells us that we are called to suffer with patience "because Christ also suffered for you, leaving you an example, so that you might follow in his steps." The language about following "in his steps" is close to the metaphor of walking. We are to walk as Christ walked. Of course, Christ did not merely set an example. He bore our sins, and no one else can do that (1 Pet. 2:24). He is more than an example, but he is never less.

So we may consider Christ's own "walk" while he was on earth. Christ physically walked about in Palestine. People followed him around. The twelve disciples followed him physically. As they did so, they had extended opportunity for personal fellowship, and this fellowship solidified their knowledge of him and their imitation of him. Or at least it should have. The disciples did not fully understand either Christ or his works until the Holy Spirit came on them (John 13:7; 16:13, 25).

The metaphor of walking occurs not only in the New Testament but also in the Old. For example, Proverbs 2:20 says concerning the person who follows wisdom,

So you will *walk* in the way of the good
and keep to the *paths* of the righteous.

Jesus Christ perfectly fulfills this Old Testament description. He uniquely fills the role of the righteous man of Psalm 1, who does not "*walk* in the counsel of the wicked" (1:1). So, just as in the case of the Christian "walk," we can correlate Christ's physical walk from place to place in Palestine with a spiritual walk in the way of righteousness.

In the broad, metaphorical sense, Christ's whole life on earth was a "walk." God the Father sent his Son in the power of the Holy Spirit to accomplish and work out on earth just this walk (Matt. 3:17; Luke 4:16). Christ's walk set an example for the Christian's walk, following "in his steps" (1 Pet. 2:21). His walk also resulted in a unique accomplishment of obedience, leading to his resurrection. His death and resurrection, as the endpoint of his "walk" on earth, granted us forgiveness, justification, and new life.

[Christ] was delivered up for our trespasses and raised for our justification. (Rom. 4:25)

But if Christ is in you, although the body is dead because of sin, the Spirit is *life* because of righteousness. If the Spirit of him who raised Jesus from the dead dwells in you, he who raised Christ Jesus from the dead will also *give life to your mortal bodies through his Spirit* who dwells in you. (Rom. 8:10–11)

The Christian walk has a Trinitarian basis. Our walk is planned and ordained and commanded by God the Father: "For we are his [God's] workmanship, created in Christ Jesus for good works, which God prepared beforehand, that we should *walk* in them" (Eph. 2:10). Our walk takes place after the pattern of God the Son in his incarnation: "We were buried therefore with him [Christ] by baptism into death, in order that, just as Christ was raised from the dead by the glory of the Father, *we too might walk* in newness of life" (Rom. 6:4). Our walk takes place as we are empowered by the Holy Spirit, who is the Spirit of Christ sent from the Father: "If we live by the Spirit, let us also *keep in step with the Spirit*" (Gal. 5:25).

Since Christ uniquely and climactically reveals God, we can infer that his walk on earth takes place as a manifestation of the eternal life that the Son shares with the Father in the Holy Spirit. Christ's *life* on earth manifests the *life* of the eternal Son with the Father. His life on earth is a *walk*. So, may we say that the life of God himself is a "walk"?

I do not think it works if we apply the word *walk* to God's eternal existence. When the word *walk* describes physical walking, it implies a change of location. God fills the universe, rather than being "located." When used metaphorically, the word *walk* suggests moving and progressing toward a goal. This kind of description suits human action in the world, and it suits Christ as a person who is incarnate and has a human nature. But God in his eternal existence does not need to "achieve" anything.

We can nevertheless see that human life on earth imitates in some respects, on a creaturely level, the eternal life of God. God is the living God. He is eternally active in love, since the persons of the Trinity love one another. We have to avoid suggesting that God's love is an "achievement" or a "goal," as if to imply that he was not always loving as an aspect of the fullness of being God. His love is an eternal activity. We imitate that eternal activity in a creaturely way when we grow in exercising love. For us as creatures, love in its fullness is a goal at which we have not yet arrived.

In addition, a walk on earth takes place in an environment. We travel from point A to point B. And we travel along a path. Both the endpoints and the path are external to the person who is taking the walk. But before the creation of the world God did not have anything "external" to him to serve as the endpoints or as a path.

Using an analogy with a physical path, Proverbs indicates that the path on earth is "the path of righteousness," in which is life: "In the *path* of righteousness is life" (Prov. 12:28). The path of righteousness on earth obviously reflects God who is righteous. The path of life reflects God who is life, eternal life. The Son as the eternal image of the Father manifests righteousness and life. He does so in the presence of the Father from all eternity, and then he does so on earth in his earthly life as the incarnate God.

Thus, Christ's walk on earth does reflect the original life and righteousness of God, which belong to God the Father, are manifest in the Son, and characterize the Spirit as life (Rom. 8:10). God does not need a created environment in order to express righteousness. He lives and acts in the "environment" that is God himself. The Father lives and loves in the Spirit in the path of righteousness, and the righteousness of which we speak consists in the Son, who is the image of the Father. This is the archetypal divine action after which God patterns our Christian walk. The Christian walk takes place in a created environment, consisting of other human beings and the challenges of situations. It also takes place in the "environment" of God—God the Father's plan, God the Son's pattern, and God the Spirit's power. God has fellowship with us, just as Christ had fellowship with the disciples on the road to Emmaus when they walked with him (Luke 24:15, 28).

God promises to walk with us:

And I will *walk* among you and will be your God, and you shall be my people. (Lev. 26:12)

. . . as God said,

"I will make my dwelling among them
    and *walk* among them,
    and I will be their God,
    and they shall be my people." (2 Cor. 6:16)

Our spiritual walk has corporate dimensions. We walk with God among us, and we walk with other people. We find a type or foreshadowing of this walk in the journey of the people of Israel through the wilderness (1 Cor. 10:6, 11). We walk with God and also with all who belong to Christ in the fellowship of his body. We encourage them in their walk, and they encourage us (Rom. 1:11–12; 1 Thess. 5:14).

Outside the Bible itself, the greatest Christian classic of all time is arguably *The Pilgrim's Progress*, by John Bunyan. The whole narrative has a structure based on the analogy between Christian living and walking on a pilgrimage. The pilgrimage begins for the protagonist "Christian" in "the city of Destruction," and ends at the "Celestial City." The Christian pilgrim walks from A to B. Bunyan's story builds on the biblical analogy of walking.

From the beginning God designed that physical walking would have analogical relation (or a relation of synecdoche) to life. The analogy goes back to God himself. God is righteous, and the authority of his righteousness determines the path of his action. God is living, and he acts with purpose. The character of God serves as a foundation and archetype both for human life as a whole and for the practice of physical walking. Thus the metaphorical relations in walking are not less "real" than other perspectival analyses.

Frame's Triad of Lordship

Next, let us use Frame's triad of lordship: authority, control, and presence. The Lord God has *authority* to prescribe the manner of the Christian walk and its path. He has *control* to empower the

Christian to accomplish his walk. God is *present* by walking with us, as we have just observed. Or we may alter the picture to say that the Holy Spirit dwells in us, expressing the presence of God in us (see John 14:23), and it is he who empowers us (Acts 1:8; Gal. 5:22–23) and guides us authoritatively (John 16:13).

We may also apply Frame's triad to physical walking. God expresses his authority in his words of creation and command, which specify the nature of human walking. God expresses his control in creating each one of us, giving each one the power to walk, and empowering every step. God expresses his presence in sustaining each one of us as we walk: "In him we live and *move* and have our being" (Acts 17:28).

Scientific Perspectives

We may analyze walking from any number of scientific perspectives. As with the case of the apple, these perspectives invite us to consider technical details.

Consider a quantitative perspective. Human beings have two feet. A walk consists in a sequence in time, according to which foot 1 and foot 2 are swung forward one after the other. So we get a numerical pattern (see fig. 4).

Figure 4

Time	1	2	3	4	5	6	7
Foot	1	2	1	2	1	2	1

We can count the total number of steps in a particular walk. We can also count the heartbeats accompanying the walk.

Using the spatial perspective, we can describe the spatial positions of all parts of the path of the walk. We may also describe the three-dimensional motions of each arm, each leg, and each foot, and rotation of the hips. We may describe the movement of the eyes as well.

Using a physical perspective, we may analyze the mechanics of muscle and bone in the movements of a walk, the energy expended during the walk, the forces on the pavement and the forces on various muscles and joints.

Using the perspectives of chemistry, biochemistry, and molecular biology, we may study the molecular metabolism that releases chemical energy of sugar for the use of the muscles, the conversion of starch and fat into sugar, the diffusion of oxygen to the muscle cells, the elimination of carbon dioxide, and the molecular-level chemical reactions proceeding in the individual muscle cells.

We may also study from the perspective of neurology and physiology the interaction of nerve, muscle, and bone, and the role of visual perception, balance, and kinesthetics in the walk. And we may consult experts in physical training.

Considering sociological aspects of walking, we may study why people walk, social perceptions of the value of exercise, and social interaction during walks involving two or more people.

We may consider the economic dimension such as sales of exercise clothing or interaction of walking with health and the economics of health, including the expenses of recovery from injuries that affect walking.

We may even consider the legal dimension of walking. It is illegal to walk on many major highways. It is legal in most other circumstances, but jaywalking may be prohibited. It is illegal to walk in places when you are trespassing—though what is illegal is not the walking as such but the fact that you have gotten yourself onto someone else's property.

As in the case of the apple, we may observe that scientific perspectives, by focusing on general patterns, may provide powerful, useful information—in this case, information that is useful for human health and human flourishing. The generalities help us because each new person does not need to start from scratch in learning about walking, and the more technical learning may help us to improve.

The various sciences give us perspectives—multiple perspectives. But so does ordinary life. God has ordained all the textures that we notice from all the perspectives. They are all "real," and in a sense all significant, because God's knowledge of them makes them significant.

14

Metaphysics of a Bookmark

As a third example of how a multiperspectival metaphysics works, we may analyze something as simple as a bookmark. I own several special bookmarks that are artistically designed. But the bookmark on which I want to focus is merely a three-by-five-inch card, which I commandeered for the purpose. It is sticking between two pages in a particular book that I am gradually reading.

We could journey through the same list of perspectives that we used in the previous two chapters. But we hope that the previous chapters give sufficient illustrations for many of the perspectives. We will therefore truncate our list and consider only a few.

Contrast, Variation, and Distribution

We first consider contrast, variation, and distribution. My bookmark contrasts with other objects on my desk: the book itself, pens, pamphlets, note pads, as well as other three-by-five-inch cards used for taking notes. We can consider variation over time. In time, my bookmark begins to show faint signs of wear. I may write notes on it having to do with the book I am reading. The addition of writing changes its appearance—it *varies* the appearance. The three-by-five-inch card varies in appearance depending on the angle at which I look at it. If it sits within a closed book, it varies in appearance depending on how much of it sticks up beyond the edge of the pages.

If we focus on the class of bookmarks, rather than my particular bookmark, we find a contrast between bookmarks and other objects. We have variation among different bookmarks. Some bookmarks are designed to be such—for example, the "artistically designed" bookmarks that I have at home. Other bookmarks, among which is my three-by-five-inch card, are objects "commandeered" for this function, even though they were not originally designed with such a purpose especially in mind. The word *bookmark* itself shows evidence of a range of uses here. On the one hand, an artistically designed variety is called a bookmark even if it is not functioning to mark a place in a book. My three-by-five-inch card is a bookmark in a second sense, in that it is so only because it is currently functioning as a bookmark. Suppose I put a pen or pencil or even a stone between the pages of a book in order to hold my place. Someone might see it and say, "What's that?" And I might rightly say, "Oh, that's my bookmark," meaning that it is temporarily functioning as one.

Suppose now that I have my book open, and I turn it face down on my chair in order to hold the place open while I step out briefly. Is the chair itself my bookmark? It seems to me that such use of the word *bookmark* would be farfetched. However, if I return with a friend, and my friend asks what the book is doing there, I might say loosely, "Oh, that's my bookmark." I do not mean that the chair itself is the bookmark, but rather that the whole setup is functioning as a kind of virtual bookmark, or a functional substitute for a physical object that would more ordinarily play the role of a bookmark.

A functional bookmark is not necessarily a physical object. It may be either a small physical object or some other means of marking out a page location within a book. We usually do that by inserting a small object between the two pages. But we have alternatives. Some people "dog ear" a page. A person might even take one book and insert it between the pages of another, so that the first book functions as a bookmark for the second.

Next, consider distribution. My bookmark is *distributed as a member of a substitution class* within the class of all my bookmarks, which in turn is included in the class of all bookmarks that anyone owns. My bookmark is *distributed as part of a structural sequence* in relation to the pages of the book. It comes after page 212, let us say, and before page 213. My bookmark is *distributed as a point in a system* when we look at a system of multiple dimensions classifying various sizes and designs of bookmarks, and classifying other paraphernalia for interacting with books.

The Poetry of a Bookmark

Can we find "poetry" in a bookmark? And would such poetry represent one aspect of the nature of a bookmark? A bookmark does not offer a particularly promising start for streams of eloquent poetry. But we can still notice symbolic associations. A bookmark such as my three-by-five-inch card functions to mark where I am in reading a book, and its meaning as a bookmark is bound up with its relation to the book and to my reading.

So we may think about my reading. I have read the part of the book preceding the location of the bookmark, and I have not read the part following that location. I continue to move the bookmark as I proceed through the reading. Reading is itself a kind of story with a beginning, a middle, and an end. I am in the middle.

Figuratively speaking, I am on a journey. The journey takes me physically through the pages of the book. Linguistically, the journey takes me through the printing and the sentences in the book. It takes me mentally and spiritually through the unfolding of ideas and/or stories in the book. At the end of the journey I have reached a destination that I intended beforehand—to have read the book. I may also have reached a destination mentally or spiritually, in that I have grown through the absorption of the ideas or stories in the book. My journey in thought is in turn part of the larger "journey" that makes my life.

So now we are considering at least two journeys, the smaller journey of reading the book and the larger journey of life. Within each of these journeys, the bookmark has a role. It marks the place where I currently sit. This "place" lies between the past and the future. The past corresponds to the part of the book that I have already read, and my memories (in the present) of this reading experience. The future corresponds to the part of the book that I have not yet read but intend to. My present corresponds to the thinness of the bookmark itself. But that thinness enjoys a relationship to past and future.

In short, temporal relationships in my life map into spatial relationships between the bookmark and the pages of the book. The bookmark itself functions like Frame's existential perspective. It is I, residing in the present, who think about past, present, and future and God's mastery over them. The bookmark metaphorically represents me in my relationships. Because we are speaking about analogies or metaphorical relationships, we might even venture to suggest that, by analogy, we can compare God to the author of the book. God has "written" beforehand the entirety of my life and even the entirety of history in his "book," namely his plan, which includes (as smaller books) the lives and destinies of all the human beings on earth (Rev. 17:8; 20:12). God knows all of history, and he also knows my current location in history.

People may react by saying that this comparison of mine is perhaps colorful or interesting in its own way, but it is *my invention*. It has nothing to do with my bookmark, really, but only with what in my imagination I *make* out of the bookmark. I *make* it into a symbol of life and time and memory and God's relation to my living my life.

Yes, in a sense I "made" the symbolic connection. I have "created" it, after a fashion. Every human being has a creativity, which is an analogue to the original creativity of God. God created the world, and he could have created other worlds as well. We are not God and we cannot literally create a world, but we can imagine a world. And we can imaginatively "create" meaning or significance within the world by creative associations like the one between my bookmark and my life.

But did my creativity take God by surprise? Of course not. My creativity is a gift from God. He thought my thoughts before I ever did. As we have emphasized, God has designed the world and the history of the world down to the level of every particularity. He has not *merely* designed its general features. He designed the association between my bookmark and my life. So in a sense I "created" nothing. I only saw what was there, something that I had not seen before. The full *reality* of my bookmark includes everything that God has specified about it. That reality includes the relation between my bookmark and my life, such as I have come to observe. I made my observations about the relationship between my bookmark and life because God first of all, prior to my understanding, created a world in which he built in a multitude of analogies by his design. In other words, I saw the analogy because he made an analogy. Time and story belong to the character of the world.[1] (For more analysis of the bookmark, see appendix C.)

---

[1] See the discussion of story in relation to world history in Vern S. Poythress, *In the Beginning Was the Word: Language—A God-Centered Approach* (Wheaton, IL: Crossway, 2009), chaps. 13, 24–29.

15

Perspectives in Combination

We have now analyzed three units from human experience: my apple, Sue's walk, and my bookmark. All three can be analyzed from multiple perspectives.

The Acronym TEAR

We can also contemplate very broad categories in which these units fall. One approach in semantics distinguishes four different kinds of entities: things ("objects"), events, abstracts, and relations. The acronym TEAR summarizes the four categories.[1] Using this categorization, an apple is a thing (T). Sue's walking is an event (E). My bookmark is a thing (T), but when we take into account its function, the significance of the bookmark lies in relations (R) with the surrounding pages.

At first glance these categories may seem to result in a clean classification. But further reflection shows that they function somewhat like perspectives. For example, we could ask ourselves what love is. At first glance we might argue that it is an abstract or a relation—if Al loves Donna, Al has a relation to Donna. But

---

[1] John Beekman and John Callow, *Translating the Word of God: With Scripture and Topical Indexes* (Grand Rapids: Zondervan, 1974), 68; Johannes P. Louw and Eugene A. Nida, eds., *Greek-English Lexicon of the New Testament Based on Semantic Domains*, 2 vols. (New York: United Bible Societies, 1988), group "relationals" together with abstracts, so that there are only three categories altogether: "objects," "events," and "abstracts" (1:vi). One may see some relationship between TEAR and Aristotle's categories. People could use TEAR as a stripped down version of Aristotle, to *reduce* meaning to fixed categories, or as a more flexible system where they admit the multidimensional nature of meanings.

we know love partly through the fact that people express love in action. When Jesus says, "Love your enemies" (Matt. 5:44), he does not mean primarily that we should have warm feelings of affection about them. We should pray for them and do good to them, and these are activities—"events," in the TEAR classification. Moreover, the Bible says that God is love (1 John 4:8, 16). So with this formulation love is a person—T in the TEAR classification. God is the origin for all human love.

In addition, the TEAR classification has a close relationship to an earlier triad—the particle, wave, and field perspectives. The particle perspective treats units in a thing-like way. It does so not only for my apple, which we readily classify as a thing, but also for Sue's walking, which is an event, and for the bookmark's relation to the book. Similarly, the wave perspective treats units as events developing in time. My apple ripens over time or gets eaten, and when we focus on this wave-like development, it is as if we were treating the apple like an event—the event of ripening or the event of getting broken up as it is eaten. Finally, the field perspective treats units as relational.

My Apple as a Perspective

Let us now expand our earlier analyses of an apple, a walk, and a bookmark into perspectives. Our previous reflections on "poetic" significance came near to making new perspectives. We can use my apple as the starting point for a perspective on the whole world. How? In considering the poetry of my apple we observed that my apple symbolically can connote love between a husband and wife. Love between husband and wife in turn connotes the love between Christ and his church. This love originates in the love between the persons of the Trinity. God is love. All of creation and all of history express his love.

My wife bought my apple at the store. But ultimately the apple came from God. He gave it to me. Why? Because he loves me. My apple gives me one particular expression of the love that God displays through the rule of Christ in all the world (Heb. 1:3). So when

I understand the significance of my apple, it offers a perspective on all the world.

Someone—I do not know whether it was a poet or a philosopher—once said that if he could actually understand one object, he would understand the world. In a sense, this is true. But we need to add two clarifications. First, what the poet or philosopher expresses as a mere possibility of understanding becomes a reality when we come to know God through Christ. The apple expresses the goodness of God and the love of God in Christ, a love that constitutes both the foundation for the world and its destiny (Eph. 1:10). By understanding the apple in relation to God, we understand everything. Second, our understanding of God never becomes *comprehension*—we do not understand God completely, nor do we understand my apple comprehensively, to the very bottom.

Sue's Walk as a Perspective

Similarly, Sue's walk offers us a perspective on God and the world. Walking becomes a metaphor for the Christian walk. The Christian walk encompasses all of life. Whether or not a person is a Christian, he "walks" through life. In the whole of history, the human race "walks" from its beginnings to its consummation. In addition, we can construe even God's actions as a "walk" if we qualify the word *walk* to indicate that God does not need an environment outside himself in order to act.

My Bookmark as a Perspective

Finally, my bookmark can serve as a perspective on everything when we use the analogy between its position in the book and my position in my life. The human race as a whole has a story, and we are now at a certain point in that story.

Can my bookmark serve as a perspective even on God? God is not subject to the limitations of time. Rather, his activity in creation and providence constitutes the character of time as we experience it. Our lives and our history take place because of foundational relationships in God himself. If we may oversimplify, we may say that God the Father is the originator, in relation to God the Son as executor, and in relation to the Holy Spirit as consummator. All three persons of the Trinity accomplish acts in time through their fellowship with one another, a fellowship that is *relational*. God's archetypal relationality is the foundation for our ectypal relationality, which is expressed in the relationship between our human execution of the task of reading at the point where the bookmark resides, our view of the origin of our reading in the past with the commencement of the book, and our view of the goal of reading in the future when we finish the book. God's eternal action in the Father's begetting the Son lays the foundation for God's actions in time as he brings about events in the world that he created. We imitate him when we read a book and use a bookmark.

Combining Two Perspectives: An Apple and a Walk

If my apple offers one perspective, and Sue's walk offers another, we can also explore the combination of perspectives. Each offers a perspective on the other. We may deepen our understanding by looking at one through the eyes of the other.[2] Let us consider how we might do so with my apple and Sue's walk.

Perspectivally speaking, my apple symbolizes love. Sue's walk symbolizes the Christian walk. Our walk should be characterized by love: "And *walk in love*, as Christ loved us and gave himself up for us, a fragrant offering and sacrifice to God" (Eph. 5:2). The language of walking in love leads in Ephesians 5:2 directly to a comparison with Christ's love, which was expressed in his "walk" through his time on earth. Christ's love and sacrifice form the heart of redemption, and we never exhaust their significance. So my apple and Sue's walk give us a fruitful combination.

When we say that our walk is to be characterized by love, we are viewing our walk from the perspective of love. Conversely, we can view our love from the perspective of our walk. Love must work out

---

[2] See Vern S. Poythress, *Symphonic Theology: The Validity of Multiple Perspectives in Theology* (Grand Rapids: Zondervan, 1987; repr., Phillipsburg, NJ: P&R, 2001), chap. 3, as well as examples, in John Frame's books, of the fruitfulness of using one perspective to deepen our understanding of another.

in action: "Little children, let us not love in word or talk but in deed and in truth" (1 John 3:18). That is to say that true love *walks*.

Just before 1 John 3:18, the Scripture appeals to what Christ did: "By this we know love, that he laid down his life for us, and we ought to lay down our lives for the brothers" (1 John 3:16). So, just as in Ephesians 5:2, Christ's work of redemption lays the foundation for our love being a love that walks.

James underlines the same reality: "But be *doers* of the word, and not hearers only, deceiving yourselves" (James 1:22). "So also faith by itself, if it does not have *works*, is dead" (James 2:17).

Combining Three Perspectives: An Apple, a Walk, and a Bookmark

If we have succeeded in deepening our understanding of ourselves and the world through combining two perspectives, we may add a third. A bookmark symbolizes the relation between a plan in the past, execution in the present, and the attainment of a goal in the future. The Christian walk, as a walk in love, has a past, a present, and a future. It has its basis in the work of Christ in his suffering, death, and resurrection. It is energized in the present by the gift of the Holy Spirit. It looks forward to the attainment of consummate communion with God in the future:

> . . . we ourselves, who have the firstfruits of the Spirit, groan inwardly as we wait eagerly for adoption as sons, the redemption of our bodies. (Rom. 8:23)

> For now we see in a mirror dimly, but then face to face. (1 Cor. 13:12)

> No longer will there be anything accursed, but the throne of God and of the Lamb will be in it, and his servants will worship him. They will see his face, and his name will be on their foreheads. And night will be no more. They will need no light of lamp or sun, for the Lord God will be their light, and they will reign forever and ever. (Rev. 22:3–5)

We are now free to walk in love, to serve God with our hearts, because Christ has freed us. This freedom has been termed the "already" aspect of redemption—the "indicative," because it has already happened, and the gospel indicatively declares it to have been accomplished. Christ's accomplishment belongs to our past. God moves us to walk in love, not only by the past, but also with hope for the future, which is the "not yet" aspect of redemption. The future corresponds to our "imperative," so called because we have imperatival commands and directives, thrusting us toward the goal. Our future is our goal. Both past and future have intricate relations to our present. Our present walk in love is affected by and receives significance from its relation to the past and future of God's purposes.

Multiple Perspectives

Can we further multiply the perspectives?

In 2012, the world population was about seven billion people. Each of these is unique. Each person has a unique background and a unique cluster of experiences, gifts, hopes, and fears. Each person has his own "perspective," in the broad sense of the word. Each person also finds distortions in his being and in his thinking because of sin. If we could all be free from sin, how would we combine perspectives? What would it be like to learn and learn and learn from how someone else sees things and from what his journey or walk has shown him?

Such learning would be like learning from the four Gospels taken together. The four Gospels have a lot in common. But each of them also has some distinctive emphases. Rightly understood, these emphases harmonize with one another. Each emphasis deepens our knowledge of and appreciation for Christ and his work. Taken together, they give us a richness greater than any one Gospel.

Similarly, Frame's three perspectives on ethics operate in harmony with one another. Each perspective affirms the others and leads to the others. If we appear to find disharmony rather than harmony, we have to continue to work. We ought not to be satisfied when pieces do not fit together. We definitely should not accept that two truths can contradict one another.

Let us consider again the seven billion people on earth. Each person, on average, uses several different perspectives during a day. We are now thinking of perspectives in a narrower sense. A single person may have a work-oriented perspective while on the job, a socially oriented perspective in interactions with friends and family, and a food-and-fellowship perspective during meals. When we combine this multiplicity with the uniqueness of the person, we get 20 billion or more perspectives. When two people talk with each other and listen with genuine sympathy, we have the potential for 20 billion times 20 billion possible combinations, which works out to 400 billion billion perspectives.

When two people have spent a lifetime exploring their mutual perspectives, we may contemplate bringing them together into larger groups. When two join another two, we get 160,000 billion billion billion billion perspectives. Is that enough for you? It is not enough, because God's wisdom encompasses far more than this.

Let us then not suppose that within this life a philosophical speculator can dissolve the mysteries and tell us once and for all what my apple really is.[3] I mean my Granny Smith apple, 2.5 inches in diameter, lying with others in a bag on my kitchen table, showing me my wife's love, which shows me the church's love, which shows me God's love for his people. The philosopher cannot supply me with the single, final, definitive, monoperspectival account about my apple, because he cannot supply a final account of God's love. Consequently, the philosopher also cannot tell me about apples in general, because the universal is entangled with the particular according to the divine pattern of one and many. The philosopher cannot specify appleness without its interlocking with my apple. And so he cannot specify it without having plumbed the depths of God's love, an expression of the Father's love for the Son in the Holy Spirit.

Yet, by common grace, the speculator may still give us food for thought. He offers a perspective, and we should respect him as a human being made in the image of God.

---

[3] "Being is not a welter of images from which essences must be wrested in an action of noetic rarefaction on the one hand, nor a chaos of the unthematizable on the other, but is an unmasterable beauty boundless in its variations" (David Bentley Hart, *The Beauty of the Infinite: The Aesthetics of Christian Truth* [Grand Rapids: Eerdmans, 2003], 141).

My Analysis as One among Many

My own analysis of metaphysics offers only one possible analysis among many. It offers a perspective (in the broad sense of perspective). Someone else—any of the seven billion people on earth—may legitimately have his or her own true approach. That does not mean, however, that "anything goes." Truth and error contrast with each other. All people should seek to know God, who is the truth, and who repudiates error. But the truth of God's mind is rich. We do not seek identity of perspective, but loyalty to the truth, from whatever perspective a person has as a starting point.

PART 5

Other Subdivisions of Philosophy

16

Ethics

We have finished our exploration of metaphysics. What about other subdivisions of philosophy?

To address each of the subdivisions in detail would take many books. In this book we can only sketch the implications. I hope that it is clear that the Bible provides resources for surpassing the entire history of secular philosophy.

By exploring the nature of what exists, we have illustrated that the Bible has resources for providing satisfying answers. God tells us what kinds of things exist. God by his word of command creates and sustains all kinds of creatures, in their unity and diversity. God by nature is Trinitarian, and the world that he created has both unity and diversity intertwined with each other. The world by nature bears the stamp of his creative wisdom, and it reflects his tripersonality in the multiplicity of its dimensions. The world specified by God's multidimensional speech is itself suitable for multiperspectival analysis. The multiplicity of ways in which we analyze it reflects the perspectival multiplicity of ways in which God has specified it by his speech.

As usual, metaphysics—the way the world is—has implications for other subdivisions of philosophy. Let us first consider ethics, which studies the nature of right and wrong.

Perspectives on Ethics

If metaphysics is multiperspectival, so is ethics. John Frame's work on ethics supplies us with resources. His book *The Doctrine of the Christian Life*[1] has addressed extensively the area of ethics, including philosophical ethics. The book interacts with and criticizes major systems of philosophical ethics, namely, deontological ethics, utilitarian ethics, and existentialist ethics.

In addressing these questions, Frame's book relies on the Bible throughout. Using the Bible, Frame is able to give straightforward, biblically based answers. God is the Lord of all. His absoluteness, his goodness, and his justice together are the ultimate source for moral standards. Human beings are made in his image, and so, by God's plan, they have in their consciences a sense of moral right and wrong.[2] Since the fall into sin, this sense can be and is perverted, buried, and otherwise evaded. But it is still there. God also rules history, so that morally good or bad behavior has consequences. Because God designed us, he knows what is best for us. True moral standards are found in what God commands in the Bible.

Since God is the ultimate authority for moral standards, he provides the norms for ethics in his word. The character of God as our ultimate authority provides the foundation for the normative perspective. God's word provides abundant instruction, so that we need not remain in doubt about answers to fundamental ethical questions, such as whether stealing is wrong and why. We know that stealing is wrong because God says so. And we know why it is wrong—because it violates God's commandment not to steal.

Since God created the world and rules over it, he also provides the situation in which we live. God therefore provides a foundation for the situational perspective, which focuses on the circumstances around us. From a situational perspective, we can give additional reasons why it makes sense that stealing is wrong. God created a

---

[1] John M. Frame, *The Doctrine of the Christian Life* (Phillipsburg, NJ: P&R, 2008); see also the shorter work by Frame, *Perspectives on the Word of God: An Introduction to Christian Ethics* (Eugene, OR: Wipf and Stock, 1999).

[2] We will not here debate the meaning of the phrase *image of God*. Genesis 1:26–28 appears to have some focus on the task of dominion that human beings are to exercise over the world on God's behalf. In this dominion, human beings are imitating God's rule over the universe. So this exercise of dominion is one of many ways in which human beings are like God and imitate God. Human distinctiveness includes many aspects of "godlikeness." I use the phrase *image of God* to include all these aspects.

world in which obedience to his commandments leads to blessing. An individual who refrains from stealing escapes the liability for stealing; he escapes a guilty conscience; and he escapes punishment that he will receive if he is caught (or punishment in the next life even if he is not caught in this life).

Not only the individual but the society benefits. A society whose members refrain from stealing avoids anger and quarreling and bad feelings and destruction of property and other consequences that stealing tends to produce. Such a society flourishes, and the people in it flourish. They receive blessings from God, both directly in a sense of his pleasure and indirectly through additional material prosperity.

Finally, God created us as human beings, who have a conscience and a sense of right and wrong. God thus provides the foundation for the existential perspective. This perspective alerts us to further reasons why theft is wrong. It is wrong because our consciences tell us it is wrong. Of course, our consciences may be corrupted by sin, so they do not provide an ultimate authority. The ultimate authority belongs to God. A Christian existential perspective is able to explain how people's internal sense of right and wrong contributes to ethics. At the same time, it avoids reducing ethics to the standards of human conscience, which would lead to relativism.

In sum, Frame's three perspectives for ethics—the normative, situational, and existential perspectives—work together because they harmonize according to God's plan. God ordained all three of them through his control over the norms, the situations, and the human persons. He also gave us the capacity, as human beings, of thinking about and appreciating all three perspectives. We can do so because God made us in his image. The three perspectives harmonize if we use them properly, in communion with God and with an appreciation for the way in which God designed them to interlock.

Within a biblically based approach, these three are perspectives on the same whole. Each leads to the others. Each implies the others and each presupposes the others.

Non-Christian Ethics

By contrast, secular philosophical ethics has found itself in conundrums. Deontological ethics is a kind of secular version of the normative perspective. It focuses on transcendent norms for ethical behavior. One such norm might be that you should do to others as you want them to do to you. For example, you should not steal because you do not want others to steal from you.

But when this perspective is detached from God who gave it, its connection with human persons and with the existential perspective tends to disintegrate. Why do we as humans have any connection with these alleged norms? Why should I commit myself to the principle of not stealing, or the more general principle of doing to others what I want done to me? Why not rather be selfish? Why not steal as long as I can get away with it? And if someone else steals from me, why not go after him out of selfishness, rather than out of a general principle that theft is wrong? And why should we think that the norms have any connection with our situation?

Utilitarian ethics (and more broadly teleological ethics, that is, ethics based on goals) is a kind of secularized distortion of the situational perspective. Utilitarian ethics says that we ought to maximize "utility," the sum of benefits for all human beings. But how do we measure utility without norms for measurement? In secular utilitarian ethics, the situation gets isolated from the norms, so that we can always ask, Why *should* I care about maximizing utility? Utility has no deontological or normative "bite" to it. For example, it might be argued that a poor person should be allowed to steal from a rich person because the poor person has more need for the money than the rich one does. Indeed, some people are in favor of schemes for "leveling the wealth." But other people would object that the relative need that a poor person has does not make it *right* for him to steal. They are thereby calling in question whether utilitarian ethics (or at least this form of utilitarian ethics) is right.

Similarly, teleological ethics says that we should choose our actions so that they lead to the best goals, the best outcomes. But who decides what outcomes are "best"? And without existentially oriented wisdom, how can a human being judge well which actions lead to which goals?

Political ethics in particular is plagued by what has been called the "law of unintended consequences." Laws that politicians put in place with good intentions have unintended consequences. For example, a law reduces the speed limit to promote safety, but it results in people wasting more time in traveling. A law puts in place standards for state-controlled education, but the law frustrates good teachers who want to teach for long-run understanding rather than merely for ability to do well on a standardized test. A law for rent control forbids landlords from increasing the monthly rent, in order to protect the renters. But the landlords, finding that rising prices gradually leave them with an unprofitable business, refuse to maintain and repair their rental properties. The renters do not suffer from higher rents but end up suffering from poor living conditions.

Finally, secular existentialist ethics is a distortion of the existential perspective. Secular existentialist ethics starts with the individual. And since it does not acknowledge God, the individual must himself generate his own ethical norms. He creates his own meanings. Here the existentialist idea of creating one's own life detaches existentially created meaning from external norms and from the situation.

By contrast, Frame's Christian approach has all three perspectives. They harmonize because one God promulgates the norms, creates the world, and creates human beings with a sense of morality. Frame also can contribute to resolving many other specialized ethical issues because the Bible is such a rich source of ethical instruction, both directly through commandments and indirectly through illustrations in its historical portions, as well as the rich knowledge of God that it promotes. Its principles have implications for the ethics of war, abortion, poverty, child rearing, state-controlled education, marriage and sexual relationships, and more.

In the study of the Bible itself, we see a kind of interaction between the three perspectives. The commandments are in focus in the normative perspective. The historical portions are in focus in the situational perspective, which helps us grow in understanding how situations call for embodiment of ethical principles. God himself as a personal God is in focus in the existential perspective, which leads to focusing not only on human persons and their motives, but also on God as a divine personal God, whose character is both source for our norms and motivation for our activity.

17

Epistemology

Now we turn to consider epistemology. If the world by nature is multiperspectival, knowledge by nature is multiperspectival. God's archetypal knowledge is tripersonal knowledge. Our human derivative knowledge involves multiple perspectives. Accordingly, a Christian approach to epistemology is multiperspectival.

Perspectives on Epistemology

John Frame works out a Christian epistemology in his book *The Doctrine of the Knowledge of God*. As its title indicates, the book focuses on human knowledge about God, rather than human knowledge of the world. But the two are related, because all knowledge of the world involves knowledge of God, as Romans 1:19–21 has reminded us. In addition, any truth that we know is a truth that God already knows and that he makes known to us (Ps. 94:10). Knowledge always involves communion with God, though for an unbeliever it involves also a struggle to escape God.[1]

Frame's book in fact discusses knowledge of the world as well as knowledge of God.[2] Frame is presenting a *general* theory of knowledge, not simply a theory about the knowledge of God.

We need not here discuss all the ins and outs in the details of Frame's approach, but we can provide an introductory sample.

---

[1] See Vern S. Poythress, *Logic: A God-Centered Approach to the Foundation of Western Thought* (Wheaton, IL: Crossway, 2013), chap. 15.

[2] John M. Frame, *The Doctrine of the Knowledge of God* (Phillipsburg, NJ: P&R, 1987), 64–72.

Frame organizes his discussion using a triad of perspectives: normative, situational, and existential. These are the three perspectives that we introduced in connection with ethics. The use of these ethical perspectives is appropriate in epistemology because our knowledge has an ethical dimension. Ethics includes in principle a consideration of what we should believe.

Frame's book on epistemology has three parts: part 1, "The Objects of Knowledge"; part 2, "The Justification of Knowledge"; and part 3, "The Methods of Knowledge." These three correspond respectively to the situational perspective, the normative perspective, and the existential perspective on knowledge. Each of the parts is further broken down, partly using the same perspectives. For example, part 1 has three chapters: (1) "God, the Covenant Lord"; (2) "God and the World"; and (3) "God and Our Studies." These correspond respectively to the normative, the situational, and the existential perspectives. It is possible to do this further breakdown because the three perspectives interpenetrate. Within one perspective we can, by looking closely, find the other two. Thus, if we consider part 1 as a use of the situational perspective, we can find *within* this part a further subdivision based on the normative, situational, and existential perspectives.[3]

Human knowledge always involves the coherent interlocking of normative, situational, and existential perspectives. Knowledge must be justified; it must have grounds. The grounds are in focus in the normative perspective. Second, knowledge must be knowledge of something, which means that it must interact with the world and requires the situational perspective. Third, knowledge involves *us* as persons. *We* are the ones who know, which involves the existential perspective, focusing on the persons who know.

We may use the case of stealing as an example. Juliet claims that stealing is wrong. She is making a normative claim. Her initial focus is on the normative perspective. If challenged, she would want to be able to give justifications. The justifications would involve further appeals to norms. Pragmatic justifications would appeal to the fact that stealing has bad consequences in human

---

[3] Note Frame's explicit discussion of perspectivalism in ibid., 89–90.

societies. So this kind of justification looks out at the world of society and considers lessons that we can learn about the situation. Finally, in the existential perspective, we focus on Juliet as the one who believes that stealing is wrong. Her motives for believing may be good or bad or mixed. She may have the belief because she is convinced that God prohibits stealing and she cares for the glory of God. Or she may believe primarily because she cares selfishly for protecting her own property and can see that a general prohibition against stealing helps to protect her.

As usual, these three perspectives work together, because God is Lord over all. They interpenetrate, so that each leads to and includes the others. For example, if we begin with ourselves as knowers, in the existential perspective, we discover that we are aware of ourselves in relation to a larger world, and so we find within ourselves a reflection of the situational perspective, which looks out on the world. For example, within ourselves we find a conviction about stealing. And then we observe that this conviction says something about what is appropriate behavior in the world at large.

We are also conscious of the fact that as creatures we are not ultimate arbiters of the world. To know rightly, we must submit to standards outside ourselves. And so the existential perspective leads to the normative perspective. When we believe that stealing is wrong, we are also presupposing that there is a transcendent norm that forbids stealing.

At the same time, we have inward intuitions about what we can trust to be true. When we are spiritually healthy in relation to God, our existential sense of what we can trust reflects the actual norms that God has for knowledge. The normative perspective affirms the importance of the existential perspective and confirms its reliability when we are in right communion with God. We believe in our hearts that stealing is wrong because God has created us with a conscience and with a sense of right and wrong, one aspect of which is the conviction that stealing is wrong. (But this observation must be qualified by the principle that people can harden their consciences and twist their sense of moral standards.)

If we begin with the normative perspective, it tells us that we who are potential knowers must be honest and circumspect in interacting with the world: so the norms specify how we act and how we must expect the world to interact with us. For example, the norms say that we must be honest about the effects of stealing on society.

The norms thus include specifications about us in the existential perspective and about the world in the situational perspective. So simple accounts of knowledge that reduce it to only one pole do not do justice to the way God has ordained knowledge to work.

Frame's work on the use of perspectives illumines the multidimensional character of the structure of knowledge, which in turn forms one aspect of the multiperspectival character of the world as created, and reflects the tripersonal character of God who created it. Frame thereby provides a redeemed view of the subject of epistemology.[4]

Philosophical Objectivism and Subjectivism

Frame's work avoids some of the difficulties that plague secular philosophical approaches to knowledge. For example, philosophies that incline to objectivist approaches to knowledge focus on either norms for knowledge or empirical data as a basis for knowledge. A focus on norms typically takes the form of *rationalism*. According to this view, human reason serves as the principal norm for knowledge. Philosophies that focus on empirical data are forms of *empiricism*. Such philosophies are using the situational perspective as their primary entryway to knowledge.

But without God, the norms end up with no coherent relation to the situation. Abstract, impersonal norms alone cannot give us

---

[4]Note also the discussion of fellowship with God in cognition, Vern S. Poythress, *Inerrancy and Worldview: Answering Modern Challenges to the Bible* (Wheaton, IL: Crossway, 2012), chaps. 19–20. Readers may also want to consider an author who interacts more with readers who do not yet accept the truth of the Bible: Esther L. Meek, *Longing to Know: The Philosophy of Knowledge for Ordinary People* (Grand Rapids: Brazos, 2003); see also the review of Meek's book: John M. Frame, "Review of Esther Meek's *Longing to Know*," *Presbyterion* 29, no. 2 (Fall 2003), http://www.frame-poythress .org/review-of-esther-meeks-longing-to-know/. K. Scott Oliphint interacts with Alvin Plantinga's "Reformed epistemology" in "The Old-New Reformed Epistemology," in *Revelation and Reason: New Essays in Reformed Apologetics*, ed. K. Scott Oliphint and Lane G. Tipton (Phillipsburg, NJ: P&R, 2007), 207–19.

knowledge. We need input from the world. To know what stealing is, we must know something about the world. For example, we must have some conception of property and of carrying off a piece of property that belongs to someone else. Thus a purely rationalist view of knowledge fails.

Conversely, the world by itself cannot give us knowledge, because we need normative guidance to know what to believe on the basis of what we are observing. If, for example, Juliet were observing a world full of robots that looked like human beings and saw one robot carrying off a book from another robot's house, she would have empirical data, but no basis for morally condemning the actions of the "thieving" robot. Theft has to be defined not merely from empirical observation, but also by using intangibles such as the idea of property, the idea of human intention, and the idea of a moral principle ("theft is wrong"). Thus a purely empiricist view of knowledge fails.

And finally, we need ourselves to do the observing. Subjectivist approaches to knowledge focus on the person who believes or knows. Subjectivism emphasizes the existential perspective, but in a distorted way, because the existential perspective is separated from the normative and the situational. Subjective beliefs and knowledge are empty unless they are beliefs and knowledge *about* something, which requires the situational perspective on the world. Juliet can subjectively believe that theft is wrong only if the idea of *theft* involves relations to a world of human action.

Finally, beliefs are groundless unless guided by norms. Theft does not become morally wrong merely because Juliet starts believing that it is; it is already so, as a norm.

Theories of Truth

Let us consider some further disputes that arise in secular philosophical epistemology.[5] One principal dispute concerns the nature of truth. What is truth? Philosophers have come up with several

---

[5] For clear summaries of several principal disputes in epistemology, I have found useful Steven B. Cowan and James S. Spiegel, *The Love of Wisdom: A Christian Introduction to Philosophy* (Nashville, TN: B&H, 2009), 33–100.

competing theories of truth. There are also variations within each of the main theories. We will confine ourselves to basic issues, ignoring variations and other complexities, in order to illustrate the difference between Frame's multiperspectival approach and the main secular approaches.

The main theories about truth are the *correspondence* theory, the pragmatic theory, and the coherence theory of truth. According to the correspondence theory, a statement is true "if it corresponds to the way things really are."[6] For example, it is true that theft is wrong only because theft is actually wrong.

Next, according to the *pragmatic* theory, a statement is true if it "works," that is, if it leads consistently to good results in practice for those who hold it to be true. According to this theory, believing that theft is wrong has good results (in restraining thievery and in giving people grounds for punishing thieves). That is why it is true. Pragmatists usually say that success must be long-run success. They realize that a particular belief could lead to a series of short-range successes and still fail later on.

Finally, according to the *coherence* theory, a statement is true if it "coheres with" and is consistent with the other beliefs that a person holds. Theft is wrong because it fits in with a larger system of moral beliefs, including general principles (such as "do to others as you would have them do to you"), practical benefits (it helps social well-being), and movements of conscience.

In evaluating these theories, we may note first that, in their usual form, they fail to distinguish between God and creatures. And that is a major failure, typical of philosophical reasoning oriented to an autonomous conception of reason. All three theories essentially assume a non-Christian view of epistemological immanence by implying that humanity, and not God, functions as the sole reference point for discussing truth. Allegedly, theft is wrong merely because "reality" as experienced by human beings in some fashion is that way, or because human beings find that it works, or because it fits other human beliefs. Apparently, God does not matter.

---

[6] Ibid., 36.

The theories are in danger of assuming a non-Christian view of transcendence as well, since the formulations of the theories leave God out. God, by implication, is irrelevant. He is "distant" and uninvolved (which is the non-Christian view of transcendence).

From a Christian point of view, we should say that there are two forms of correspondence theory. In a non-Christian version, truth corresponds to a state of affairs in the world, in virtual independence of God. According to this version, theft is wrong because it is actually wrong "out there." The state of affairs is treated as if it were "brute fact" or self-sufficient fact, instead of being dependent on the mind and plan of God. But this version leads to a difficulty, because no human being is able to achieve a transcendent viewpoint, a viewpoint encompassing (1) himself and his statement, (2) the reality of the fact, and (3) the correspondence between (1) and (2). How can a non-Christian know the correspondence itself, or even talk about it, without leaping out of his skin and pretending to have a transcendent, godlike viewpoint? Moreover, since the fact in question (for example, the fact that theft is wrong) is treated as independent of God, it is completely impersonal, and one cannot know that it actually has the character that would allow it to be digested by a person.

By contrast, in a Christian version of the correspondence theory, what is true for human beings corresponds to what is true according to the mind of God, and God's knowledge is the standard for truth. Theft is wrong because it is wrong in God's mind, according to God's moral judgment. God's knowledge must be distinguished from human knowledge. Human beings can know truth (according to the principle of God's immanence), but they do not know everything; they are situationally limited. In addition, they do not serve as the ultimate standard; they are normatively limited. Finally, they do not know in the same way that God does; they are existentially limited.

If there were no God, the limitations in human beings would threaten to undermine knowledge. How could anyone know that theft is wrong? Their knowledge might fail because of the *situation*. Might there not be some special obscure situation, unknown to them, that would be an exception to the general principle that theft is wrong? Their knowledge might fail because the norm escapes them. If they know a moral norm imperfectly, might there not be a norm above the norm, so to speak, that specifies some exceptions about theft? And knowledge might fail because of existential limitations. Might not human beings' consciences be skewed, so that they cannot see properly whether theft is wrong?

God, by contrast, knows everything, is authoritative in his knowledge, and knows existentially as the ultimate personal knower. He does not have the human limits. If God makes his will known in Scripture, and if in addition we have some general revelation from him through human conscience and circumstances, we can lean on his infinite knowledge and on his gracious provision for us. By this means we have an answer to the suspicions that the limited character of our knowledge undermines all knowledge.

Next, there are two forms of pragmatic theory. The non-Christian version looks only at what "works" for limited human purposes within this life, and considers only what "works" for man and not for God. A Christian version distinguishes God and man. All of what God knows harmonizes with what he achieves, and he always achieves what he purposes to achieve. So all the truth that God knows "works" for God.

Human beings, as usual, do not serve as an ultimate standard. But what works for human beings can be defined as what works in the long run, and the long run includes the last judgment and the consummation of all things. Then, in the presence of God and under the inspection of his judgment, we will see what beliefs from this life "work" in the sense that they pass God's judgment. This principle has an obvious application to the question of whether theft is wrong. The idea that theft is wrong works at the last judgment, because at the last judgment God confirms it.

Finally, consider the two forms of the coherence theory of truth. In the non-Christian version, truth means coherence with a person's other beliefs. But this makes truth relative to the person. Since God has been removed from the picture, there is no transcendent God who can serve as a superhuman standard and judge between the claims from two different persons, each of whom claims to have coherent beliefs within his own system.

In a Christian version of coherence theory, we distinguish God from human beings. All truth coheres perfectly within the mind of God and among the three persons of the Trinity. Christ is the truth and is self-coherent and self-consistent. Human belief about a particular truth should indeed cohere with other beliefs if those beliefs also are true. God created us in such a way that we sift through truth claims partly on the basis of a background of other beliefs. But since human beings are not the ultimate standard for truth, we cannot merely assume that all the other beliefs that a particular human being has will always be true.

Among those beliefs, however, there is knowledge of the true God, according to Romans 1:19–21. Unbelievers "suppress the truth" (Rom. 1:18). Consequently, all unbelieving thought is incoherent. For example, thieves are incoherent in their conviction that their own theft is okay; their conviction does not match their knowledge of God, which they are suppressing. A thorough coherence would include not only coherence with all that a person consciously knows about God, but also coherence with God himself, whom the person knows. In other words, it would be coherence with all the truth of God. Of course, human beings do not know all these truths, and within this life they do not achieve perfect coherence. But a thorough coherence, including coherence with God himself, would guarantee the truth of the particular belief that a person initially singled out for inspection.

A Christian, then, can have a Christian version of all three theories at once. How can that be? The three theories are perspectives on one another.

- The correspondence theory expresses the normative perspective. Truth in God's mind is the norm for sifting truth as we conceive it. Our ideas are true if they correspond to the norm in God's mind.
- The pragmatic theory expresses the situational perspective. Truth makes a difference in results in the world, which is the natural focus of the situational perspective.

- The coherence theory expresses the existential perspective. It focuses on what persons believe in their personal commitments. That focus is existential, personal. Because all human beings know God, coherence implies that beliefs must cohere with the personal mind of God, and when they do, they are sound and cohere within the minds of individuals as well.

The normative, existential, and situational perspectives interlock. They lead to one another rather than being in competition or excluding one another as irreconcilable alternatives. We cannot operate without beliefs. And beliefs always rely on a deep sense of reliability: reliability of ourselves and our minds, reliability of the world, and reliability of norms from God. Neither can we hold beliefs or grow in beliefs in a sound way without interacting with the world and thereby seeing what "works." When we see what is working, it is still *we* who see it; and we are responsible, subject to the norms of God's presence, to respond with beliefs in accord with what works, that is, beliefs that *cohere* with what works. Because it is God's world, we can also believe—as one belief that enjoys coherence with our other beliefs about God—that God has made the world and us. He has made us so that by observing what works we can actually find out what the world is like, in which case our beliefs correspond to the world. Coherence, pragmatic effectiveness, and correspondence go together as perspectives.

Kinds of Knowledge

We may observe that human knowledge can be knowledge of persons (acquaintance), knowledge as skill (know-how), or knowledge of particular truths expressed in language. Stephanie says, "I know Betty" (acquaintance); "I know how to send a text message" (know-how); "I know that Paris is the capital of France" (a truth). Secular philosophical epistemology usually focuses primarily or exclusively on knowledge of truths. But the three types are involved in one another and can serve as perspectives on one another.

Knowledge of persons is the focus of the existential perspective. To know God in a saving way involves knowing a person (God as a personal God), knowing facts about him (truths), and beginning to know how to conduct oneself in a godly way in the world (know-how). Knowing that Paris is the capital of France involves knowing how to answer a geography question about the capital of France, which is know-how. It also involves knowing that God knows all about Paris and has providentially ordained it to be the capital of France. This knowledge about God is an aspect of knowing him personally (acquaintance). (Unbelievers, however, typically suppress personal knowledge of God.)

Stephanie also knows herself, both that she has a general capacity for knowledge and that she knows in particular that Paris is the capital of France. She also knows that many of her acquaintances may possibly know the same truth. In the case of a truth like the fact that Paris is the capital of France, there is a strong *social* component in knowledge. Stephanie probably learned about Paris from a schoolteacher or a textbook or some personal source. In this process, she has to understand what it means to be a person and how she can appropriately relate to other persons in their knowledge claims in order to get started with a propositional truth about Paris. Knowledge of propositions in this way presupposes knowledge of persons—a lot of knowledge of persons, accumulated in a long process of growing up as a child.

Secular epistemology has often tried to isolate knowledge of true propositions so that such knowledge could be analyzed thoroughly and philosophers could perhaps master the nature of knowledge. The attempt already misconstrues the nature of knowledge, because knowledge of truths cannot be so isolated. To think that it can is to conceal the presence of God and to engage in a reduction.

At the bottom we may suspect that there are idolatrous religious motivations. Reductionism as an intellectual movement comes from a desire to have a substitute for God. Something else rather than God, namely, the endpoint of the process of reduction, serves as the unifying and final explanation. If a philosopher can eliminate God, who is personal, he may hope to have an impersonal substitute, in the form of an abstract theory, abstract concepts of which allegedly allow a reduction of knowledge to a masterable impersonal pattern.

We may note also that the interlocking of acquaintance, know-how, and knowledge of truths shows the indispensability of what Michael Polanyi has called *tacit knowledge*.[7] Human beings cannot bring to full expression in consciousness everything that they know through personal acquaintance. If Donna knows Tim well, she may be able to talk at length about all kinds of facts that she knows about Tim, including his personality quirks and mannerisms and attitudes. But she always knows more—she knows a whole person. Similarly, know-how is not fully expressible. The carpenter training his son to hammer a nail cannot simply give him verbal instruction, however extensive. The son must get the feel of the hammer and the proper coordination in his arm muscles.

Tacit knowledge always lies in the background of even the simplest, most explicit, most self-consciously-aware knowledge of a truth. The presence of tacit knowledge, including especially the knowledge of acquaintance and the knowledge of God, frustrates the ideal philosophical goal of transparent knowledge through rational analysis.

The Justification of Knowledge

Next, consider the philosophical discussion of the justification of knowledge. The mainstream of twentieth-century analytic philosophy has found attractive one formulation in particular: knowledge is "justified true belief." What do we say about this formulation?

This particular formulation can be seen as a kind of condensation of Frame's triperspectival discussion of knowledge. The word *justified* leads to the normative perspective, which focuses on the justification of knowledge. The word *true* leads to the situational perspective, which focuses on the world and its states of affairs—how things actually are in the world. The word *belief* leads to the existential perspective, which focuses on a person who knows and is believing. In Frame's treatment, these three aspects are perspec-

---

[7] Michael Polanyi, *The Tacit Dimension* (Garden City, NY: Anchor, 1967).

tives. They all involve one another and lead to one another. No one aspect can be isolated, and the whole discussion of knowledge can be richly in accord with the richness of the world and the human beings that God has created.

But we may wonder whether it is quite the same way when the idea of justified true belief is discussed within secular philosophical circles, especially the circle of analytic philosophy. Do these circles rather tempt people to think that they can isolate each of the three separate factors that together make up knowledge? And does the formulation mean the same thing that it would within a context like Frame's?

Moreover, not every tradition in Western philosophy has been equally attracted to tight, rigorous-sounding single-sentence formulations. So we might ask what presuppositions underlie the preference for this particular kind of answer to people's big questions about knowledge. The kind of answer that a person gives, as well as the substance of the answer, reveals things about the person who is answering (see also chap. 25).

And yet, the persons who participate in saying that knowledge is justified true belief are very much in the background. Why? Perhaps a philosophical tradition longs for (strongly, personally, existentially) rational justification and objective, religiously neutral grounds for its claims. Analytic philosophy can tempt us to conceal the personal assumptions that go into the whole project. But persons are indispensable for the project even to exist.

We can show some of the difficulty if we ask what kind of knowledge we are discussing. Are we discussing knowing persons (acquaintance), knowing a skill (know-how), or knowing truths? The focus is on knowing truths. But tacit knowledge lies in the background: we cannot make completely explicit the justifications for our beliefs or even what those beliefs are. Nor can we make truth completely explicit to ourselves. Any particular truth presupposes a tacit background. Ultimately it also presupposes the background of God's mind, which is incomprehensible.

We may also observe that when we reckon with the Creator-creature distinction, we bring in a distinction that disrupts univocal thinking (one-level thinking) about knowledge. What is "belief"? It depends, of course, on what we mean by belief. Belief for a human being, or belief for God? Does God have beliefs? What if we include in our meaning the idea that a person who believes is dependent on something outside his mind as a source for belief (whether someone's testimony, or an empirical observation, or just an intuitive hunch)? Since God is not dependent, he has no beliefs in this particular sense, though of course God has knowledge. So, if we use this particular sense of the word *belief*, God's knowledge is not justified true belief, and the whole formulation does not work.

What do we mean by *true* in the formula "justified true belief"? Do we use God's knowledge of truth as our reference point, or human knowledge? And what does "justified" mean? Who is doing the justifying, God or man?

Each of these questions can be fleshed out when we deal with any particular knowledge claim, such as whether Juliet knows that theft is wrong. First, what does it mean for her to believe that theft is wrong? Is it clear? Romans 1:32 indicates that even unbelievers "know God's righteous decree" concerning moral principles. That is, they know, deep down, that theft is wrong because they are made in God's image. But they may suppress this knowledge. They may approve practices that violate God's moral law. They may say that they *do not believe* that theft is wrong.

So do they or do they not? They are trapped between what they are as creatures made in the image of God and what they desire to be in rebellion—autonomous sources of law who can specify that theft is not wrong. Their belief structure is deeply incoherent. But it certainly makes sense to say, in some sense, that they know that theft is wrong and yet they do not believe it—at least in their conscious beliefs and in their actions.

Is it true that theft is wrong? We need to ask whether the question seeks to find a foundation for truth in the world or in God. If it is in the world, how can morality derive merely from data?

One possible secular answer to these questions would be to say that a discussion about God is irrelevant, or that it misunderstands the meaning of "justified true belief." The secular answer would continue by observing in the context of philosophical discussion that people are talking about human beliefs and human knowledge, not about God's knowledge. But since human knowledge is knowledge only by imitating God's knowledge, God cannot be eliminated from the concept of knowledge. The move to eliminate him is a version of non-Christian transcendence, which treats God as irrelevant. The philosophical discussion also appears to invite us to treat human knowledge and belief on its own terms—as if we could, without reference to God, use our own minds in the analysis. In practice, our own minds become the ultimate standard for judgment, and then we have fallen into non-Christian immanence.

The Gettier Problem

We may further illustrate the application of multiple perspectives by considering a particular difficulty called the "Gettier problem." Starting with the formulation that knowledge is "justified true belief," Edmund Gettier in 1963 produced two counterexamples.[8] The second of his two counterexamples offers the following propositions:

1. Jones owns a Ford.
2. Either Jones owns a Ford or Brown is in Barcelona.

Gettier invites us to imagine a scenario in which a third man, Smith, has good grounds for believing proposition 1. "Smith's evidence might be that Jones has at all times in the past within Smith's memory owned a car, and always a Ford, and that Jones has just offered Smith a ride while driving a Ford."[9] So Smith is justified in believing 1, and by deduction he also believes proposition 2 and is justified in doing so (by the inference known as addition). But, as it turns out, Jones was driving a rental car, and proposition 1 is false. Proposition 2 is nevertheless true, because, unbeknownst to Smith, Brown is in fact in Barcelona. Smith's belief in proposition 2

---

[8] Edmund Gettier, "Is Justified True Belief Knowledge?," *Analysis* 23 (1963): 121–23, accessed December 10, 2012, http://www.ditext.com/gettier/gettier.html; see discussion at Matthias Steup, "The Analysis of Knowledge," in *The Stanford Encyclopedia of Philosophy*, Fall 2012 ed., ed. Edward N. Zalta, accessed December 20, 2012, http://plato.stanford.edu/archives/fall2012/entries/knowledge-analysis/; Cowan and Spiegel, *Love of Wisdom*, 64–72.

[9] Gettier, "Justified True Belief."

satisfies all three conditions: it is justified, it is true, and it is, of course, Smith's belief. Nevertheless, Smith does not *know* that 2 is true, because the truth of 2 is only accidental, compared with the reasons or justifications that Smith could give for believing in 2.

Most philosophers accept that Gettier's counterexamples are convincing. But they disagree on how best to respond to this difficulty.[10] One possible response might be simply to say that Gettier's counterexamples show that the account in terms of justified true belief is not complete or adequate. Moreover, maybe there is no particular reason why *any* condensed account should be complete, since God has made us and the world in a complex way.

Yet Frame's three perspectives show that the formula "justified true belief" has promise of some insight in it. The three words correspond to Frame's three perspectives, normative, situational, and existential, and together these perspectives do give us insight into the nature of knowledge.

If we wish, we might go a step further and suggest that the Gettier problem shows the entanglement or interlocking between justification and belief, or better, between the normative, situational, and existential perspectives on knowledge. Smith's relationship to proposition 2 is problematic because the reasons that Smith could give for his believing do not mesh thoroughly with the account that we would give from the situation as to why proposition 2 is true. That is, Smith's justifications, from the normative perspective, do not match what we find out when we focus on the situational perspective.

The reasons, corresponding to the normative perspective, involve evidence and information that Smith has about Jones and his driving a Ford. Smith's personal beliefs, corresponding to the existential perspective, involve a synthesis from this variety of evidence, leading not only to the conclusion in the form of proposition 1, but also to a further conclusion in proposition 2. Smith's reasons support proposition 2 only because they support exactly one of the simpler propositions out of which proposition 2 is composed. Smith believes and knows that proposition 1 has this kind

---

[10] Steup, "Analysis of Knowledge," section 2.

of support, and therefore also that proposition 2 has exactly the same kind of support. In Smith's view the support that his belief has is not related to Brown's location. By contrast, the situation verifies the truth of proposition 2 precisely by supporting the other embedded proposition (about Brown), not the one for which Smith has the reasons and the more robust beliefs.

This approach focuses more on the issue of what kind of justifications Smith has. But we could also focus on belief. Could a more robust, "thick," perspectivally informed conception of belief help answer the problem? Smith believes proposition 2, not merely as a whole, but in the context of other beliefs and knowledge, including beliefs about Jones's habits and including an awareness that Smith has no idea of Brown's whereabouts. This context of personal knowledge, some of which may be tacit, qualifies the manner in which Smith is personally committed to proposition 2. Given this robust understanding of Smith's belief, the manner of his belief does not lead to the conclusion that Smith's belief in proposition 2 is "justified true belief" in a way that does full justice to a wider context of belief. It is not true that Jones owns a Ford, and this is an indispensable aspect in Smith's belief in proposition 2. If Smith himself were to focus on this larger, robust context of belief, he might end up saying that though proposition 2 is true as an abstract proposition, his own *beliefs* about 2 are not completely true, because of the entanglement of complexity in his beliefs.

Some philosophers have in fact suggested that we add a fourth condition: that a "person's justification for a belief not be derived from a false belief."[11] But this response differs from mine in that it does not seem to recognize that part of the difficulty lies in the word *belief* and its inseparability from the persons and context of believing. Instead, the response "patches up" the difficulty by adding things about *further* beliefs, but still within a framework where each belief is treated as if it could be isolated from the context of the person.

We could also suggest that we could introduce a more robust treatment of what it means to be true. It requires a reduction to

---

[11] Cowan and Spiegel, *Love of Wisdom*, 68.

a merely one-dimensional analysis of natural language to use the word *true* with respect to disembodied, isolated propositional formulations.[12] If Smith had a chance and were responding as a full person, we might hear him observe that, yes, proposition 2 turns out to be true, but it is true by means of another kind of correspondence to the world than what Smith really had in mind. Given this difference, it is not true in the way that Smith thought it was true, and his belief in that respect is not true, though the compound proposition itself is true.

Philosophers have also tried to patch up the theory of justified true belief by a situational approach. They have suggested that we add a fourth condition, to the effect that the belief in question cannot have its justification undermined by a person's coming to have knowledge of some other truth (such as Smith's coming to know that Jones does not own a Ford).[13] This attempt addresses the fact that truths are related to one another and to propositional formulations. But it appears still to tempt us to treat each particular truth as if it were isolatable, both from other truths and from the persons who are believing. It appears to be evading the full perspectival relation between justification, truth, and belief, or between normative, situational, and existential perspectives on knowledge.

Reliabilism

Philosophers may also attempt to provide a remedy for the Gettier problem by loosening the normative pole in the formula, one's understanding of justification. Instead of justification, we have "reliability": "For the reliabilist, it does not matter so much whether a person can give an adequate account of his reasons for a belief. What matters is that his beliefs be produced in a reliable way."[14]

The expression "produced in a reliable way" just pushes the problem back to determining how we judge what is reliable. We could say that reliability is determined by having reasons (a normative focus), by truth (as reliable interaction with the world, a

---

[12] Poythress, *Logic*, chaps. 17–23.
[13] For a more precise formulation, see Cowan and Spiegel, *Love of Wisdom*, 69.
[14] Ibid., 70.

situational focus), or by the reliability in belief commitments (an existential focus). But then are we back where we started, with the interaction of a normative perspective (having reasons), a situational perspective (interaction with the world), and an existential perspective (belief commitments)? Moreover, if we try to isolate reliable production of belief from a person's tacit knowledge of reasons for belief, we may easily end with a belief that is successful because reliably produced, but in which the person who believes does not know whether or why it might be successful, and so has no real grounds for belief internal to his mind. We have mistakenly tried to isolate the normative perspective (reliability) from the existential perspective (confidence in reliability).

The Location of Justification

We may consider still another question about justification of knowledge, the question of the "location" of that justification. There are at least three main approaches. (1) "Internalism" says that "a person's justification for a belief must be internal to his mind."[15] For example, Juliet may say that she knows that theft is wrong because she has reasoned it out, either by looking at the effects on society or by appealing to a general principle that you should "do to others what you would have them do to you." She can provide justifications for what she believes, and these justifications are "internal": they are part of the furniture of her mind. (2) "Externalism" says that justification is external to the mind; it lies in whether the belief is "caused or formed in an appropriate way."[16] For example, the impulse of her conscience may lead to Juliet's believing that theft is wrong, even though she cannot provide further reasons for her belief. We as onlookers may nevertheless conclude that Juliet's belief is justified because God has given her a good conscience. (3) "Virtue epistemology" says that "the key to knowledge is intellectual *virtue*."[17] Intellectual virtues include honesty, open-mindedness, diligence in inquiry, and others. Juliet believes that theft is wrong

---

[15] Ibid., 73.
[16] Ibid.
[17] Ibid., 78.

because she is honest enough not to suppress the voice of conscience or the evidence of social consequences from theft.

A quick inspection of these approaches shows yet another use of perspectives. Internalism, by focusing on what goes on in the mind, represents an existential perspective. Externalism, by focusing on processes external to the mind, represents a situational perspective. Virtue epistemology, by focusing on the "virtues" or norms for intellectual work, represents a normative perspective. As usual with perspectives, each of these requires the others. But secular philosophers usually see them as alternatives. It makes one wonder once again whether the desire for a reductionism or for a masterful answer to the question tempts people to ignore the rich context for any one perspective on knowledge.

The Structure of Justification

Finally, let us consider briefly another problem in epistemology, the problem about the "structure" of knowledge. There are at least three main views.

Foundationalism says that certain kinds of knowledge are "basic" and need no further justification. Other knowledge is built up as a superstructure on the basis of the foundation. For example, *empiricism* is a form of foundationalism, because it says that the knowledge of sense experience is basic, and that everything else derives from it. Other forms of foundationalism may argue that other kinds of knowledge are basic.

How does foundationalism approach a specific knowledge claim, like the claim that theft is wrong? It depends on which kinds of knowledge are basic. The idea that theft is wrong could be treated either as a basic form of knowledge (an intuitive dictate of conscience) or as a result built on the basis of a lot of reasoning about social benefits. This reasoning about social benefits would in turn be based on a foundation of previous knowledge about human beings and societies, which would eventually go back to sense data. At least for empiricism, the steps in tracing back to foundations would stop at that point, because empiricism thinks that sense data are basic.

A second view, *coherentism*, says that no beliefs are absolutely "basic" or foundational. All beliefs are justified by coherence with other beliefs. We have already met a similar approach in dealing with the nature of truth. How does this work out in practice? Juliet believes that theft is wrong because that belief harmonizes with other moral beliefs, all of which affirm the importance of respecting other people, and because it harmonizes with her observations about social benefits of not stealing. The difficulty here is the obvious one: how do we avoid subjectivism, in which Juliet's beliefs are internally coherent within her mind, but may not necessarily have any relation to the outside world?

A third view, *contextualism*, says that we seek justifications for belief only within relatively specific *contexts*. We take for granted most of what we believe and test a particular idea only within the context in which testing is appropriate. For example, Juliet tests her belief that theft is wrong within the context of other moral principles. She takes for granted many of her beliefs about other persons and their motivations and the ways that society functions. These beliefs offer a broader context in which she can draw conclusions about how theft impacts society.

Evaluating Theories of the Structure of Knowledge

Now how do we evaluate these three approaches to the structure of knowledge?

From a Christian point of view, humans are dependent and are not the ultimate standard for knowledge. So a foundationalism that locates the foundation in something in the world or in the human mind is idolatrous—it replaces God with some created thing or some aspect of creation. For example, empiricism idolizes sense experience.

Yet a Christian does have a "foundation" in a sense. God is the ultimate source of knowledge and also the standard for knowledge. But it is also important to say that our knowledge of him is *mediated* through revelation. So we are always in a position of dependence, in which we depend not only on God himself, but also on tacit knowledge that God has given us. Our knowledge includes acquaintance with other persons, and that acquaintance, especially with parents, brothers, sisters, teachers, and school classmates, has been instrumental in bringing us to the state of knowledge in which we currently live as adults.

What about coherentism? A Christian should of course reject any coherentism that never acknowledges a more ultimate standard than the ideas in one's own mind. Yet we can also see a grain of truth in coherentism, because the process of growing up from childhood involves coherent interaction with parents, teachers, and the world. This interaction takes place according to God's design and God's providence, and in the midst of God's presence. Our beliefs change and grow as they interact with one another and with the beliefs of those around us. (So we should take into account the *social* dimension of knowledge.) In this process, we are interacting with divinely given norms. We are not imprisoned within our own "house" of belief, as a secular form of coherentism might suggest.

Finally, contextualism makes some sense against the background of ordinary experience. Most of the time we take our beliefs for granted. Our critical inspection of a particular idea or belief usually takes place within some kind of limited context. Contextualism could be seen as simply a kind of observation about typical human experience in ordinary situations. But contextualism is wrong if it pretends that we never ask more ultimate questions, such as how we justify knowledge as a whole, as opposed to how we justify a particular belief that theft is wrong. People do, after all, have the experience of asking more and more ultimate questions. If theft is wrong, it must be because there are moral standards that can be known. So what are moral standards, and how can they be known? When Juliet thinks that theft is wrong, is she just listening to her own preferences? Contextualism ignores such larger questions, or gives up on answering them, or becomes a form of coherentism.

If we like, we can see here a hint that several perspectives are at work. Foundationalism is like a particle perspective, at least with respect to basic knowledge. Each bit of basic knowledge is like a particle, distinct and not in need of further support. Coherentism, by contrast, is akin to a field perspective. Each belief makes sense only when tested by means of its relations—coherent or incoherent?—with respect to an ever-widening circle of other beliefs. Contextualism is field-like as well, inasmuch as it appeals to contexts. But the contexts are limited; they are the contexts relevant to "local" problem solving. In this respect contextualism is suggestive of problem solving and has an affinity with the wave perspective, which asks about progress in time toward answering a question about knowledge.

These three approaches actually belong together. They are each useful perspectival starting points for considering the structure of knowledge. But each is inadequate when it is used to ignore the others.

18

The Soul, the Mind, and Psychology

At an early point (chap. 1), I mentioned metaphysics, epistemology, and ethics as major subdivisions within philosophy. The *Encyclopaedia Britannica* of 1910 offers us a more expansive list of subdivisions: "psychology [which here means the study of the mind or soul], epistemology or theory of knowledge, and metaphysics, then logic, aesthetics and ethics."[1] In addition, there are some more-specialized areas, such as philosophy of law, philosophy of religion, philosophy of language, philosophy of history, and philosophy of science.

We will dip briefly into each of these areas in order to illustrate how a biblically based approach provides distinctive answers. We begin with psychology.

The Existence of the Soul

In 1910 the *Encyclopaedia Britannica* classified psychology as a subdivision of philosophy. But nowadays the word *psychology* is primarily used to describe one of the social sciences. However, philosophers continue to discuss some foundational issues about humanity. Is there such a thing as the *soul*? Or are we just biological

---

[1]Andrew Seth Pringle-Pattison, "Philosophy," in *Encyclopaedia Britannica*, 11th ed. (Cambridge: University of Cambridge, 1910), 21:440.

machines? What is the mind? Is it distinct from the body, and if so how?

As usual, metaphysical views make a difference. We earlier discussed materialism, which says that all of reality reduces to matter and motion. This metaphysical position automatically leads to the conclusion that there is no such thing as a soul. In an attempt to be consistent, some materialists also deny the reality of the mind. They would say either that consciousness is an illusion or that it is a reflection of underlying neuronal physical processes in the brain as a physical organ of the body.

In a Christian view, by contrast, we acknowledge that God created a world with many dimensions, and he created us with many dimensions. We also know, from a number of explicit texts in the Bible, that human beings continue to live spiritually after their bodies die and become nonfunctional (Luke 16:19–31; 2 Cor. 5:8; Phil. 1:23; Rev. 6:9–11). People continue to exist as they await the time of bodily resurrection (John 5:28–29). Thus, in a fundamental way not only are we *more* than bodies, but we can come to a state where we are *other* than functioning bodies.

God does not provide us with the details about *how* people continue to live when their bodies disintegrate. But it is not a problem for God. It is a problem for us, because all our scientific information about the functioning of human bodies belongs—naturally enough—to this life. If we try to extrapolate from this life to another life, we do so using the pictures belonging to this life. And those pictures do not provide details about how the next life *differs* in decisive ways from this world. It is mere arrogance to claim that God could not arrange things in ways that we cannot conceive.

The instruction that God does provide about life after death has implications for this life, because it reorients our evaluation of what is really important and lasting: "And do not fear those who kill the body but cannot kill the soul. Rather fear him who can destroy both soul and body in hell" (Matt. 10:28). It also has a bearing on reductionistic approaches to human nature. We should acknowledge that human beings are rich creatures, with many dimensions in their thinking, their motivations, and their behavior.

Human nature is not reducible to matter in motion. Human beings are responsible to God, and they continue to bear responsibility after they die.

Resistance to reductionism also helps in relation to the philosophy of the mind. In philosophical discussion, the word *mind* can serve almost as a synonym for the soul or for everything significant about distinctively human experience, involving consciousness, sense experience, reflection, conscience, emotions, dispositions, and so on. But the term *mind* is subject to a liability in that it may tempt us to concentrate wholly on *conscious* awareness, leaving to one side *tacit* knowledge, sleep, dreams, and other aspects of human experience. We are more than consciousness. We have personalities. We have moral commitments. We can experience communion with God. We can talk to God in prayer, and listen to him by reading the Bible. People can be moral or immoral, not only in their outward behavior but also in inward dispositions and desires. The world is complicated, and people are complicated. Thus a philosophy of the *mind* cannot capture human nature in its fullness.

Modern Psychology

We also have to consider psychology as a social science. A Christian approach to psychology—and, more broadly, to an understanding of human nature—has developed under the auspices of the movement called *biblical counseling*.[2] Informed by Van Til's presuppositional apologetics, a number of counselors and students of the Bible have constructed their own biblically based approach to personal human struggles and their healing. Biblical counselors appropriate common-grace insights from secular psychology, cognitive science,

---

[2] In the first generation, this movement was called *nouthetic counseling* by its principal founder, Jay Adams (see Jay Adams, *Competent to Counsel: Introduction to Nouthetic Counseling* [Grand Rapids: Ministry Resources Library, 1986]). In the second generation, principal works include David Powlison, *Seeing with New Eyes: Counseling and the Human Condition through the Lens of Scripture* (Phillipsburg, NJ: P&R, 2003); Edward T. Welch, *Counselor's Guide to the Brain and Its Disorders: Knowing the Difference between Disease and Sin* (Grand Rapids: Zondervan, 1991); and Welch, *Blame It on the Brain? Distinguishing Chemical Imbalances, Brain Disorders, and Disobedience* (Phillipsburg, NJ: P&R, 1998). A historical analysis is found in Powlison, *The Biblical Counseling Movement: History and Context* (Greensboro, NC: New Growth, 2010), a revision of Powlison, "Competent to Counsel? The History of a Conservative Protestant Anti-Psychiatry Movement" (PhD diss., University of Pennsylvania, 1996). There are now many shorter publications addressing specific problems and challenges.

psychotherapy, psychiatry, neurophysiology, and neurology. But they do so from within their own distinctive framework, based on biblical presuppositions. And they do not do so uncritically. They sift what they read in order to distinguish valid insights from distortions produced by sin and by ill-grounded secular assumptions. They acknowledge the rich, multifaceted nature of human persons, rather than trying to reduce human nature to learned behavior or a medical model.

The medical model for understanding human functions is an important alternative to biblical counseling. The medical model, in its purest form, says that human failures of all kinds stem from biological dysfunctions, whether these originate from defective genes, from bodily damage inflicted by the environment or invasive organisms, from hormonal imbalances, or from neurological malfunctions. The medical model virtually reduces everything to biology. It has an affinity to philosophical materialism, which reduces everything to matter and motion.

By contrast, biblical counselors adopt a richer, multidimensional approach. They acknowledge that we have bodies. They know that hormones and neurology each have a role in the way we function. But they also know about sin and righteousness, about responsibility to God and man. It is not always easy to figure out why people do what they do, but a multidimensional approach—or multiperspectival approach, if you will—has more ability to help people, if indeed people are metaphysically complex beings who function in many dimensions. By contrast, a one-dimensional biological approach may help when the root problem is biological, but it will misfire with respect to any other kind of human failure and suffering.[3]

---

[3] Biblical counseling provides further resources through several channels. See the bibliography in note 2, above, and at http://www.ccef.org/.

19

Logic

Our exploration of metaphysics also has implications for logic. Logic must reckon with the multiperspectival character of the world and of human knowledge of the world, rather than trying to reduce truth to one dimension. How does this reckoning change our view of logic?

We can only touch on a few main points here. A full discussion would require much more space.[1]

The Creator-Creature Distinction

First, our metaphysical analysis includes the Creator-creature distinction. This distinction has implications for logic. We must distinguish God's logic from human conceptions of logic. And what is God's logic? God is the source and archetype for human logic. Ultimately, his "logic" means his consistency with himself. This consistency has many dimensions. He is faithful; he cannot deny himself (2 Tim. 2:13).

Logic has a close relationship to rationality as it comes to expression in language. And we know that God speaks. He speaks to us in Scripture. But preeminently he speaks in eternal speech, his Word, which was with God and was God from the beginning (John 1:1). God's speech in God the Son shows his rationality, his "logic."

---

[1] See Vern S. Poythress, *Logic: A God-Centered Approach to the Foundation of Western Thought* (Wheaton, IL: Crossway, 2013).

The Stoic philosophers before the time of the New Testament speculated about reason or a "word" that was the supreme rational source behind the observable order in the world. They used the Greek word *logos* to designate this natural order. The Gospel of John uses the same word *logos* to designate the second person of the Trinity, the divine Son of God. The Son, as God's Word, is the source for the order in the created world.

In view of John 1:1, we can say that God's rationality or self-consistency is summed up in the Son, who is the Word, or the Logic, of God. This Son is a person, not an impersonal abstraction. He is incomprehensible, just as God is incomprehensible. The Father's love for the Son implies that the Father will always be faithful to the divine rationality of the Son. This person, as the rationality of God, is the foundation for human rationality. We have two levels for logic, the divine level and the human. The divine level, which is incomprehensible to us, is also the source for our derivative understanding. Our understanding includes human understanding of logic, which we have only as a gift from God, through communion with God the Logos.

Logic is both two-level and personal. These fundamental characteristics result in a two-level and personal character to *every* logical principle, including what people have regarded as the most fundamental principles, such as the law of identity (A is A), the law of noncontradiction (a statement cannot be both true and false at the same time and in the same way), and the law of excluded middle (a statement is either true or false). For instance, owing to the personal character of law in general and logic in particular, logical principles cannot be neatly isolated from the persons who hold them and know them.

For one thing, each person brings the coloring of his own understanding. And his own understanding is indeed colored not only by his background and ordinary experience, but also by his attitude toward God. Does he acknowledge that the logical principles come from God, or does he try to imagine that they are just "out there" as impersonal abstractions?

Perspectives on Logic

Knowledge of logical principles, like other kinds of knowledge, involves the normative, situational, and existential perspectives. We know that noncontradiction is a norm, but we also understand it by seeing it embodied in ordinary situations. And it is *we* as persons who know and understand, and for whom the principle seems undeniable. We are so constituted as persons that we can understand. Thus, our knowledge of the norm involves us, and our involvement constitutes the existential perspective on logic. The normative, situational, and existential perspectives interact.

The change to a Christian viewpoint thus includes a multiperspectival approach to logic. We acknowledge the relation of logic not only to the existence of norms for reasoning, but also to our minds and to the world, a world that contains innumerable instances where logical principles hold true. We acknowledge the multidimensional relations of logic to language, to spatial representations, to computers, and to other mathematical representations.

We can also see that the usual procedure, in the kind of formal logic that imitates Aristotle, is to reduce truth to isolatable propositions. It turns out that a single proposition is not really isolatable, any more than one feature of an apple, or one truth about an apple, is isolatable. One truth makes sense in relation to many other truths, and against the background of tacit knowledge. And these truths have intimate relations to the persons who know them. A recognition of the multidimensional character of language, especially divine language, leads to a recognition of limitations belonging to any procedure to express truth in a formalized, artificially restricted "language."

This change has implications for the entire project of philosophical exploration, since traditional philosophy and modern analytic philosophy depend on the use of logic. And for much philosophy, formal logic has become an ideal model that shapes how philosophers think about knowledge, reasoning, and rationality in general. So revising logic leads to revising philosophy as a whole.

20

Aesthetics

One of the remaining subdivisions of philosophy is *aesthetics*.

Defining Aesthetics

What is aesthetics? *Merriam-Webster's New Collegiate Dictionary* offers three meanings for the word *aesthetic(s)*; the first offered is "a branch of philosophy dealing with the nature of beauty, art, and taste and with the creation and appreciation of beauty."[1] But what is "beauty" and what is "art"? The discussion threatens to become circular if we say that beauty is what is *aesthetically* good, or that art is a product with *aesthetic* value. In the *Stanford Encyclopedia of Philosophy*, the main article "The Concept of the Aesthetic" indicates that some philosophers wonder whether the concept is "inherently problematic."[2] Philosophers do not agree about its meaning.

What contribution can we make to this area from a Christian point of view firmly rooted in the Bible? I am not sure. I do not have a firm sense of what the subject matter is, or how to go about discussing it profitably. It is some comfort to know that the *Stanford Encyclopedia of Philosophy* reveals similar difficulties among other people.

---

[1] *Merriam-Webster's New Collegiate Dictionary*, 11th ed. (Springfield, MA: Merriam-Webster, 2008).
[2] James Shelley, "The Concept of the Aesthetic," in *The Stanford Encyclopedia of Philosophy*, Fall 2009 ed., ed. Edward N. Zalta, accessed January 28, 2012, http://plato.stanford.edu/archives/fall2009/entries/aesthetic-concept/.

Multiple Perspectives from Participants in Art

May I nevertheless suggest that a multiperspectival approach may help? People often have very personal responses to art. Two people may agree about the basic plot content of a movie, or the subject matter or style of a painting, or the genre of a piece of music. They may also agree about technical competence or incompetence in the execution of an artistic work. They may nevertheless pointedly disagree in their personal reaction to the work. If art draws out personal responses, and if *aesthetics*, whatever it is, is somehow closely related to art, the relation to art suggests that different people may have different personal viewpoints in such an area.

Thus, the appearance of confusion about the nature of aesthetics may have a partial explanation in the existential perspective and in the multiplicity of people who bring the personal coloring of their own lives into interaction with aesthetics. The lack of agreement and the feeling of confusion may actually suggest something about the existential orientation that plays a key role in this area. God-given diversity among cultures and among people within any one culture may lead to healthy diversity in the treatment of aesthetics.

However, beauty does not reside *merely* "in the eye of the beholder." The beholder beholds beauty that is "out there" (in the situation), and which conforms to norms. As usual, the existential, situational, and normative perspectives coherently harmonize. The beholder's existential reaction, the stable work of art in the situation, and normative standards for beauty and technique function together.

Each person can, if he wishes, produce his own definition of aesthetics and then develop a personal perspective based on that definition. (But, as usual, each person must beware of including false assumptions or commitments within his starting point.) Multiple perspectives by multiple persons can enhance our knowledge and appreciation if we can once free ourselves from the baleful influence of sin.

Interlocking of Aesthetics with Contexts: The Tabernacle

Furthermore, our conclusions about metaphysics suggest that, however we end up defining aesthetics, it offers one dimension out of many as we experience the world. Artistic and literary craftsmanship appear in the Bible in the construction of the tabernacle. The skill for construction is given by the Holy Spirit:

> The LORD said to Moses, "See, I have called by name Bezalel the son of Uri, son of Hur, of the tribe of Judah, and I have filled him with the *Spirit of God*, with ability and intelligence, with knowledge and all craftsmanship, to devise artistic designs, to work in gold, silver, and bronze, in cutting stones for setting, and in carving wood, to work in every craft. (Ex. 31:1–5)

The special holy garments that Bezalel made for Aaron and his sons for ministry in the tabernacle are specifically said to be "for glory and for *beauty*" (Ex. 28:2).

Beauty, artistry, and craftsmanship thus appear in the Bible as gifts from God. They appear not in isolation, but as part of a larger project—the description of the tabernacle and its construction. The "aesthetic," whatever it may be, belongs to a larger whole that has many features. The same holds true for Solomon's temple, described in 1 Kings 5–8, Ezekiel's temple vision in Ezekiel 40–48, and the new Jerusalem in Revelation 21:1–22:5.

The New Testament makes it plain that the Old Testament tabernacle pointed forward to the climax of redemption. God comes to dwell with his people supremely and climactically in Christ. Christ is named Immanuel, "which means, *God with us*" (Matt. 1:23). John 1:14 announces that "the Word [the second person of the Trinity] became flesh and dwelt among us." The Greek word translated "dwelt" in this verse is unusual and alludes to the Old Testament tabernacle dwelling of God, so that John 1:14 might even be translated, "the Word became flesh and *tabernacled* among us." John also indicates that Jesus's body is the final temple: "he [Jesus] was speaking about the temple of his body" (John 2:21).

Thus the climactic beauty and artistry of God appears in Christ. On this basis we may infer that God is indeed beautiful (as one can see also in Rev. 4:3). His beauty is the original, archetypal beauty. Beautiful things in this world possess beauty ectypally. Their beauty has been specified by Christ, who is the Word of God.

Nowadays, art does not always involve a representation of beautiful things, but sometimes calls attention to ugly things. Our world today is not wholly beautiful, partly because it suffers under the effects of the fall into sin (Rom. 8:20–21). Artists may sometimes choose to represent in their art the tensions found in a world contaminated by sin.

Further Development

These observations represent simple beginnings. I have already confessed my own lack of clarity about aesthetics, so I will leave the work to others.[3]

---

[3] See Philip Graham Ryken, *Art for God's Sake: A Call to Recover the Arts* (Phillipsburg, NJ: P&R, 2006); David Bentley Hart, *The Beauty of the Infinite: The Aesthetics of Christian Truth* (Grand Rapids: Eerdmans, 2003); see also the brief remarks on art forms in Vern S. Poythress, *Redeeming Sociology: A God-Centered Approach* (Wheaton, IL: Crossway, 2011), chaps. 31–33. Hart situates himself in the context of Eastern Orthodoxy rather than in orthodox Protestantism and understands how folds of context influence theologizing. My mention of his work should be understood in this context. Hart's heart is in the right place: "But if the Christian story is to be offered to the world as the gift of peace, it must be told in its fullness, without conceding any ground to the other narrative" (ibid., 34). Yet it is very hard for a person in modern society to avoid unwittingly conceding ground in some area or other. I think I see concessions in Hart. He, doubtless, would see concessions in my work. These dangers confirm the importance of using multiple perspectives of multiple people to correct as well as enrich one another.

Specialized Branches of Philosophy

It remains for us to consider several specialized branches of philosophy: philosophy of law, philosophy of religion, philosophy of language, philosophy of history, philosophy of science, and the study of the history of philosophy. We will consider these one at a time.

Philosophy of Law

First, consider the philosophy of law. The archetype for human law is God's law. When we use the term *law* with respect to God, we can treat the term as a perspective on everything that God says. Everything that God says is "law" in a sense, because it is always the authoritative speech of the divine king and lawgiver. But the term *law* suggests a focus on God's *commandments*, and more specifically on commandments regarding human conduct and life.

Subordinate to God's commandments, we have to deal with human commandments given by legislatures, employers, parents, and others in authority. Human beings can give commandments because they imitate God, who made human beings in his image. These human commandments represent an exercise of human authority, which is authorized by God.

Frame's book *The Doctrine of the Christian Life* expounds the subject of human authority, especially under the discussion of the fifth commandment, which gives guidance concerning the meaning and nature of human authority. The fifth commandment, through its implications, also provides a context for understanding man-made laws. Such laws are produced by human authorities. We need to evaluate them using God's law as the ultimate standard. The human authorities, whether in civil government or education or communications media or business or family or church, have their authority because God has appointed them (Rom. 13:1). The reality of God's appointment, as well as the reality of his standards, forms the context for understanding laws and regulations not only in civil government but also in other areas of society.[1]

By contrast, secular philosophy has a problem in explaining the origin of law, because (with few exceptions) it does not want to appeal to God. Even philosophers who do appeal to God may want to avoid appealing to the Bible as the word of God. But without such an appeal, their own ideas of God may go astray, and they may then also go astray in the way they evaluate both the law as a whole and the examples of particular laws. For example, they may attribute to God their own desire for abstract equality and use it as an argument for redistributing the wealth. Or an exploitive rich person may make excuses for himself by telling himself that those under him are there by God's appointment and therefore may be freely exploited.

Some people would say that law originates merely from human consensus. But this view does not give any individual human being a moral reason for obeying a law with which he disagrees. True, he may still obey out of fear of bad consequences. But then again, he may disobey if he thinks he can get away with it. In addition, this view does not protect the individual from the tyranny of the majority. The danger of such tyranny is evident from historical examples. Hitler came into power by constitutional means. And many within German society, carried along by his rhetoric, agreed with the political directions that he chose. But does might make right? Does the will of the majority make right? God says no.

---

[1] See also Vern S. Poythress, *Redeeming Sociology: A God-Centered Approach* (Wheaton, IL: Crossway, 2011), chap. 25.

Other philosophers might try to trace law back to utility: law should be whatever helps human flourishing. But there are difficulties here. Once again, does this view give an adequate moral basis for individual obedience? Could not an individual argue that he should work for his own individual flourishing and not for everyone else? And once again, the will of the majority threatens to become tyranny. What if the flourishing of the majority can take place better by the nonflourishing or elimination of a minority? Hitler wanted to get rid of the Jews because he thought that they were a problem to society as a whole.

From these simple examples we can see how it is difficult to give an adequate basis for law by focusing merely on a human level.

Philosophy of Religion

Next, consider the philosophy of religion. In a sense we have been addressing questions related to the philosophy of religion all along, because we attempt to reckon at every point with the reality of God. But because we use the Creator-creature distinction, and because we are willing to use the Bible, our way of approach is notably different from a good deal of discussion in the philosophy of religion.

In the last half of the twentieth century and into the twenty-first, much has taken place in analytic philosophy of religion. We cannot enter into it in detail. We can find fascinating insights in this field, but dangers may creep in through the back door.

If we do not pay attention to the Creator-creature distinction and to our need for God's verbal instruction about himself in the Bible, we run the danger of turning into a path where we reason autonomously or otherwise compromise with the desires for autonomous reason. If we try to reason out the character of God, we may succumb to non-Christian thinking about God's transcendence and immanence. In a non-Christian view of God's immanence, human rationality is thought to deal adequately with God, and God is on the same rational level with man. Or in a non-Christian notion of transcendence, God is inaccessible and unknowable by rational means.

Pluralism and Exclusivism in Religion

In addition, the Bible has a notable emphasis that religion can be either true or false. God is the only true God. In his holiness he detests false worship of substitutes for God. Idolatry insults him. Moreover, idolatry betrays the knowledge all human beings everywhere have about God by virtue of creation (Rom. 1:18–23).

The Bible's distinction between the true God and false gods, and between true and false religion, does not sit well with some philosophy of religion. If a person devotes himself to universal rationality, his devotion may tempt him to "level out" all religions and to avoid the distinction between true and false. The pluralism that is common in modern life further reinforces this avoidance.

Philosophy of Language

Next, consider the philosophy of language. What do we say about the nature of language? As we have already made clear in our discussion of metaphysics, God speaks. He is the original or archetypal speaker. So language exists on two levels, the divine level and the human. And the two levels interact, according to God's design. Language as we know it is not *merely* human. It is a gift from God, and the gift expresses the character of the giver. God himself ordains all the regularities of all the languages of the world through his sovereign determination in his speech, specifying the nature of all languages. God designed natural languages as means for him to speak to us and for us to speak to him, not merely so that we can speak to fellow human beings. Our thinking about language needs to adjust to this reality. We cannot pursue the matter in detail here. But I direct readers to a book-length discussion, *In the Beginning Was the Word*.[2]

Philosophy of History

What can we say about a philosophy of history? The Bible has much to say about history. The Bible begins at the beginning, with the cre-

---

[2] Vern S. Poythress, *In the Beginning Was the Word: Language—A God-Centered Approach* (Wheaton, IL: Crossway, 2009).

ation of the world. It ends at the consummation, with the creation of
the new heavens and the new earth. It explains God's purposes from
beginning to end. In the middle it places Christ's work of redemption. When we take all these things together, we have a basic philosophy of history, because we understand what history is about.[3]
Much in the secular philosophy of history really expresses discontent with the Bible's picture, and discontent leads to quests for a
replacement that could be built up through autonomous thought.

Philosophy of Science

What about the philosophy of science? God's comprehensive rule
over the world has implications for our understanding of science.
Once again, the Creator-creature distinction makes a difference.
Our understanding of science is subordinate and derivative in comparison to God's understanding of the world and his rule over it.
Since God rules the whole world through his word (Heb. 1:3), his
word of command specifies everything about the world. Human sciences explore aspects of the regularities that God has appointed in
his wisdom. Human beings engaged in science are therefore thinking God's thoughts after him analogically in the area of science.
Their thoughts and their theories are derivative: human beings
are giving their best guesses and approximations, which reflect the
real laws. The real laws are God's words. We can make progress in
understanding the foundations of science if we start with God and
the Bible's teaching about God. These matters are addressed more
fully in the book *Redeeming Science*.[4]

The History of Philosophy

In addition to all these subdivisions of philosophy, some academic
classes in philosophy adopt primarily a historical approach. The

---

[3] For more details about history, see ibid., chaps. 11–19, 24–29; Poythress, *Redeeming Sociology*,
chaps. 11–18; and Poythress, *Inerrancy and Worldview: Answering Modern Challenges to the Bible*,
chaps. 5–6. These sketches can be supplemented by many works on redemptive history, such as
Geerhardus Vos, *Biblical Theology: Old and New Testaments* (Grand Rapids: Eerdmans, 1948; repr.,
Eugene, OR: Wipf and Stock, 2003); Richard B. Gaffin Jr., *Resurrection and Redemption: A Study
in Paul's Soteriology* (Phillipsburg, NJ: P&R, 1987); Edmund P. Clowney, *The Unfolding Mystery:
Discovering Christ in the Old Testament* (Colorado Springs, CO: NavPress, 1988).
[4] Vern S. Poythress, *Redeeming Science: A God-Centered Approach* (Wheaton, IL: Crossway, 2006).

teacher leads the class in examining some particular philosopher or group of philosophers from the past. The class devotes itself primarily to trying to understand the philosopher, rather than evaluating whether he is right on this or that issue. After all, how would a student be able to give a definitive answer to the question of right or wrong without having himself *solved* the difficulty in question, and thereby having done a very significant piece of philosophizing himself?

How might a Christian respond to all this philosophizing? To respond in detail would take many books.[5] But the general principles are easy to summarize. We may recognize several principles. (1) All human beings live in God's world and cannot escape knowing God (though they may suppress their knowledge of God—Rom. 1:18). (2) Human beings receive many benefits from God by common grace, and these benefits include intellectual benefits in the form of insights and knowledge of many truths. (3) Because of principles 1 and 2, we may learn much from others, particularly those whom God has richly gifted.

(4) The history of philosophy is full of cases where philosophers have adopted a commitment to autonomous reason and failed to distinguish the rationality of the Creator from the rationality of themselves as creatures. They go astray at the foundations. At root, their thinking is *antithetical* to Christian faith. (5) Most philosophers fail to submit to the teaching of Scripture. Even Christians can be tempted in this way, when they adopt the ground rules of autonomy in order to have dialogue with unbelievers.

(6) Sifting through the good and bad in a particular philosophy is not easy. The good is thoroughly mixed with the bad, partly because even the bad, if it is to appear plausible, must counterfeit something good.

---

[5] For an extended response to the history of philosophy, see John M. Frame, *A History of Western Philosophy and Theology: Spiritual Warfare in the Life of the Mind* (Phillipsburg, NJ: P&R, forthcoming), title subject to change.

PART 6

Interacting with Defective Philosophies

22

The Challenge of Philosophies

The basic idea of Christian philosophy is simple: in whatever you are thinking about, pay attention to God and to what he says in the Bible. Receive its instruction as God's instruction, giving you wisdom.

It is easier said than done. But the Bible itself does provide a resource. God's provision in his word is most valuable, because God's speech is pure (Ps. 12:6). We do not need critically to sift it for good and bad. We need to have it sift us, for our purification: "Sanctify them [disciples] in the truth; your word is truth" (John 17:17).

The Challenge of Critical Appropriation

Interacting with previous philosophies is not simple. Human sin contaminates all merely human works. Works of philosophy have some positive insights, by virtue of common grace. But they also have some distortions, because of the effects of sin on human thinking. Sorting the good from the bad is not easy.

Writings by other people are always potentially valuable, because each person brings to his writing the uniqueness of who he is. Philosophers frequently offer new, creative perspectives on the world or on some subject within philosophy. Many of them are outstandingly brilliant people. Their perspectives may supplement our own, and by interacting with multiple perspectives we may grow in knowledge, in depth, and in wisdom.

We may grow, I say. But we may also be led astray. Much in the history of Western philosophy has been driven by underlying religious desire for autonomy. This desire shows itself in the very fact that a writer ignores what the Bible says. Or he treats the Bible as merely one more human writing. Much work done in the name of philosophy has been overtly or covertly hostile to the Christian faith.

Attempts by Christians

Through the ages Christians have reflected on philosophy. We in our day may build on what they have done. Some Christians have indeed been aware of the contrast between Christian faith and the offerings of philosophers, and have engaged in critical appropriation of philosophical ideas, rather than mere acceptance. Augustine interacted critically with Platonic philosophy. Thomas Aquinas interacted critically with Aristotle.

We may be grateful for these attempts. But some of them were not critical *enough*. The critic who wants (rightly) to appropriate positive insights may at the same time swallow more than he intends. He may be corrupted at the same time that he is learning. John Frame discusses discerningly the issue of appropriating insights from ancient Greek philosophy. He issues this caution in the light of the previous history of attempts:

> Combining the Christian perspective with the Greek is not advisable. We can learn today from the questions the Greeks asked, from their failures, from the insights they express in matters of detail. But we should rigorously avoid the notion of rational autonomy and the form-matter scheme as a comprehensive worldview. Unfortunately, during the medieval period and beyond, Christian theologians relied extensively on Neoplatonism and (beginning with Aquinas) Aristotelianism. Aquinas, for example, distinguished between natural reason (which operates apart from revelation) and faith (which supplements our reason with revelation). Then he referred over and over again to Aristotle as "the Philosopher" who guides us in matters of natural reason.[1]

---

[1] John M. Frame, "Greeks Bearing Gifts," in *Revolutions in Worldview: Understanding the Flow of Western Thought*, ed. W. Andrew Hoffecker (Phillipsburg, NJ: P&R, 2007), 33.

The Contribution of Cornelius Van Til

Cornelius Van Til, in his development of presuppositional apologetics, has pioneered a more thoroughgoing critical interaction with philosophy. Van Til's own works provide examples,[2] and the work continues among his followers.[3] Recently, Frame has produced a major work interacting with the history of philosophy, and it can serve as a key resource.[4] Not everyone can do it well. It takes people with strong faith and special gifts, and sometimes a strong stomach, to recognize folly when it takes very appealing forms, to reject it thoroughly, and yet to appropriate every last bit of positive insight.

---

[2] See, for example, Cornelius Van Til, *A Survey of Christian Epistemology*, In Defense of Biblical Christianity 2 (n.p.: den Dulk Christian Foundation, 1969); Van Til, *A Christian Theory of Knowledge* (n.p.: Presbyterian and Reformed, 1969); Van Til, *Christianity and Barthianism* (Philadelphia: Presbyterian and Reformed, 1965); Van Til, *The New Modernism: An Appraisal of the Theology of Barth and Brunner* (Nutley, NJ: Presbyterian and Reformed, 1973); Van Til, *The New Hermeneutic* (Nutley, NJ: Presbyterian and Reformed, 1974).

In my judgment, Van Til's work is very important, and yet also hard to read. Van Til believes in an antithesis between Christian and non-Christian thinking, and this antithesis comes out clearly in his analysis of the works of others. He also believes in common grace, but it is harder to discern from his works how positively to appropriate grains of truth within the works of non-Christian thought.

[3] See the essays of John Frame on the subject catalogued in "Bibliography," in *Speaking the Truth in Love: The Theology of John M. Frame*, ed. John J. Hughes (Phillipsburg, NJ: P&R, 2009), 1044–45.

[4] John M. Frame, *A History of Western Philosophy and Theology: Spiritual Warfare in the Life of the Mind* (Phillipsburg, NJ: P&R, forthcoming), title subject to change.

23

Immanuel Kant

As an example, consider Immanuel Kant (1724–1804).[1] Kant is a complex and subtle philosopher, so we will consider only a tiny piece, the opening lines from his *Critique of Pure Reason*:

> There can be no doubt that all our knowledge begins with experience. For how should our faculty of knowledge be awakened into action did not objects affecting our senses partly of themselves produce representations, partly arouse the activity of our understanding to compare these representations, and, by combining or separating them, work up the raw material of the sensible impressions into that knowledge of objects which is entitled experience? In the order of time, therefore, we have no knowledge antecedent to experience, and with experience all our knowledge begins.
>
> But though all our knowledge begins with experience, it does not follow that it all arises out of experience. For it may well be that even our empirical knowledge is made up of what we receive through impressions and of what our own faculty of knowledge (sensible impressions serving merely as the occasion) supplies from itself. If our faculty of knowledge makes any such addition, it may be that we are not in a position to

---

[1] Cornelius Van Til, *Survey of Christian Epistemology*, In Defense of Biblical Christianity 2 (n.p.: den Dulk Christian Foundation, 1969), 106–14; Vern S. Poythress, *Logic: A God-Centered Approach to the Foundation of Western Thought* (Wheaton, IL: Crossway, 2013), appendix F1; John M. Frame, *A History of Western Philosophy and Theology: Spiritual Warfare in the Life of the Mind* (Phillipsburg, NJ: P&R, forthcoming), title subject to change.

distinguish it from the raw material, until with long practice of attention we have become skilled in separating it.[2]

Kant goes on to explain that an addition that comes from our "faculty of knowledge" would be *a priori* knowledge, which is "distinguished from the *empirical*, which has its sources *a posteriori*, that is, in experience."[3]

In this early discussion, Kant is already working toward establishing a distinction between the contribution from the mind (*a priori*) and the contribution whose sources are in experience (*a posteriori*). For Kant this distinction is important for establishing positive foundations for the exercise of reason in science, and for establishing the limitations of the scope of reason. Kant's argument here plays a significant part in his entire system.

Common Grace in Kant

First, we may see an element of common grace. Kant is viewing the whole project of human knowledge from the perspective of the knower. He is asking how we, as human subjects, have the subjective experience that we have. He is operating in a manner similar to what Frame has called the *existential perspective*. This perspective is indeed a perspective on all things that human beings know, including God. In a Christian worldview, the existential perspective harmonizes and interlocks with the normative and situational perspectives. God (the focus of the normative perspective) and the world (the focus of the situational perspective) can both be viewed from the perspective of what we as human persons can experience and know about them. It is insightful to view God and the world from that perspective, and John Frame does so (in those parts of *Doctrine of the Knowledge of God* that employ the existential perspective).

Kant does likewise. When we use a perspective, we notice things that we may not have noticed before via other perspectives. We

---

[2] Immanuel Kant, *Immanuel Kant's Critique of Pure Reason*, trans. Norman Kemp Smith, unabridged ed. (New York: St Martin's, 1965), 41–42 (B1–B2, i.e. pp. 1–2 from Kant's second edition).
[3] Ibid., 42–43 (B2).

experience new insights. Kant's observations become particularly apt when we consider the development in the twentieth century of experimental psychology, experimental neuroscience, and experimental examination of the intricacies of the sensory organs in human beings. We find that a massive amount of physiological and neurological processing takes place in the production of human experience. Kant's statements about sensory experience and the later twentieth-century investigation contain many positive insights that are due to common grace.

The remaining difficulty is the one we have already discussed about perspectives. Particularly in a non-Christian context, one perspective can be used as the exclusive key. The user then gives the impression that everything can be *reduced* to the dimensions specified by the one perspective. In particular, Kant thinks that the distinction between *a priori* knowledge and knowledge from experience (*a posteriori*) is a *fundamental* insight that gets us to the roots of the world. He thinks he has a precise distinction, and he thinks monoperspectivally. But Kant ends up denying that we can know God, at least by "pure reason," and he denies that we can know the world in the form of "the thing in itself." God and the world are reduced to the dimensions of the existential perspective, as Kant construes it.

Even here Kant's thinking contains grains of truth. We cannot know God in the same manner and in the same depth as God knows himself. Neither can we know the world in the same depth that God does. What Kant says is tantalizing, because he is playing off genuine insights into some of the limitations of human knowledge. But distortions may creep in. In fact, in Kant's case they do creep in. Perhaps "pure reason" ends up being *autonomous* reason, which makes itself into a false god or false absolute and then pronounces that any "god" that cannot fit into its expectations for human mastery in knowledge must not be knowable at all.

But we are getting far ahead of ourselves by glancing forward to some of the conclusions that come out later in the development of Kantian philosophy. Our point is not to consider all the arguments and conclusions in detail, but to point out that a construal of the meaning of the existential perspective at the beginning of Kant's philosophical operations can have a big influence on the end. The beginning sounds plausible because it has grains of truth in it. But, already at the beginning, the nature of the existential perspective may be misconstrued in a decisive way, yet subtly so that the average reader—and Kant himself—does not detect it. The conclusions are built into the starting point.

Analysis of Terms

So let us begin to analyze Kant's starting argument by looking at key terms. These terms may have vagueness or ambiguity, which make it possible to introduce a distorted view of the existential perspective. The terms appear to promise to give us the deep structure of reality, or at least of the epistemological side of reality. But they contain difficulties because they are not perfectly precise.

What key terms occur in Kant's opening lines? Several: "knowledge," "experience," "faculty of knowledge," "objects," "our senses," "representations," "our understanding," "combining or separating," "the raw material of sensible impressions," "that knowledge of objects which is entitled experience." None of these expressions is precisely defined. All are pretty general. We are not talking about knowledge of Sally the horse or the apples that my wife brought home from the grocery store. We are talking on a high level of generality. How do we know the relation of the one, the general term, to the many, the particular experiences of horses and apples?

We can observe a tension or a puzzle as to what constitutes "knowledge." Consider the second sentence in the first paragraph of the quote from Kant. Near the end of this sentence, Kant tells us about "that knowledge of objects which is entitled experience." "Experience" is almost a synonym for knowledge. But prior to that, we are told about "objects affecting our senses," on which the activity of our understanding operates and works "up the raw material of the sensible impressions."

The Narrative of Producing Knowledge of Objects

There is a narrative here, a story of how we come to have the "experience" that constitutes knowledge. There are several stages in the story. The story begins with "objects affecting our senses." First, we have "objects." The objects act; they are a cause of an effect. They are "affecting our senses." Then they "produce representations." What are "representations"? Perhaps Kant means something akin to mental concepts. The objects also "arouse" something. Another causal term, the term "arouse," occurs here. What is aroused is "the activity of our understanding." That activity undertakes to "compare," and engages in "combining or separating them," that is, combining or separating the representations. There are more causal acts here. In the last part of the sentence, there appears to be a summary: the activity of understanding "work[s] up the raw material of the sensible impressions." There is more causal activity here in the event of "working up." What is worked up is "the raw material of the sensible impressions." The product after this "working up" is that the raw material gets transformed or changed into something else, namely, "that knowledge of objects which is entitled experience."

One of the obvious questions is about "knowledge." If "knowledge" belongs only to the final stage or final product of the narrative, how does Kant *know* all the rest? How does he expect us to know? In particular, how do we know what is "the raw material of the sensible impressions" *before* it is "worked up" and transformed into knowledge? If Kant knows all the stages before the narrative arrives at the goal, namely, the achievement of knowledge, maybe it is because we *also* have knowledge of sense experience of the kind that is alleged to exist before it is "worked up."

For example, people can, by an effort of concentration, suppress their knowledge that they are looking at an apple and consider only the blotches of color and brightness. The effect is something like the artistic effect of pointillism, a style of painting in which a scene is reduced to tiny dots of color. But it takes considerable intellectual concentration and single-mindedness to "think away" the presence of an apple and just think about the colors and their spatial arrangement. The use of intellectual concentration seems to be in tension with Kant's expression "raw material." The experience of blotches of color and brightness is not literally "raw material," but a rather sophisticated intellectual effect of consciously "thinking away" every other dimension of experience, and focusing single-mindedly on color and brightness belonging to various spots in the visual field. That method of thinking away is possible only because of deep personal motivations that empower a person to want to look at "experience" in a creative new way. Similarly, the neurological study of sensory nerves and the sensory cortex of the brain takes considerable intellectual firepower. It is not very "raw." So perhaps Kant does not want to go this way. Perhaps he might say that we know by inference the things that he mentions.

Multiple Assumptions, Multiple Perspectives

What inferences lead to Kant's narrative? Might different people have different narratives? In addition, might their intellectual firepower be used in several different ways, to produce several different attempts to analyze human life down to its metaphysical skeleton? The empiricists want to have irreducible pieces of sense experience. What they mean by "experience" is experience prior to our "working it up" into "objects." Objects are a later construction, rather than things that are "affecting our senses." The idealists want to begin with knowledge or concepts or ideas—entities of some kind in the mind—because they do not think that we can get behind them. According to their viewpoint, talking about "the raw material" is nonsense, because we have no access to it. They might wonder whether Kant's narrative about a quest for knowledge is pure speculation, exceeding the bounds of reason.

Modern physiologists and neurologists who study human perception have their own narratives, which are useful situational perspectives on the functioning of human body parts. But do these narratives have a metaphysical priority to everything else? Does Kant's narrative? Or may we as Christians say, as one perspective, that God gives me my current experience and gives me knowledge of him?

What is an "object"? Kant wants to confine "experience" to "sense" experience. So the "objects" that are part of this experience can only be sense objects, such as chairs, apples, and horses. For an empiricist, however, the real "sense experience" consists of blotches of color in various locations; objects like chairs and apples are highly structured through the use of prior concepts of chairs and apples. If we ignore the empiricist objection and start with chairs and apples, Kant's approach is still reductionistic. We experience the presence of God, though we may suppress it. We also digest other people's ideas as we listen to them or read their writings. We are "experiencing" people and their ideas, not merely "senses." Kant excludes God, language, and people at the beginning when he focuses on "senses."

Kant is thus already making moves in the direction of laying down the tracks that will determine what is metaphysically ultimate. He does so by assumptions, not by argument. Assumptions are concealed in the vocabulary and in the opening narrative. There is hardly any other way to do it, since philosophers have to use language, and use of language always depends on assumptions. But it seems so innocent, so obvious, and so attractive because it utilizes a perspective—the existential perspective. At the same time, it is a distorted use, because it claims to be ultimate rather than partial.

Deconstruction

Deconstruction has had its fun deconstructing narratives like Kant's. Deconstructors are aware that words can slip around. In addition, philosophical narratives have the conceptual baggage of narrative structure, with its typical phases of plot development. We can catalog some phases in the plot inherent in Kant's narrative: (1) desire (the observer thinking, I want knowledge that I do not have yet); (2) plot movement (cause-and-effect, then more cause-and-effect, combining or separating—will we arrive at our goal?); (3) test ("work up . . . into"); and (4) resolution ("here it is; we have arrived; we have achieved knowledge").[4]

---

[4] Vern S. Poythress, *In the Beginning Was the Word: Language—A God-Centered Approach* (Wheaton, IL: Crossway, 2009), chaps. 24–29.

Deconstructors have made themselves aware of language, and this has made them realize that Kant and other classical philosophers are bringing in a host of assumptions. The deconstructors have some good observations by common grace. But it should be clear that when we inspect language from a Christian point of view, we have different assumptions.[5]

In his subsequent discussion in *Critique of Pure Reason*, Kant goes further. He wants to distinguish carefully between the achievements of the mind and the achievements accomplished by the object. The mind and the external object become like two characters in a story. Kant evaluates what effects belong to each of the two "characters." Like the storybook figure of the father of the princess in a Vladimir Propp folktale,[6] Kant wants to reward the hero figures in his story according to their accomplishments. His narrative follows a conventional plot.

In a Christian worldview, mind and object are correlative; mind is in focus with the existential perspective, and objects are in focus with the situational perspective. Because of ectypal coinherence, either mind or object can be used as a perspective. But we cannot achieve a perfect mental separation between their contributions. The archetype for the mystery of the relation between subject and object is the divine original. God knows himself. The Father knows the Son. Both Father and Son are simultaneously subject and object.

---

[5] There is much to say about a critical analysis of deconstruction, far more than the beginning I attempted in ibid., appendix I.

[6] Vladimir Propp, *The Morphology of the Folktale*, 2nd ed. (Austin: University of Texas Press, 1968), 79.

24

Edmund Husserl

Edmund Husserl (1859–1938) may serve as our next example. Husserl is another complex, subtle, powerful philosopher, and we cannot enter into an extensive discussion of his approach (he is the father of *phenomenology* and influenced Martin Heidegger, Maurice Merleau-Ponty, and Paul Ricoeur). We may illustrate a critical analysis of Husserl using several small pieces from his key work *Ideas*.[1]

The first piece is from the introduction to *Ideas*: "[To understand phenomenology] *a new way of looking at things* is necessary, one that contrasts *at every point* with the natural attitude of experience and thought."[2] This language seems to promise a new perspective. In fact, phenomenology, as Husserl develops it, is one form of an existential perspective: we start from a person and consider his consciousness of the world around him as well as his consciousness of himself. But there are many possible perspectives and many ways of proceeding within an existential focus. More questionable is Husserl's claim that "Pure Phenomenology" is going to be set forth "as the most fundamental region of philosophy."[3] This sounds like an ambition to find the deep structure of the world.

Because the phenomenological standpoint is so unlike "the natural attitude," Husserl undertakes to proceed toward it by gradual

---

[1] Edmund Husserl, *Ideas: General Introduction to Pure Phenomenology* (London: Allen & Unwin; New York: Humanities, 1931).
[2] Ibid., 43, italics original.
[3] Ibid., 41.

steps. The procedure is complex. But in the process, what do we do with the fact that the terms and discussions contain analogies and are not perfectly stable? Consider the first lines in the first chapter:

> Natural knowledge begins with experience (*Erfahrung*) and remains *within* experience. Thus in that theoretical position which we call the "natural" standpoint, the total field of possible research is indicated by a *single* word: that is, the *World*. The sciences proper to this original standpoint are accordingly in their collective unity sciences of the World.[4]

What is "natural"? What is "experience"? Does it include "experience" of God? What is "the World"? Does it include God?

The explanation continues by talking about "perception":

> In "outer perception" we have primordial experience of physical things, but in memory or anticipatory expectation this is no longer the case; we have primordial experience of ourselves and our states of consciousness in the so-called inner or self-perception, but not of others and their vital experiences in and though "empathy." We "behold the living experiences of others" through the perception of their bodily behavior.[5]

This discussion distinguishes between what is "primordial" and what is not. By doing so, it prioritizes certain aspects of "experience." Why should we make this distinction, and why should we think that one aspect is more "primordial"? Husserl assumes rather than demonstrates the ultimacy of an individual and his consciousness in comparison to a group of people and their interactions. He appears to bias the discussion in favor of Western individualism. One might in reply point out that babies interact with their parents and siblings in the process of learning who they are, learning how to interact socially, and learning language. Interpersonal interaction is in this sense "primordial" in comparison with individual adult self-consciousness and adult experience of perception.

---

[4] Ibid., 51, italics original.
[5] Ibid., 51–52.

In addition, we run the danger, as Husserl's rhetoric flows into us, of confining "outer perception" to *sense* perception. In a manner similar to Kant, we may reduce "experience" to "sense experience" and leave out our robust social interaction with other human persons and with God. Husserl has spoken about "the perception of their bodily behavior" as a means by which we obtain knowledge of others. This expression appears to leave out linguistic communication. One of the keys to understanding other people is listening to them. We are not merely listening to their lips uttering sounds (a reduction to sense experience). We are listening to the people.

Husserl has engaged in a certain selectivity. This selectivity is a perspective. Yes, we can observe that through sounds we listen to persons. But the selectivity can come back to bite us later on. Do we produce the philosophical problem of solipsism, the problem of other minds? Having eliminated other people at the beginning, can we retrieve them later on, or do we remain prisoners within our own minds? Do we think that we are interacting not with other people, but with our "perceptions" and "ideas" that "constitute" "people" as objects of our consciousness? We can perspectivally focus on such a point of view, but it is only one perspective. Treating it as foundational is a reduction.

Husserl continues by indicating a little more about what he has in mind when he talks about "the World": "The World is the totality of objects that can be known through experience (*Erfahrung*), known in terms of orderly theoretical thought on the basis of direct present (*aktueller*) experience."[6] The ambiguities here do not permit us to say clearly what sort of view of God is compatible with these expressions. Do we meet God in "experience" because he is everywhere present in the world, as a Christian view of divine immanence understands? Do we meet him especially in "religious experience," certain spiritually intense moments? If so, do we, by singling out "religious" experience, unwittingly imply that God is absent most of the time, in ordinary experience?

Or we can move in the opposite direction. Is God absent, because "experience" is being conceived as experience of created

---

[6] Ibid., 52.

things by themselves, independent of the presence of God? Or if God is present, is he present in such a way that we may master him with "orderly theoretical thought," as non-Christian immanence would imply? Or is God present as the Lord who governs "experience"? If we are not careful, a non-Christian view of transcendence and immanence gets smuggled in even when we are reading the first few lines of the book. I do not presume to judge Husserl's motives, but I am suggesting at the very least what may happen to readers. Having once read into the work a non-Christian view of "the World," readers can corrupt their reading of the whole rest of the book.

Husserl continues:

> The acts of cognition which underlie our experiencing posit the Real in *individual* form, posit it as having spatio-temporal existence, as something existing in *this* time-spot, having this particular duration of its own and a real content which in its essence could just as well have been present in any other time-spot.[7]

Now "the Real" turns out to have "spatio-temporal existence," which apparently excludes God. Is this further explanation a narrowing, or is it simply the further clarification of what was meant earlier on the page? Husserl also introduces the idea of "essence," which is a key term. What does it mean? This term takes us back to our discussion of essence and accidents in chapter 11, and difficulties that are entrained when we think too quickly that we know exactly what we mean. Husserl's concern for essences is closely related to his interest in "pure" categories, which we have earlier characterized as a problematic ideal.

In short, even this brief exploration of Husserl shows that the opening pages of his discussion contain a thicket of difficulties once we start asking questions about the meanings of key terms. We can also see selectivity at work—the selectivity in talking about "experience" in a way that largely ignores or puts into the background language and interpersonal relationships; the selectivity of "the

---

[7] Ibid.

World," apparently conceived of independently of God; the selectivity in the choice to see "essence" as a key; and the selectivity in the claim that "Pure Phenomenology" is "the most fundamental region of philosophy." As with Kant, building such a philosophy depends on language that has not secured its own foundations.

25

Analytic Philosophy

Philosophers in the analytic tradition might be sympathetic with some criticisms of Plato or Kant, but distinguish the analytic tradition as one that is aware of language and exercises care. Yes, there is care of a certain kind. But many questions can still be raised. For instance, is that same analytic care exercised when analytic philosophers attempt to address larger questions?[1]

Bertrand Russell

We may take as an example Bertrand Russell. He did his technical work within the tradition of analytic philosophy, but he also explored larger implications. In discussing some of the implications, he says, "It is taken for granted that scientific knowledge, in its broad outlines, is to be accepted."[2] That seems commonsensical, and Russell talks later about "scientific common sense."[3] Russell knows well enough that a search for human wisdom cannot get off the ground without assumptions. In his judgment, the products of science offer the most reliable starting point. So he will build on them. And here is one of the conclusions at which he arrives:

---

[1] On analytic philosophy, see also Vern S. Poythress, *Logic: A God-Centered Approach to the Foundation of Western Thought* (Wheaton, IL: Crossway, 2013), appendix F2.
[2] Bertrand Russell, *Human Knowledge: Its Scope and Limits* (New York: Simon and Schuster, 1948), xi.
[3] Ibid.

That man is the product of causes which had no prevision of the end they were achieving; that his origin, his growth, his hopes and fears, his loves and his beliefs, are but the outcome of accidental collocations of atoms; that no fire, no heroism, no intensity of thought and feeling, can preserve an individual life beyond the grave; that all the labors of the ages, all the devotion, all the inspiration, all the noonday brightness of human genius, are destined to extinction in the vast death of the solar system, and that the whole temple of man's achievement must inevitably be buried beneath the debris of a universe in ruins—all these things, if not quite beyond dispute, are yet so nearly certain that no philosophy which rejects them can hope to stand. Only within the scaffolding of these truths, only on the firm foundation of unyielding despair, can the soul's habitation henceforth be safely built.[4]

In reply, we should certainly affirm that modern science is a marvelous product of common grace. But Russell's confidence in science passes over virtually all the important questions about the nature of this world. Could it be that religious bias and flawed assumptions lie underneath the structure of twentieth-century secularism in science? Could it also be that people are in danger of arguing in a circle to come to materialistic conclusions?

If we may oversimplify this materialist view, science starts with a decision to focus on the material—matter and motion and energy. It then achieves results about the behavior of matter and motion and energy. People are amazed at the results, and so they think these results are the heart of knowledge. They then conclude that at bottom the world is merely matter and motion and energy. The conclusion follows from the nature of the original decision, not from the nature of the world.[5]

The Theory of Speech Acts

Or we may consider the theory of speech acts. Here is a more modest program within the tradition of analytic philosophy, a program

---

[4] Bertrand Russell, "A Free Man's Worship," in *Why I Am Not a Christian*, ed. Paul Edwards (New York: Simon & Schuster, 1957), 107.
[5] For further discussion, see Vern S. Poythress, *Redeeming Science: A God-Centered Approach* (Wheaton, IL: Crossway, 2006), especially chap. 1, on religious bias, and chaps. 15–16, on the nature of reality.

to understand commitments and social transactions accomplished by human speech. We can find insights here that are due to common grace. We can also see simplifications and reductions. The focus is on simple sentences, not on complex, multiparagraph discourse. The focus is on simple speech acts with simple purposes, not on communication with more complex and multidimensional purposes.

Such reductions are relatively harmless if we admit to ourselves that we are reducing matters to one or a few dimensions. But if we make an analysis of speech acts a piece in a philosophical platform that we will leverage in order to know reality, we have the same problem that Kant and Husserl had. Our categories become the pillars on which we build metaphysics.[6]

Tacit Assumptions

The tradition of analytic philosophy has busied itself with the task of critical analysis of philosophical issues. But has it busied itself equally with critical analysis of the basic assumptions of its own tradition? Has it really taken to heart what Michael Polanyi wrote, or Hans-Georg Gadamer, or cosmonomic philosophy, or deconstruction, or romanticism? These alternatives exist for a reason. Those inhabiting these traditions are quite convinced that analytic philosophy has serious deficiencies in its foundations.

Do analytic philosophers see these deficiencies? It will not do for analytic philosophers to respond merely by criticizing alternatives with arguments that tacitly rely on uninspected assumptions belonging to their own tradition. If irrationality is self-refuting, it does not follow that only their understanding of rationality survives.

Thus, challenges to a particular philosopher or to a broader philosophical tradition can arise not only as we critically inspect key terms, but also as we critically inspect hidden assumptions, such as assumptions that inevitably belong to the very idea of rationality and the texture that philosophical reasoning will imitate.

---

[6] Vern S. Poythress, *In the Beginning Was the Word: Language—A God-Centered Approach* (Wheaton, IL: Crossway, 2009), appendix H.

Conclusion

Philosophy started as the pursuit of wisdom. Wisdom is still worth pursuing. The book of Proverbs affirms the importance of wisdom:

> *Get wisdom*; get insight. (Prov. 4:5)

> The beginning of wisdom is this: *Get wisdom*,
>   and whatever you get, get insight.
> Prize her highly, and she will exalt you;
>   she will honor you if you embrace her.
> She will place on your head a graceful garland;
>   she will bestow on you a beautiful crown. (Prov. 4:7–9)

The Bible goes beyond this kind of urging and inviting by instructing us in wisdom. God speaks, so what we hear is the wisdom of God. This wisdom is summed up in Christ (1 Cor. 1:30; Col. 2:3), who is the Logos of God (1 John 1:1).

From this source we may grow in wisdom. We get answers to the big questions, including answers touching on the concerns of the tradition of Western philosophy. In previous generations, and in previous work within this generation, much has been done already in explaining the Bible's answers in ways that help to make those answers clear and accessible. So in this book we have been able to make a quick tour that consolidates what has been done. In addition, we have addressed at more length the question of metaphysics. We have asked what exists and how it exists. Trinitarian perspectivalism, as developed by John Frame and me, offers resources for moving beyond the reductionisms characteristic of much philosophy, and moving into a healthy philosophy, which according to Frame can be defined as theology.

Other Areas?

Learning continues during this life, from generation to generation. We enjoy contributions from the past, but we can always learn more, explore more, and learn more deeply. We can correct what we find has been done amiss by previous generations. So what we have explored in this book, as well as what has been achieved in other books cited here, does not bring us to an endpoint. I hope that it offers a beginning by suggesting directions and encouragements to those who come after.

> For the weapons of our warfare are not of the flesh but have divine power to destroy strongholds. We destroy arguments and every lofty opinion raised against the knowledge of God, and take *every thought captive to obey Christ*. (2 Cor. 10:4–5)

> So, whether you eat or drink, or whatever you do, do all to the glory of God. (1 Cor. 10:31)

Cosmonomic Philosophy

I have learned from many others in coming to the point of writing this book. I single out Abraham Kuyper, who emphasized that Christ is Lord of all of life. Kuyper argued that Christians should have a distinctive approach to academic studies, and I am endeavoring to do what he envisioned. I also owe a debt to Cornelius Van Til, who learned from Kuyper and who became a more immediate source for much in this book that is similar to Kuyper's thinking. The influence of John Frame is also evident throughout.

The Founders of Cosmonomic Philosophy

In addition, during the years 1967–1973 I read literature from the "neo-Kuyperian" tradition, including Herman Dooyeweerd (1894–1977), Dirk H. Th. Vollenhoven (1892–1978), Hendrik van Riessen (1911–2000), and Hendrik G. Stoker (1899–1993).[1] These men wanted to build on the heritage of Abraham Kuyper and wanted to see the growth of a genuinely Christian philosophy. They developed a line of thinking that has been called *cosmo-*

---

[1] For a historical introduction, see Bernard Zylstra, introduction to *Contours of a Christian Philosophy: An Introduction to Herman Dooyeweerd's Thought*, by L. Kalsbeek (Toronto: Wedge, 1975), 14–33. Kalsbeek's book may serve as an entry-level introduction to the substance of Dooyeweerd's thought. See also Roy Clouser, *The Myth of Religious Neutrality*, 2nd ed. (Notre Dame: University of Notre Dame Press, 2005); and Jeremy G. A. Ive, "A Critically Comparative Analysis and a Trinitarian, 'Perichoretic' Reconstruction of the Reformational Philosophies of Dirk H. Th. Vollenhoven and Herman Dooyeweerd" (PhD diss., King's College, London, 2011).

nomic philosophy.[2] I learned from them, and I honor them for their attempts. I particularly appreciate Vollenhoven, because his writings included the discussion of a Christian approach to mathematics and to logic.[3] He and the other cosmonomic philosophers challenged me to be completely Christian in my thinking, including those areas that most of the world considers to be religiously neutral.

Emphases of Cosmonomic Philosophy

What were some of the emphases of cosmonomic philosophy?

Religious Roots to Thinking

First, cosmonomic philosophers argued that religious roots and commitments of the heart influence all theoretical reflection. This idea goes back to Kuyper, Calvin, and Augustine, who discussed the difference that arises because of the Holy Spirit's work of regeneration. Cosmonomic philosophers attempted to trace out in more detail how fundamental religious commitments influenced the direction of thinking.

The Trap of Dualisms

Second, cosmonomic philosophers criticized *dualisms*, artificially absolutized bipolar oppositions in thought. Greek philosophy had a form-matter dualism. Medieval philosophy had a nature-grace dualism. Enlightenment thinking had a science-freedom dualism. Dualisms typically arise because thinkers have lost hold of the re-

---

[2] Sometimes the term *cosmonomic philosophy* is more narrowly associated with Herman Dooyeweerd, who wrote the foundational text, *A New Critique of Theoretical Thought*, 4 vols. (Amsterdam: H. J. Paris; Philadelphia: Presbyterian and Reformed, 1955–1958; repr., Lewiston, NY: Edwin Mellen, 1997), in which the idea of God's cosmic law plays a leading role. Dooyeweerd's original Dutch title, *De wijsbegeerte der wetsidee*, translates literally as "The Philosophy of the Law-Idea." (The term *cosmonomic* derives from the Greek word *kosmos*, meaning "world," and the Greek word *nomos*, meaning "law." In more modern terms, we might speak of "laws for the universe." Or, if the word *universe* is inappropriate because it suggests only the physical universe, we might speak of "laws for the cosmos.")

[3] Dirk H. Th. Vollenhoven, *De wijsbegeerte der wiskunde van theïstisch standpunt* (Amsterdam: Van Soest, 1918); Vollenhoven, *De noodzakelijkheid eener christelijke logica* (Amsterdam: H. J. Paris, 1932); Vollenhoven, "Problemen en richtingen in de wijsbegeerte der wiskunde," *Philosophia Reformata* 1 (1936): 162–87; Vollenhoven, "Hoofdlijnen der logica," *Philosophia Reformata* 13 (1948): 58–118. I should also mention D. F. M. Strauss and Marinus Dirk Stafleu, who endeavored to apply cosmonomic philosophy to mathematics and physics.

ality of God, whose personal unity and comprehensive plan unify all of creation.

The Trap of Reductionisms

Third, cosmonomic philosophers criticized all forms of *reductionism*. Reductionism typically arises when human beings lose sight of God. Without God in the picture, they attempt to explain all of the created world by *reducing* it to some one fundamental layer. For example, philosophical *empiricism* regards sense experience as foundational. It endeavors to "build up" everything else from the foundational layer of sense experience. So empiricism *reduces* reality to the layer of sense experience. Psychologism *reduces* all of life to human psychology. Reductionistic forms of sociology reduce all of life to social interaction. Marxism reduces life to structures of material production and economics. Materialism or naturalism reduces the universe to matter and motion. Idealism reduces the universe to mental ideas. Over against all these views, cosmonomic philosophy emphasized the irreducible richness and multidimensional character of the created world.

I agree with all three of these emphases, and I trust that they appear in my own discussion of metaphysics.

The Distinction of "Modal Spheres"

Fourth, in cosmonomic philosophy, the antireductionist approach went together with the practice of distinguishing between "modal spheres." According to cosmonomic philosophy, several distinct modal spheres belong to the cosmos. Each modal sphere has its own meaning, and none is reducible to another. Different cosmonomic publications give slightly different lists of the modal spheres, but here is a common one: first is the quantitative sphere, then the spatial sphere, then the kinetic, physical, biotic (having to do with organic life), psychic (sensitive and sensory), logical, historical, lingual, social, economic, aesthetic, juridical, ethical, and pistical (fiduciary, pertaining to faith and certainty). They come in a fixed order, from lowest (quantitative) to highest (pistical) spheres, as follows.

- pistic
- ethical
- juridical
- aesthetic
- economic
- social
- lingual
- historical
- logical
- psychic
- biotic
- physical
- kinetic
- spatial
- quantitative

When I started reading cosmonomic philosophy, the idea of modal spheres interested me right away. I felt that in some respects it was accessible and valuable for giving concreteness and specificity to the antireductionist thrust of the philosophy. At the same time, none of the spheres was precisely defined—at least in the literature that I read. I had difficulty knowing whether I understood them properly.

Sphere Universality

Fifth, cosmonomic philosophy spoke of *sphere universality*. In addition to each sphere having its own meaning, each sphere has connections with the rest. Cosmonomic philosophy used the expression *sphere universality* to describe connections where one sphere seems to be reflected in another. For instance, a person can represent numbers spatially by writing them one after the other on a line. The quantitative sphere is thereby reflected in the spatial sphere. This idea lies next door to the idea that each sphere is like a starting motif or theme that can be used as a perspective on God and the world and the self. Thus, cosmonomic philosophy has an affinity with the multiperspectivalism that Frame and I use. But it is no more than an affinity. In our multiperspectivalism we have gone our own way.

Differences with Cosmonomic Philosophy

And why have we gone our own way? I admire the Christian motivation of the cosmonomic philosophers, so most of the differences are perhaps best left in silence. But a few differences need discussion in order to set our work in the context of the past.

Using the Bible

One difference can hardly escape notice. John Frame and I freely quote from the Bible, and we expect the Bible to guide our thinking about the big questions. Frame even proposes as one possible perspective that we simply identify philosophy and theology. He and I think that historically philosophy has made a ghastly mistake by virtually excluding the direct use of the Bible and trying to get somewhere by merely general reasoning. God never intended us to operate that way. And after the fall it becomes all the more crucial that we receive the instruction in the Bible with all meekness, because it serves to purify us from sin, including sinful effects on the mind.

We are supposed to apply Scripture to every aspect of life. In no area are we free to ignore it. Neither are we supposed to set boundaries beforehand concerning what God will or will not choose to say in Scripture. Cosmonomic philosophy rightly emphasized that Scripture is the word of God and has a foundational message addressed to our hearts. But then it seemed to Frame and me that in practice some of the cosmonomic writings narrowed this "message": they implied that Scripture spoke *only* to the "heart" and *not* to any specific questions that crop up in the study of a single modal sphere. Do the pages of Scripture say something about the physical resurrection of the body (physical sphere), the origin of human life (biotic sphere), the nature of ethical standards (ethical sphere), the historicity of the exodus from Egypt (historical sphere), or the foundation of logic (logical sphere)? Let us go and study the Scripture faithfully and follow where it leads, rather than coming to it with prejudgments about what questions it will or will not address.[4]

---

[4] Representatives of cosmonomic philosophy have rightly expressed fears that readers seeking answers in the Bible might miss its actual purposes in their desire to find immediate answers, and

I hope that cosmonomic philosophy wanted to do this. But did it succeed? Frame and I want to do it. Have we succeeded? None of us as fallen human beings is going to succeed perfectly. Others should sift what we have done, with a view to serving our Master.

The Distinction between Creator and Creature

We need also to consider the Creator-creature distinction. God is Creator and is unique. Everything that he has made is a creature. All creatures are dependent on him and finite. The distinction between Creator and creature can be summed up in Frame's square, as discussed in chapter 8. This square illustrates not only how we ought to think about our relation to God, but also how *not to think*—that is, we ought to avoid non-Christian views of God. It is crucial that we maintain both the subordination of our knowledge to God's (which is the Christian view of transcendence, corner 1) and the genuineness of our knowledge of God (which is the Christian view of immanence, corner 2).

In this context, the status of the word of God has importance. Frame and I have emphasized that when God speaks, his speech shows his character. His speech has divine wisdom, power, authority, righteousness, and truth. When God speaks to us as creatures, he structures his speech so that it can actually reach us. By the power of the Holy Spirit, we can come to understand it. But his speech is not *merely creaturely*. It is divine—it has divine attributes. It is not a third kind of "thing," distinct from God and distinct from creatures. It is God speaking.

God's speech to us is mysteriously mediated by the Son and by the Spirit. In addition, when God speaks to us as creatures, he utilizes created media, whether stone tablets or sound waves coming from Mount Sinai. Technically speaking, the sound waves and the stone tablets, treated as if they were merely physical objects, are not the word of God. They are the vehicle by which the word of God comes to us. The stone tablets are the recorded media

might force it to speak to questions that it does not directly address (such misreading is called the "encyclopedic assumption" in Roy A. Clouser, "Genesis on the Origin of the Human Race," *Perspectives on Science and Christian Faith* 43, no. 1 [March, 1991]: 2–13). But there is an opposite error in which we insufficiently estimate the implications of Scripture for understanding the particulars.

through which God wrote down his word permanently for all generations. When God's word comes to us, we hear *God*, not simply sound waves. When we read the Bible, we hear God; we also see paper and ink, but we look, as it were, *through* the paper and ink to what the Bible *says*. The paper and ink allow us to understand the words and the sentences and the message: the words are the words of God.[5]

The climactic revelation of God is in Christ incarnate. Christ is both God and man, both Creator and creature. He is not a third thing that is neither Creator nor creature. So this climactic revelation confirms the principle that there is no third-thing intermediate between Creator and creature.

These reflections have relevance not only for our understanding of the Bible, but also for our understanding of the words that God speaks to govern creation (Heb. 1:3). These words also are divine in their characteristics. They are the real "law" for the universe.

Cosmonomic philosophy tried to reckon with the Creator-creature distinction. But in discussing the law, some of the writings of cosmonomic philosophy do not seem to have been as clear as they could be. Cosmonomic philosophy has as one of its fundamental categories the idea of *law*, a "cosmic" law for the universe (not just the moral law as promulgated on Mount Sinai). The status of this law makes a difference. Is the law *divine*? Is it God speaking? Or is it a third thing? And if we say (as I think we should *not*) that it is a third thing, does it end up separating us from God and promoting a picture where God threatens to be an unknowable God behind the law? If the cosmic law is a third thing, the law, and not God, becomes the only thing to which we have real access. This conclusion would be contrary to the deepest intentions of the founders of cosmonomic philosophy. But such a conclusion can nevertheless creep in unwittingly if we do not make clear the status of law.

Consider a particular illustration: is cosmic law the source of our idea of justice (according to the juridical "sphere")? Is this "jus-

---

[5] Further discussion is found in John M. Frame, *The Doctrine of the Word of God* (Phillipsburg, NJ: P&R, 2010), and Vern S. Poythress, *In the Beginning Was the Word: Language—A God-Centered Approach* (Wheaton, IL: Crossway, 2009).

tice" an attribute of God himself, or just a creaturely product? If we say that it is an attribute of God himself, we can still fall into the pattern of corner 4 of Frame's square and try to make God *subject* to our limited human notions about what justice might be. For example, some philosophers have argued that it is "unjust" of God to punish Christ for the sins of others. They take themselves and not Scripture as their standard.

If, on the other hand, we say that justice belongs *merely* to creation, then our words have unwittingly placed God *beyond* justice. We make God unknowable, as in corner 3 of Frame's square. We contradict Scripture, which says, in God's own speech, that he is just. Clearly it is easy to fall into forms of non-Christian thinking without realizing it. In fact, to the degree that our hearts are still contaminated with sin, we all have temptations in this area.

The idea of justice is only one case where the challenge exists. Each of the modal spheres in cosmonomic philosophy can be treated from either a Christian or a non-Christian view of knowledge. The non-Christian view makes ethics and language and logic and family structure merely creaturely. If that were so, God would have no ethics and could not speak and could not be consistent and could not be our Father. He would be unknowable (corner 3). Or the non-Christian view identifies human conceptions of ethics and language and logic and family with the absolute standard. It tries to subject God to human conceptions, as if these were ultimate (corner 4).

We need the instruction of Scripture and the work of the Spirit of Christ to lead us into a thoroughly Christian conception, where we know God *through* scriptural instruction. This instruction shows us how God reveals himself truly in general revelation, through justice and ethics and language and logic and social interaction and every aspect of life.[6]

---

[6]This need for a Christian conception instructed by Scripture is one reason why I have undertaken to write books fleshing out the meaning of God's transcendence and immanence in a number of areas: science (*Redeeming Science: A God-Centered Approach* [Wheaton, IL: Crossway, 2006]), language (*In the Beginning Was the Word*), society (*Redeeming Sociology: A God-Centered Approach* [Wheaton, IL: Crossway, 2011]), logic (*Logic: A God-Centered Approach to the Foundation of Western Thought* [Wheaton, IL: Crossway, 2013]), and chance (*Chance and the Sovereignty of God: A God-Centered Approach to Probability and Random Events* [Wheaton, IL: Crossway, 2014]).

Flexibility concerning Perspectives

The perspectives that John Frame and I use have an affinity with the modal spheres of cosmonomic philosophy. Within our perspectival approach we can certainly distinguish various foci, as is illustrated in my discussion of the metaphysics of an apple (chap. 12). The common cosmonomic list of modal spheres offers a valuable starting point if we see it as one possibility for a list of perspectives. But I have wondered since my first encounter with cosmonomic philosophy how one would justify settling on this list and no *other* one.[7] Does it have some foundational uniqueness to it in contrast to any other list of multiple perspectives? As I have grown in appreciating the value of perspectives, including possible perspectives not yet included in a formally organized mental toolbox, I wonder whether a fixed list ends up being confining. Can we not always add more perspectives? What about a "pedagogical" perspective associated with education? An "epistemic" perspective that reflects on knowledge and the process of coming to know? A "manufacturing" perspective that focuses on making and crafting? An "informational" perspective that focuses on the informational aspect of communication?[8] In addition, it is not clear to me what is the meaning of the claim within cosmonomic philosophy that there is a fixed order in the modal spheres, from lower to higher.[9]

---

[7] Hendrik Stoker should be mentioned for his endeavor to see the structure of modal spheres as one among several cross-cutting structures. Herman Dooyeweerd spoke of individuality structures and enkaptic interlacements. So cosmonomic philosophers have tried to do justice to the richness of creation. Questions still remain as to whether we could add to or restructure the list of modal spheres.
[8] It is possible to consider education and epistemology and making and crafting and farming as illustrations of activity tied to the "historical" sphere, which has also been called the "technical" sphere or "formative" sphere. But we can distinguish various kinds of "formation" and historical development—development of personal skills, personal knowledge, institutions, ideas, farms, homes, nation-states, manufactured objects, and artistic objects. If the distinctions are real and not "reducible," what determines how many modal spheres we have? Similarly, if communication includes information and expression and personal purposes and poetic allusions, all of which are distinguishable, do they or do they not belong to a single, broader lingual modal sphere? Dooyeweerdian philosophy provides answers of a sort by allowing us to make distinctions within any one sphere through what it calls "anticipations" and "retrocipations" of other spheres, and through "individuality structures." But does the appeal to other spheres and to individuality tempt students to adopt a kind of "reductionism" that does not do full justice to finer distinctions? No analysis dissolves mystery.
[9] We cannot enter into all the details. The quantitative aspect in the created world is analogous to the quantitative aspect in the one and three of one God in three persons. The logical aspect of the world is analogous to the self-consistency of God. The lingual aspect in the world is analogous to the fact that God speaks, and the second person of the Trinity is the Word. The ethical aspect of the world, which is to be characterized by love, is analogous to the love between the persons of the Trinity. The juridical aspect of the world is analogous to the righteous character of God. In God himself, it does not appear to me to make sense to say that the quantitative aspect (threeness) is

It seems to me that my use of perspectives embraces all the modal spheres of cosmonomic philosophy by affirming them as possible perspectives. At the same time, I add other perspectives as well. This form of antireductionism seems to me to go further than cosmonomic philosophy, because not only each modal sphere but each perspective in a broader, extensible list has its own distinctiveness. And each individual created thing has its distinctiveness (my apple). Each equation in physics or chemistry has its own distinctiveness. The list of modal spheres helps, because it fights many prominent forms of reductionism. But I remain uneasy if the list is understood as complete. The list leaves open the temptation to practice subtler versions of reductionism, as long as the reduction or reductionist explanation takes place *within* a single modal sphere.

The Freedom of the Christian

Cosmonomic philosophy offers a form of systematic philosophy. This book offers a form of systematic philosophy too, but it is somewhat different because of its commitment to affirming multiple perspectives. I invite people to treat cosmonomic philosophy as a perspective on the world, or perhaps several overlapping and intersecting perspectives—one from Dooyeweerd, one from Vollenhoven, one from Stoker, and so on. That does not mean that cosmonomic philosophy is completely flawless, even when treated as

---

prior to or subsequent to the ethical aspect (love), nor is the logical aspect (self-consistency) prior to or subsequent to the biotic aspect (God is the living God). The origin of the modal spheres in God himself makes problematic the claim that one sphere is somehow "above" or "below" another.

We can make some sense of higher and lower with respect to major groups of creatures (in distinction from the Creator). Plants and animals function actively at the chemical and physical level in a way analogous to the chemical and physical activities in rocks. In addition, plants and animals are biologically active in a way that nonliving things are not. So can we say that this biological activity shows that they are "higher"? Many animals interact by moving and sensing, activities that for the most part find only dim reflections in plant life. So these animals would be "higher" than plants. Cosmonomic philosophy builds on these everyday observations to infer that the psychic sphere, in which many animals are subjectively active, is "higher than" the biotic sphere, which in turn is higher than the physical sphere characteristic of rocks. According to cosmonomic philosophy, only human beings are subjectively active in the modal spheres above the psychic sphere.

Since human beings are active in all the spheres above the psychic, it is not so clear what provides the basis for the linear ordering of the higher spheres among themselves. Cosmonomists say that the higher spheres in some sense "presuppose" the lower. But do not the lower also "presuppose" the higher—does not logic as a human focus presuppose language and human history leading to the use and investigation of logical patterns? Does it not also presuppose that we have a sense of certainty (pertaining to the pistical sphere)?

a perspective. It means only that it offers resources, some of which may need to undergo refinement, reform, or removal. Its resources would then offer one possible starting point for a perspective on the world.

John Frame and I also offer a perspective. But it is admittedly a perspective. It is not the only one that is compatible with truth. Let others freely build their own variations, subject to the teaching of Scripture.

If I am right about the metaphysics of the world, other perspectives also, when developed in obedience to God's word, can set forth truth. The truth of God is rich enough to unfold more and more as we develop new perspectives and use these in deepening our appreciation of older perspectives. In this process, distinct perspectives do not simply stand side by side as alternatives. Rather, we should endeavor to see each perspective through the others, and use one perspective to deepen and correct our understanding achieved through another.[10] We affirm the equal ultimacy of unity and diversity in truth, and unity and diversity in knowledge of the truth. We resist, on the one hand, the reductionistic rationalism of modernism, which reaches for a totalized truth of a monolithic, monoperspectival sort. We resist, on the other hand, the reductionistic irrationalism of postmodern pluralism, which despairs of peaceful truth and, in the name of peaceful coexistence, lets competing claims to truth stand side by side without rational unification.[11]

---

[10] Vern S. Poythress, *Symphonic Theology: The Validity of Multiple Perspectives in Theology* (Grand Rapids: Zondervan, 1987; repr., Phillipsburg, NJ: P&R, 2001), discusses the process. John Frame and I illustrate it in a number of writings. Perhaps the most outstanding and elaborate is Frame, *The Doctrine of the Christian Life* (Phillipsburg, NJ: P&R, 2008).

[11] On modernism and postmodernism, see also the scattered remarks in Poythress, *In the Beginning Was the Word*.

Perspectives on the Trinity

God in the Scripture gives us quite a few passages and verses that discuss one or another aspect of his Trinitarian character. The Bible presupposes a knowledge of God's character even in passages that do not directly expound it. We are supposed to use all these passages together as we grow in knowledge. Each passage functions like a perspective on God. The Bible offers no single "model" that enables us to capture everything. If we had a single comprehensive model, it would bring God down to the level of our understanding.

The Speech Analogy

Though the whole Bible offers us instruction about God, God uses a few primary analogies in expounding the nature of his Trinitarian character. One such analogy occurs in John 1:1–5, namely, an analogy with *speaking*. The second person of the Trinity, God the Son, is called *the Word*. Part of the background is Genesis 1, where God creates the world by speaking. He speaks specific utterances, such as "Let there be light" (Gen. 1:3). We may infer that these specific utterances express and reflect a more profound reality in God, a reality that has always been the case. "In the beginning was the Word" (John 1:1). John is saying that there is an original or archetypal Word of which the particular utterances in Genesis 1 are an expression. We as human beings also speak words, ectypal words that imitate God's speech and derive from the pattern of who he is.

Thus we have a pattern where God is the archetypal speaker, and his archetypal speech is the Word, the second person of the Trinity. Who is the speaker? Preeminently it is God the Father who stands as representative for God. So we can say that God the Father is the speaker. The second person of the Trinity is the Word that the Father speaks. And is the Holy Spirit active? John 1:1–5 does not mention the Holy Spirit explicitly, but elsewhere the Bible likens his work to the breath of God (see Ezek. 37:6, 9–10, 14). The Holy Spirit is the breath of God bringing the speech to its destination. We may call this complete analogy the *speech* perspective on the Trinity.

The Familial Analogy

A second important passage is John 3:34–35. Verse 35 says that "the Father loves the Son and has given all things into his hand." The giving of all things expresses his love. The relation among the persons of the Trinity is expounded here in terms of love—more specifically, familial love, the love between the Father and the Son. Human families with fathers and sons who love one another imitate this love at an ectypal level.

Once again, we can ask whether the Holy Spirit has a role. The preceding verse, John 3:34, indicates his role. He is the gift: "He [God] gives the Spirit without measure." To whom does God give the Spirit? The context shows that the Father gives the Spirit to the one described as "he whom God has sent," that is, the incarnate Son. This giving focuses on the Son's redeeming work as one sent to the earth. But God acts in Christ's earthly life in accordance with who he always is. So we can infer that there is an eternal giving of the Spirit: the Father gives the Spirit to the Son. This giving, as John 3:35 indicates, expresses love. The Spirit, as Augustine observed, is like the bond of love between the Father and the Son. So we have a *familial* analogy or *love* analogy that expounds the nature of the Trinity.

We may note already that the common designations for the three persons of the Trinity fit into our analogies. The designations *Father* and *Son* clearly evoke an analogy between God and human families. Into this picture we can also fit the language about the Son being begotten. *Begetting* is an old-fashioned English word for fathering. Adam *fathered* a son, Seth (Gen. 5:3). By analogy, God the Father *fathered* the Son. But we must make distinctions. God's act of fathering is the original and archetypal fathering, which Adam's imitates. Second, God's action is eternal. The Son always existed, as John 1:1 indicates. He is not created.

Finally, the designation "Holy Spirit" for the third person of the Trinity uses the word *Spirit*, which occurs in Ezekiel 37:14 in the analogy between the Spirit and breath. The same Hebrew word *ruach* can mean "spirit" or "breath" (or "wind"), depending on the context. Usually the context singles out one meaning exclusively, but Ezekiel 37:14 picks up on the earlier occurrences of the word *ruach* with the meaning "breath" (37:6, 9–10). The word *spirit* has built into it a reminder of an analogy between the Holy Spirit and the breath of God, an analogy that belongs to the *speech* analogy for the Trinity.

The Theophanic Analogy

A third kind of analogy is found in Ezekiel 1 and other passages where God appears to human beings. The appearance of God in visual form is called a *theophany*. In the theophany that God gave to Ezekiel in Ezekiel 1, at the center of the picture is the human-like figure on the throne (Ezek. 1:26–27). A comparison between Ezekiel 1:26–27 and the appearance of Christ in Revelation 1:13–16 shows that Ezekiel 1:26–27 gives us an anticipation or foreshadowing of the coming of Christ. It anticipates both Christ's incarnation, his becoming man, and his glorification, as he is presented in Revelation 1:13–16. The same is true for all theophanies in the Old Testament. They all look forward to the coming of Christ, who is Immanuel, "God with us" (Matt. 1:23). Jesus himself confirms this conclusion when he says to Philip, "Whoever has seen me has seen the Father" (John 14:9). Thus, theophanies in the Old Testament anticipate in temporary form what we see to be permanently true with the incarnation. The Son reveals the Father. We see the Father through the Son and in the Son.

Does the Holy Spirit have a role in theophany? Aspects of the theophany in Ezekiel symbolize the character of God. For example, the fire that appears in Ezekiel 1:4, 13, and 27 symbolizes God's ability to purify or to consume evil. (It also brings to remembrance the presence of fire when God appeared on Mount Sinai [Ex. 19:18], and the burning bush in which God appeared to Moses [Ex. 3:2].) The function of fire in judgment is confirmed later in Ezekiel when burning coals from the presence of God are thrown on the city of Jerusalem in judgment (Ezek. 10:2). The loud sound in Ezekiel 1:24 symbolizes God's power and his ability to speak, and is confirmed by the voice that then speaks from the throne (Ezek. 1:28).

All of this symbolism has an association with the Holy Spirit. At Pentecost the descent of the Holy Spirit is symbolized by tongues of fire (Acts 2:3–4), a theophanic fire. The loud sound in Ezekiel corresponds to the "sound like a mighty rushing wind" in Acts 2:2. (It is doubtless also associated with the loud sounds at Mount Sinai when God appears to Israel—Exodus 19.) The Holy Spirit empowers the apostles to speak the message of the gospel and to speak in other languages. The speech with power corresponds to the power of God and the speech of God in Ezekiel and other Old Testament theophanies.

We can then begin to extend these observations to include the human-like features that belong to the human figure in Ezekiel 1:26–27 and that the Bible elsewhere associates with God. The language about the "eyes" of God indicates his knowledge (2 Chron. 16:9; Pss. 11:4; 80:14; Prov. 15:3; Jer. 32:19). His "mouth" indicates his ability to speak (Isa. 40:5). His "arm" and his "hand" indicate his power (Ps. 44:3; Isa. 49:2; Ezek. 8:1; 37:1; Luke 1:51). His "feet" indicate his dominion (Isa. 60:13; 63:3). His "face" indicates his presence (Ex. 33:9–11, 18–23).

The Bible associates each of these characteristics of God with the Holy Spirit. The eyes of the Lamb are identified with the Holy Spirit in Revelation 5:6 (from Rev. 1:4–5 we can confirm that "the seven spirits of God" is a reference to the sevenfold fullness of the Holy Spirit). The mouth of God is associated with his breath, and so with the Holy Spirit. The inspiration of the Old Testament is ascribed to the Holy Spirit who speaks (Acts 1:16). The hand of God functions in the same way as the Holy Spirit, when we compare Ezekiel 8:1 and 11:5. The finger of God is parallel to the Holy Spirit when we compare Matthew 12:28 to Luke 11:20 and 2 Corinthians 3:3. The power of God is associated with the Holy Spirit in Luke 1:35. The face of God and the presence of God are parallel to the Holy Spirit in Psalms 51:11 and 139:7.

We may summarize by saying that the Bible associates particular attributes or characteristics of God, such as his power, knowledge, and ability to speak, with the Holy Spirit. The attributes come together in the multifaceted, powerful vision of the human-like figure in Ezekiel 1:26–27, and in the appearance of Christ in Revelation 1:13–16. Christ in his person combines the attributes into a whole figure. In addition, theophany reveals *God*. God the Father is revealed through the Son and the Spirit. This appearance of God finds its climax in the incarnation and the glorification of Christ the Son. It is adumbrated or foreshadowed in Old Testament theophanies. Thus, theophany gives us an analogical understanding of the distinct persons of the Trinity.

Theophanies also give us insight into what it means for human beings to be made in the image of God. We imitate God by speaking and by thinking and by having personal communion (among other things). Some people have thought that we imitate God only in our "spiritual" side, and not in our bodies. But we express ourselves through our bodies, with our mouths and hands and feet. God is spirit and does not have a physical body (John 4:24). But we have mouths in imitation of his ability to speak. We have hands in imitation of his ability to act. We have eyes in imitation of his ability to see. God made our bodies, and not merely our spiritual aspect, in imitation of who he is and the abilities that he has.

Redemptive-Historical Analogy

Finally, we may consider a redemptive-historical analogy that expounds the character of the persons of the Trinity. We are dealing here not so much with a particular passage, but with a larger complex, the patterns of God's actions through time, structuring the course of history. The Father sends the Son, who accomplishes the work of the Father on earth through the power of the Holy Spirit. The Holy Spirit acts in power in healing (Luke 4:18), in casting out demons (Matt. 12:28), and supremely in the resurrection of Christ from the dead: "If the Spirit of him who raised Jesus from the dead dwells in you, he who raised Christ Jesus from the dead will also give life to your mortal bodies through his Spirit who dwells in you" (Rom. 8:11; cf. 1:4).

We could say that the Father is the planner; the Son is the executor of the Father's plan; the Holy Spirit is the empowerer, and also the consummator who applies the benefits of the Son's work. Such a description helps to indicate a subtle differentiation in roles among the persons of the Trinity. But the description simplifies in its schema, since the persons of the Trinity indwell one another and all three actively participate throughout the history that works out redemption.[1]

We can see a relationship between the redemptive-historical analogy and the speech analogy. Speaking is a perspective on everything that God does. We can say that he does everything by speaking. In his speaking, God the Father acts more like a planner. God the Son as the one associated with the speech itself is the one who puts the plan or thought into execution. The Holy Spirit as the breath of God is the one who brings the word in power to its destination and works effects on those who hear. That is to say that he is the empowerer and consummator. Thus, God's actions in history express the speech of God, which has innately Trinitarian structure.

We can also see the redemptive-historical analogy as an expression of the familial analogy. The Gospel of John, which emphasizes the love between the Father and the Son, is also the Gospel that emphasizes the Father's sending the Son to accomplish the work of redemption. The Father gives the Holy Spirit to the Son not only as an expression of his love, but also as a gift enabling the Son to ac-

---

[1] See also the Trinitarian analogy in Vern S. Poythress, *In the Beginning Was the Word: Language—A God-Centered Approach* (Wheaton, IL: Crossway, 2009), chaps. 24–25.

complish his work. Thus we can say that the redemptive-historical activity of God is an expression of his action in love, which is also an expression of the Father-Son relation (in the Spirit).

Finally, the redemptive-historical analogy expresses the theophanic analogy. The theophanic analogy appears most obviously in the special appearances of God called theophanies, and in the climactic, permanent theophany in Christ as incarnate Son. But in a more extended sense, God "shows himself" or reveals himself in all his acts in history. In these acts, we learn who God is, thus receiving a revelation of the Father's character. We see a specific work of redemption or judgment. In the Old Testament, such works foreshadow the future work of Christ, and in the New Testament they manifest or apply his work. In both the Old Testament and the New, God reveals himself through our seeing Christ: "Whoever has seen me has seen the Father" (John 14:9). In these works, the Holy Spirit participates actively and makes the work of Christ in its specific characteristics metaphorically or literally visible to believers.

Thus, the three primary analogies, from speaking, loving, and appearing, interlock and offer perspectives on one another.[2] Perhaps the redemptive-historical analogy is not so much a fourth analogy as a temporal pattern that expresses all three. One or the other of the three may appear more prominently in any particular act, but all three are presupposed. For example, Jesus's miracles show him and so offer an *appearing* of redemption—they are

---

[2] One might suggest that in the speech analogy, the speaker, the Father, is most in focus (normally people listen to speakers through words, rather than focusing on the words themselves as a linguist would do). In the familial analogy, the Holy Spirit as the expression of love is in focus; in the theophanic analogy, the Son as the image who appears is in focus. Yet in each of these analogies all three persons actively participate. As we receive the gift of God, we know all three persons of the Trinity in their communion and coinherence. In the familial analogy, the Spirit expresses the relationship between Father and Son; in the speech analogy, the Son as Word travels from speaker to destination and so expresses the relationship between Father and Spirit; in the theophanic analogy, both Son and Spirit express the character of the Father, and thus the Father explicates their unity. Any one of these analogies, let alone all of them together, shows the necessarily Trinitarian character of God. God as personal is speaker, lover, and imager; God as speaker has speaker, speech, and destination; God as lover has lover, love, and beloved; God as imager has archetype, image, and character. However, all these observations offer simplifications and one-dimensional summaries of infinite mystery. Whatever may be the depths of limitations on our human understandings, the radiance of the glory of God in his necessarily Trinitarian character radiates in all his works, because his character first radiates in the infinite glory of the Father, the Son, and the Spirit, who infinitely glorify one another (John 13:31–32) in eternal communion. If we know these things and yet do not delight in them and in their incomprehensibility, we are like "a noisy gong or a clanging cymbal" (1 Cor. 13:1). We are missing communion with God in the midst of knowing facts.

theophanies. Jesus's teachings offer speech and so manifest God's speech; Jesus's compassion to the sick and the outcasts shows love—the Father's love in the Spirit. Jesus's miracles also presuppose that he is the Son who executes the plan of the Father according to the love between the Father and the Son. Jesus's miracles also function like a kind of metaphorical speech that explains the nature of God's saving kingdom. So they presuppose the speech analogy.

In sum, God in his Godhead makes himself known through analogies or perspectives. And he also employs analogies in making known his Trinitarian character. These analogies give us real knowledge of who God really is. A biblical view of the world affirms the validity and solidity of this knowledge, because God himself, in his almighty power, is its author, and the Holy Spirit brings the reality of this knowledge home to us as he works in us. The idea of analogy has as its archetype the Son, who is the image of the invisible God (Col. 1:15).[3]

---

[3] See Vern S. Poythress, *In the Beginning Was the Word*, 283–84; Poythress, *God-Centered Biblical Interpretation* (Phillipsburg, NJ: P&R, 1999), 36–47.

The Structure of a Bookmark

We may further illustrate the analysis of a bookmark, which we began in chapter 14. Since divine speech determines the metaphysics of a bookmark, we may fruitfully use triperspectival categories originally developed for the analysis of verbal discourse.[1] In this appendix we make only a beginning. This beginning will, I hope, at least increase appreciation for the enormous complexity and wonder of God's world.

Hierarchy

In our discussion of walking, we introduced the idea of hierarchy. A hierarchy consists in smaller and larger wholes, where the smaller wholes are embedded in the larger ones in a structured way. For example, the apple is a small unit within the bag of apples, which is a larger unit. The bag of apples is a smaller unit among the various items on the kitchen table. And the table together with its contents is a smaller unit within the kitchen as a whole unit. Each smaller unit is embedded within the larger ones.

Likewise, the bookmark is a smaller unit within the whole that is composed of the book, plus the bookmark, plus the physical position of the bookmark at a location between two consecutive pages. The book plus bookmark is a single unit among the various items

---

[1] Vern S. Poythress, "Hierarchy in Discourse Analysis: A Revision of Tagmemics," *Semiotica* 40, no. 1/2 (1982): 107–37.

on my desktop. The items on my desktop together with the desk and the contents of its drawers constitute a larger unit. And this unit in turn belongs to the larger unit that is my office. Thus, the bookmark is an item that is embedded in a multilayer hierarchy.

A hierarchy—actually multiple interlocking hierarchies—exists in language, including the language that I use to talk about the hierarchy for the bookmark. My language with its hierarchies imitates God's speech, which specifies all the hierarchies.

A hierarchy is a cluster of embeddings, each of which is a distribution of units in sequence. These have their ultimate archetype in the Trinity, as can be seen from the fact that the three persons of the Trinity make one God.

Filler, Prominence, and Function

A hierarchical structure can be triperspectivally analyzed using the triad of *filler*, *prominence*, and *function*. (These three are reflections of particle, wave, and field views, as discussed elsewhere.)[2] We can best explain these three related categories by example. Consider the bookmark in relation to the larger whole constituted by book plus bookmark plus physical location in the book. The bookmark is a *filler*. It is one of several bookmarks that can *fill* the location between consecutive pages.

Next, *prominence* focuses on the question of what item or items have the principal role in a larger whole. In the structure of book plus bookmark, the bookmark together with its location is the key to the whole. Without the bookmark, we are dealing with another kind of unit, namely, an unmarked book. An unmarked book has no physical prominence given to any one of its pages or any chapter or section within it. A marked book, by contrast, has extra structure. Within this extra structure, the bookmark itself, together with its location, has the prominent role. The pages on either side are necessary to the total function of the bookmark, but within that total function it is the bookmark, not the neighboring pages, that stands out intuitively. And we can even say in this case that it stands out

---

[2] Ibid.; Vern S. Poythress, *In the Beginning Was the Word: Language—A God-Centered Approach* (Wheaton, IL: Crossway, 2009), chap. 7.

physically. The neighboring pages are identified first by the bookmark rather than vice versa.

Finally, let us focus on the *function* of the bookmark. The word *function* in the context of hierarchy has a specific meaning; it designates the empty *slot* or structural location filled by the filler. The idea of an empty slot is more abstract than either filler or prominence. It is a meaningful relationship between whatever fills the slot and the material around the slot.

We may illustrate the meaning of *slot* using language as an example. In the sentence "The boy fed the dog," the expression *the boy* is a noun phrase filler that fills the subject slot. The slot of subject is an empty space in the sentence, to be filled with whatever the speaker chooses as the subject of the sentence. The speaker could put in *the man*, or *Donna*, or *a neighbor*, or some other phrase. Similarly, the expression *the dog* fills the object slot. Other objects—such as *the cat, the guinea pig*, or *my fish*—could also fit into the same empty slot.

With the bookmark, the slot is the place between consecutive pages. But we see this space not merely as a physical space, but as a possible location where items could be inserted. The item inserted could function as a bookmark even if the item is not a specially designed bookmark but a pencil or another book. But the items could also be inserted with other purposes or other functions. For example, we could put leaves from trees between the pages in order to press them and dry them out. The physical structure of consecutive locations is similar to having one or more bookmarks in a book. But because the human intention is different, they are not functioning as bookmarks. So, from the standpoint of human intention, the "meaning" of the structure as a whole, namely, book plus inserted leaves, is quite different from the "meaning" of book plus one or more bookmarks. The leaves can function "as a bookmark" or can be inserted "for pressing and drying."

As is usual with triperspectival categories, filler, prominence, and function go together. Each presupposes the presence of the others. A filler is a filler only if it fills some slot and thus has a function. In this slot, the filler is either prominent or nonprominent in relation to the larger structure for which it is a filler. Similarly, a piece is prominent only if it is prominent as a piece within a larger whole, in which capacity it functions as a filler for a slot with a function.

We can look at these three—filler, prominence, and function—from the perspective of the larger unit in which they are embedded, rather than from the perspective of the smaller unit that does the embedding. In the case of the bookmark, instead of starting with the embedding unit, namely, the bookmark, we can start with the unit in which it is embedded, namely, the whole consisting of book plus bookmark plus physical location for the bookmark within the pages of the book. This larger whole is a unit. We can then proceed to analyze the unit for its contrastive features, its variation, and its distribution. Its distribution focuses on its relation to still larger units, and this aspect leads us in other directions. But its contrastive features include the features of internal structure. It consists in the book's front cover, pages, bookmark, more pages, and back cover, all in a particular physical order. A book plus mark consists in just such a structure, and the aspects of the structure are features of the larger unit. One feature out of this whole is the bookmark itself. The bookmark has then to be understood as filler within a function defined by the slot plus its role in the total structure consisting of the succession of pieces. The relative prominence assigned to the bookmark also functions as one feature of the whole. For understanding the meaning of the whole, we have to understand the crucial, prominent role played by the bookmark. Otherwise, we may fall back to just considering the book plus bookmark as if it were not that but book plus something extraneous stuck in it (maybe purely by accident).

It should go without saying that filler, prominence, and function have their archetype in the Trinity. Each person in relation to the Godhead is a "filler," with functions in relation to the other persons. God the Father is the most prominent person of the Godhead and frequently represents God as a whole.

Physical and Referential Subsystems

Analysis of language can uncover three subsystems, namely, the phonological, grammatical, and referential subsystems.[3] In smaller systems of meaning, like the bookmark, the distinction between subsystems may be more difficult to see.[4] But in the case of a bookmark, we can at least begin. The bookmark is a physical object and enjoys spatial and tactile relations to the pages between which it lies. The pages also have physical relations to one another by means of their being glued or sewn into the spine in a particular order. This arrangement, along with the relations between parts that it includes, constitutes the physical subsystem, which is analogous to the phonological or graphological subsystem in language.

The bookmark also has meaning in relation to the meanings represented by the words and sentences and paragraphs on the pages of the book. It functions to remind the reader, "Here is where you are in relation to the meanings created by the author." Or perhaps it marks a place where he intends to copy a quotation. A single reader might even use several bookmarks at once to mark different pages of interest. Or each of several people reading through the same book at overlapping times could have his own personal bookmark. Several bookmarks might be physically differentiated by differing designs, so that each reader can tell which is his. In such a case, the bookmarks are differentiated in two ways—by appearance and by meaning. For one bookmark to be "mine" and another to be "hers" is a differentiation in meaning, which is identified by means of an underlying differentiation in appearance. Thus we can detect two distinct "subsystems" of structure, one in appearance and one in meaning. Both are systems, because each one involves the bookmark and its relation to surrounding pages and a larger, systematic pattern with respect to how bookmarks function in other books.

---

[3] Poythress, *In the Beginning Was the Word*, chap. 32.
[4] Vern S. Poythress, *Redeeming Sociology: A God-Centered Approach* (Wheaton, IL: Crossway, 2011), chaps. 31–33.

A Grammatical Subsystem for Bookmarks?

Is there a third subsystem for a bookmark, a subsystem analogous to the grammatical subsystem for language? It is not so clear. The grammatical subsystem may be fused with the other two, rather than clearly distinct. Yet we may be seeing the beginnings of a subsystem if we consider more complex cases of bookmarks.

A flat bookmark whose two sides are identical can only mark a location within a two-page limit—the left-hand page and right-hand page where the bookmark sits. A bookmark with distinct front and back sides can be used more precisely, so that its front side faces the page where the reader left off. Or it can be used less precisely, without paying attention to the difference between front and back. A paper clip or another kind of clip can be used to mark not only the page, but also the position on the page where the reader left off. Or a paper clip can clip together several pages, perhaps to mark a whole section of the book that the reader wishes to copy or reread. There are still other complex ways of using marks. The different ways of marking are different structures that affect both the physical appearance and the meaning, and they affect the two sides in an interlocking way. The set of options can be considered as the beginning of a third kind of subsystem.

Segmental, Transformational, and Oppositional Subdivisions of Hierarchy

We can consider briefly one more form of subdivision for analyzing bookmarks, namely, the subdivision that distinguishes segmental, transformational, and oppositional structures in hierarchy.[5]

First, a segmental structure is one that depends on an order in space or in time. If a reader uses several bookmarks to mark the successive sections of the book, or successive points in a developing argument, the order of the bookmarks clearly makes a difference, because the order marks the order in the meanings within the book.

Second, a transformational structure is a structure independent of order. Highlighting or underlining is a form of marking that is

---

[5] For a general definition, see Poythress, "Hierarchy," 112–20.

usually employed in an order-independent way. A reader may mark with yellow or green highlighting or underlining all the passages that bring up a single theme. The theme is a meaning within the book that is independent of the order of expression—or at least the reader is focusing on an aspect that is independent of order.

Third, oppositional structure is a regularity in the contrasts between more than one theme or structure of the other two types. For example, if a reader uses yellow highlighting for theme 1 and green highlighting for theme 2, the contrast between the two is called *oppositional*. If a reader uses a complex system of marks in an analysis of a book, each mark can be viewed as a "bookmark," in a broad sense, and the system as a whole will probably show segmental, transformational, and oppositional structures in an interlocking fashion.

Significance before God

In a sense these systems of marking are created by an individual reader. Readers are made in the image of God, and so they have a creativity in imitation of divine creativity. But the creativity also has structure. The fact that we can describe and understand a system of marking created by another reader shows that features of the system can be shared. In the providence of God, these systems are available as possibilities before any reader decides to use them. As usual, God's word of command has specified all the structures involving not only the actual use of a bookmark but also its *potential* uses.

We have talked about some of the general structures of meaning and appearance in which bookmarks may function. But each reader may make particular choices about what themes he wants to highlight. Or in his own mind he may assign a particular significance to a particular passage in the book, a passage that he singles out by placing a bookmark. He may choose to write a short note on the bookmark to remind him of the significance that he saw in the passage. Or he may make no note and simply rely on his memory. If he makes no note and says nothing to anyone, the significance that he has found may remain individual. No one knows except him and God. Yet there is still a structure of meaning, enabled by God, that attaches to the bookmark for him as an individual. This structure is ordained by God both in its uniqueness and in the features that it shares with other instances where other readers use bookmarks in idiosyncratic ways.

By virtue of the fact that God's specifications provide metaphysics, we can conclude that the "metaphysics" of a bookmark includes the complexities for how human beings may use it with significance. The world is complicated. God made it so. The complexities fit together into a whole world because of the wisdom of God's plan, not because one aspect can be "reduced" to another.

Bibliography

Adams, Jay E. *Competent to Counsel: Introduction to Nouthetic Counseling*. Grand Rapids: Ministry Resources Library, 1986.

Aristotle. *The Categories: On Interpretation*. Translated by Harold P. Cooke. And *Prior Analytics*. Translated by Hugh Tredennick. Cambridge, MA: Harvard University Press, 1962.

Beekman, John, and John Callow. *Translating the Word of God: With Scripture and Topical Indexes*. Grand Rapids: Zondervan, 1974.

Clouser, Roy A. "Genesis on the Origin of the Human Race," *Perspectives on Science and Christian Faith* 43, no. 1 (March 1991): 2–13.

———. *The Myth of Religious Neutrality: An Essay on the Hidden Role of Religious Belief in Theories*. 2nd ed. Notre Dame: University of Notre Dame Press, 2005.

Clowney, Edmund P. *Preaching and Biblical Theology*. Grand Rapids: Eerdmans, 1961.

———. *Preaching Christ in All of Scripture*. Wheaton, IL: Crossway, 2003.

———. *The Unfolding Mystery: Discovering Christ in the Old Testament*. Colorado Springs, CO: NavPress, 1988.

Collins, C. John. *Genesis 1–4: A Linguistic, Literary, and Theological Commentary*. Phillipsburg, NJ: P&R, 2006.

Cowan, Steven B., and James S. Spiegel. *The Love of Wisdom: A Christian Introduction to Philosophy*. Nashville, TN: B&H, 2009.

DeWeese, Garrett J. *Doing Philosophy as a Christian*. Downers Grove, IL: InterVarsity, 2011.

Dooyeweerd, Herman. *A New Critique of Theoretical Thought*. 4 vols. Amsterdam: H. J. Paris; Philadelphia: Presbyterian and Reformed, 1955–1958. Reprint, Lewiston, NY: Edwin Mellen, 1997. Originally in Dutch, *De wijsbegeerte der wetsidee*. 3 vols. Amsterdam: H. J. Paris, 1935–1936.

Frame, John M. *Apologetics to the Glory of God: An Introduction*. Phillipsburg, NJ: P&R, 1994.

———. "Backgrounds to My Thought." In *Speaking the Truth in Love: The Theology of John M. Frame*, edited by John J. Hughes, 9–30. Phillipsburg, NJ: P&R, 2009.

———. "Bibliography." In *Speaking the Truth in Love: The Theology of John M. Frame*, edited by John J. Hughes, 1029–63. Phillipsburg, NJ: P&R, 2009.

———. *Cornelius Van Til: An Analysis of His Thought*. Phillipsburg, NJ: P&R, 1995.

———. *The Doctrine of God*. Phillipsburg, NJ: P&R, 2002.

———. *The Doctrine of the Christian Life*. Phillipsburg, NJ: P&R, 2008.

———. *The Doctrine of the Knowledge of God*. Phillipsburg, NJ: P&R, 1987.

———. *The Doctrine of the Word of God*. Phillipsburg, NJ: P&R, 2010.

———. "Greeks Bearing Gifts." In *Revolutions in Worldview: Understanding the Flow of Western Thought*, edited by W. Andrew Hoffecker, 1–36. Phillipsburg, NJ: P&R, 2007.

———. *A History of Western Philosophy and Theology: Spiritual Warfare in the Life of the Mind*. Phillipsburg, NJ: P&R, forthcoming. Title subject to change.

———. *Perspectives on the Word of God: An Introduction to Christian Ethics*. Eugene, OR: Wipf and Stock, 1999.

———. "A Primer on Perspectivalism." May 14, 2008. Accessed January 26, 2012. http://www.frame-poythress.org/frame_articles/2008Primer.htm.

———. "Recommended Resources." In *Speaking the Truth in Love: The Theology of John M. Frame*, edited by John J. Hughes, 1063–70. Phillipsburg, NJ: P&R, 2009.

———. "Review of Esther Meek's *Longing to Know*." *Presbyterion* 29, no. 2 (Fall 2003). http://www.frame-poythress.org/review-of-esther -meeks-longing-to-know/.

———. *Salvation Belongs to the Lord: An Introduction to Systematic Theology*. Phillipsburg, NJ: P&R, 2006.

———. *Van Til, the Theologian*. Phillipsburg, NJ: Pilgrim, 1976.

Gaffin, Richard B., Jr. *Resurrection and Redemption: A Study in Paul's Soteriology*. Phillipsburg, NJ: P&R, 1987.

Geisler, Norman L., and Paul D. Feinberg. *Introduction to Philosophy: A Christian Perspective*. Grand Rapids: Baker, 1980.

Hart, David Bentley. *The Beauty of the Infinite: The Aesthetics of Christian Truth*. Grand Rapids: Eerdmans, 2003.

Hoffecker, W. Andrew, ed. *Revolutions in Worldview: Understanding the Flow of Western Thought*. Phillipsburg, NJ: P&R, 2007.

Hughes, John J. "The Heart of John Frame's Theology." In *Speaking the Truth in Love: The Theology of John M. Frame*, edited by John J. Hughes, 31–74. Phillipsburg, NJ: P&R, 2009.

———, ed. *Speaking the Truth in Love: The Theology of John M. Frame*. Phillipsburg, NJ: P&R, 2009.

Husserl, Edmund. *Ideas: General Introduction to Pure Phenomenology*. London: Allen & Unwin; New York: Humanities, 1931.

Ive, Jeremy George Augustus. "A Critically Comparative Analysis and a Trinitarian, 'Perichoretic' Reconstruction of the Reformational Philosophies of Dirk H. Th. Vollenhoven and Herman Dooyeweerd." PhD diss., King's College, London, 2011.

Kalsbeek, L. *Contours of a Christian Philosophy: An Introduction to Herman Dooyeweerd's Thought*. Edited by Bernard and Josina Zylstra. Toronto: Wedge, 1975. Originally in Dutch, *De wijsbegeerte der wetsidee: Proeve van een christelijke filosofie*. Edited by Johan Stellingwerff. Amsterdam: Buijten & Schipperheijn, 1970.

Kant, Immanuel. *Immanuel Kant's Critique of Pure Reason*. Unabridged edition. Translated by Norman Kemp Smith. New York: St. Martin's, 1965.

Keller, Timothy. *The Reason for God: Belief in an Age of Skepticism*. New York: Dutton, 2008.

Kline, Meredith G. *Images of the Spirit*. Grand Rapids: Baker, 1980.

Kruger, Michael J. *Canon Revisited: Establishing the Origins and Authority of the New Testament Books*. Wheaton, IL: Crossway, 2012.

Kuyper, Abraham. *Lectures on Calvinism: Six Lectures Delivered at Princeton University under Auspices of the L. P. Stone Foundation*. Grand Rapids: Eerdmans, 1931.

————. "Sphere Sovereignty." In *Abraham Kuyper: A Centennial Reader*, edited by James D. Bratt, 463–90. Grand Rapids: Eerdmans; Carlisle, PA: Paternoster, 1998.

Louw, Johannes P., and Eugene A. Nida, eds. *Greek-English Lexicon of the New Testament Based on Semantic Domains*. 2 vols. New York: United Bible Societies, 1988.

Meek, Esther L. *Longing to Know: The Philosophy of Knowledge for Ordinary People*. Grand Rapids: Brazos, 2003.

————. *Loving to Know: Covenant Epistemology*. Eugene, OR: Wipf and Stock, 2011.

Merriam-Webster's New Collegiate Dictionary. 11th ed. Springfield, MA: Merriam-Webster, 2008.

Moreland, J. P., and William Lane Craig. *Philosophical Foundations for a Christian Worldview*. Downers Grove, IL: InterVarsity, 2003.

Moser, Paul K. "Christ-Shaped Philosophy: Wisdom and Spirit United." Accessed November 20, 2012. http://www.epsociety.org/userfiles/art-Moser%20(Christ-Shaped%20Philosophy).pdf.

Murray, John. "The Attestation of Scripture." In *The Infallible Word*, edited by N. B. Stonehouse and Paul Woolley, 1–54. Philadelphia: Presbyterian and Reformed, 1946.

Naugle, David K. *Philosophy: A Student's Guide*. Wheaton, IL: Crossway, 2012.

Oliphint, K. Scott. *Reasons for Faith: Philosophy in the Service of Theology*. Phillipsburg, NJ: P&R, 2006.

Oliphint, K. Scott, and Lane G. Tipton, eds. *Revelation and Reason: New Essays in Reformed Apologetics*. Phillipsburg, NJ: P&R, 2007.

Pike, Kenneth L. "Language as Particle, Wave, and Field." *The Texas Quarterly* 2, no. 2 (1959): 37–54. Reprinted in *Kenneth L. Pike: Selected Writings to Commemorate the 60th Birthday of Kenneth*

Lee Pike, edited by Ruth M. Brend, 117–28. The Hague/Paris: Mouton, 1972.

———. *Language in Relation to a Unified Theory of the Structure of Human Behavior*. 2nd ed. The Hague/Paris: Mouton, 1967.

———. *Linguistic Concepts: An Introduction to Tagmemics*. Lincoln: University of Nebraska Press, 1982.

———. *Phonemics: A Technique for Reducing Languages to Writing*. Ann Arbor: University of Michigan Press, 1947.

———. "Toward the Development of Tagmemic Postulates." In *Tagmemics*. Vol. 2, *Theoretical Discussion*. Edited by Ruth M. Brend and Kenneth L. Pike, 91–127. The Hague/Paris: Mouton, 1976.

Plantinga, Alvin. *Where the Conflict Really Lies: Science, Religion, and Naturalism*. Oxford: Oxford University Press, 2011.

Polanyi, Michael. *Personal Knowledge: Towards a Post-Critical Philosophy*. Chicago: University of Chicago Press, 1958.

———. *The Tacit Dimension*. Garden City, NY: Anchor, 1967.

Powlison, David. *The Biblical Counseling Movement: History and Context*. Greensboro, NC: New Growth, 2010.

———. "Competent to Counsel? The History of a Conservative Protestant Anti-Psychiatry Movement." PhD diss., University of Pennsylvania, 1996.

———. *Seeing with New Eyes: Counseling and the Human Condition through the Lens of Scripture*. Phillipsburg, NJ: P&R, 2003.

Poythress, Vern S. "A Biblical View of Mathematics." In *Foundations for Christian Scholarship: Essays in the Van Til Perspective*, edited by Gary North, 159–88. Vallecito, CA: Ross House, 1976.

———. *Chance and the Sovereignty of God: A God-Centered Approach to Probability and Random Events*. Wheaton, IL: Crossway, 2014.

———. "A Framework for Discourse Analysis: The Components of a Discourse, from a Tagmemic Viewpoint." *Semiotica* 38, no. 3/4 (1982): 277–98.

———. *God-Centered Biblical Interpretation*. Phillipsburg, NJ: P&R, 1999.

———. "Hierarchy in Discourse Analysis: A Revision of Tagmemics." *Semiotica* 40, no. 1/2 (1982): 107–37.

———. *Inerrancy and the Gospels: A God-Centered Approach to the Challenge of Harmonization*. Wheaton, IL: Crossway, 2012.

———. *Inerrancy and Worldview: Answering Modern Challenges to the Bible*. Wheaton, IL: Crossway, 2012.

———. *In the Beginning Was the Word: Language—A God-Centered Approach*. Wheaton, IL: Crossway, 2009.

———. "Kinds of Biblical Theology." *Westminster Theological Journal* 70, no. 1 (2008): 129–42.

———. *Logic: A God-Centered Approach to the Foundation of Western Thought*. Wheaton, IL: Crossway, 2013.

———. "Multiperspectivalism and the Reformed Faith." In *Speaking the Truth in Love: The Theology of John M. Frame*, edited by John J. Hughes, 173–200. Phillipsburg, NJ: P&R, 2009. Accessed January 26, 2012. http://www.frame-poythress.org/poythress _articles/AMultiperspectivalism.pdf.

———. "Philosophical Roots of Phenomenological and Structuralist Literary Criticism." *Westminster Theological Journal* 41, no. 1 (1979): 165–71.

———. *Redeeming Science: A God-Centered Approach*. Wheaton, IL: Crossway, 2006.

———. *Redeeming Sociology: A God-Centered Approach*. Wheaton, IL: Crossway, 2011.

———. "Reforming Ontology and Logic in the Light of the Trinity: An Application of Van Til's Idea of Analogy." *Westminster Theological Journal* 57, no. 1 (1995): 187–219.

———. Review of *Essays on Biblical Interpretation*, by Paul Ricoeur. *Westminster Theological Journal* 43, no. 2 (1981): 378–80.

———. Review of *Interpreting God and the Postmodern Self: On Meaning, Manipulation and Promise*, by Anthony C. Thiselton. *Westminster Theological Journal* 59, no. 1 (1997): 131–33.

———. Review of *Is There a Meaning in This Text? The Bible, the Reader, and the Morality of Literary Knowledge*, by Kevin J. Vanhoozer. *Westminster Theological Journal* 61, no. 1 (1999): 125–28.

———. Review of *Narrative, Religion and Science: Fundamentalism versus Irony, 1700–1999*, by Stephen Prickett. *Westminster Theological Journal* 65, no. 2 (2003): 392–96.

———. Review of *Story, Sign, and Self: Phenomenology and Structuralism as Literary-Critical Methods*, by Robert Detweiler. *Westminster Theological Journal* 41, no. 1 (1978): 210–11.

———. Review of *The Two Horizons: New Testament Hermeneutics and Philosophical Description with Special Reference to Heidegger, Bultmann, Gadamer, and Wittgenstein*, by Anthony C. Thiselton. *Westminster Theological Journal* 43, no. 1 (1980): 178–80.

———. *The Shadow of Christ in the Law of Moses*. 1991. Reprint, Phillipsburg, NJ: P&R, 1995.

———. "Structuralism and Biblical Studies." *Journal of the Evangelical Theological Society* 21, no. 3 (1978): 221–37.

———. *Symphonic Theology: The Validity of Multiple Perspectives in Theology*. Grand Rapids: Zondervan, 1987. Reprint, Phillipsburg, NJ: P&R, 2001.

Pringle-Pattison, Andrew Seth. "Philosophy." In *Encyclopaedia Britannica*. 11th ed., 21:440–45. Cambridge: University of Cambridge, 1910.

Ridderbos, Herman. *Redemptive History and the New Testament Scriptures*. Phillipsburg, NJ: P&R, 1988.

Rushdoony, Rousas J. *The One and the Many: Studies in the Philosophy of Order and Ultimacy*. Nutley, NJ: Craig, 1971.

Russell, Bertrand. *Human Knowledge: Its Scope and Limits*. New York: Simon and Schuster, 1948.

———. *Why I Am Not a Christian: And Other Essays on Religion and Related Subjects*. Edited by Paul Edwards. New York: Simon & Schuster, 1957.

Ryken, Philip Graham. *Art for God's Sake: A Call to Recover the Arts*. Phillipsburg, NJ: P&R, 2006.

Sayers, Dorothy L. *The Mind of the Maker*. New York: Harcourt, Brace, 1941.

———. *Zeal of Thy House*. New York: Harcourt, Brace, 1937.

Shelley, James. "The Concept of the Aesthetic." In *The Stanford Encyclopedia of Philosophy*. Fall 2009 ed. Edited by Edward N. Zalta. Accessed January 28, 2012. http://plato.stanford.edu/archives/fall2009/entries/aesthetic-concept/.

Silva, Moisés. "The Case for Calvinistic Hermeneutics." In *Revelation and Reason: New Essays in Reformed Apologetics*, edited by K. Scott Oliphint and Lane G. Tipton, 74–94. Phillipsburg, NJ: P&R, 2007.

Stonehouse, N. B., and Paul Woolley, eds. *The Infallible Word: A Symposium by the Members of the Faculty of Westminster Theological Seminary*. 3rd ed. Philadelphia: Presbyterian and Reformed, 1967.

Van Til, Cornelius. *Christian Apologetics*. 2nd ed. Edited by William Edgar. Phillipsburg, NJ: P&R, 2003.

———. *Christianity and Barthianism*. Philadelphia: Presbyterian and Reformed, 1965.

———. *Christian Theistic Ethics*, In Defense of Biblical Christianity 3. N.p.: den Dulk Christian Foundation, 1971.

———. *A Christian Theory of Knowledge*. N.p.: Presbyterian and Reformed, 1969.

———. *Common Grace and the Gospel*. Nutley, NJ: Presbyterian and Reformed, 1973.

———. *The Defense of the Faith*. 4th ed. Edited by K. Scott Oliphint. Phillipsburg, NJ: P&R, 2008.

———. *An Introduction to Systematic Theology: Prolegomena and the Doctrines of Revelation, Scripture, and God*. 2nd ed. Edited by William Edgar. Phillipsburg: P&R, 2007.

———. *The New Hermeneutic*. Nutley, NJ: Presbyterian and Reformed, 1974.

———. *The New Modernism: An Appraisal of the Theology of Barth and Brunner*. Nutley, NJ: Presbyterian and Reformed, 1973.

———. *A Survey of Christian Epistemology*. In Defense of Biblical Christianity 2. N.p.: den Dulk Christian Foundation, 1969.

Vollenhoven, Dirk Hendrik Theodoor. "Hoofdlijnen der logica." *Philosophia Reformata* 13 (1948): 58–118.

———. *De noodzakelijkheid eener christelijke logica*. Amsterdam: H. J. Paris, 1932.

———. *De wijsbegeerte der wiskunde van theïstisch standpunt*. Amsterdam: Van Soest, 1918.

Vos, Geerhardus. *Biblical Theology: Old and New Testaments.* Grand Rapids: Eerdmans, 1948. Reprint, Eugene, OR: Wipf and Stock, 2003.

Warfield, Benjamin B. *The Inspiration and Authority of the Bible.* Edited by Samuel G. Craig. Philadelphia: Presbyterian and Reformed, 1967.

Welch, Edward T. *Blame It on the Brain? Distinguishing Chemical Imbalances, Brain Disorders, and Disobedience.* Phillipsburg, NJ: P&R, 1998.

———. *Counselor's Guide to the Brain and Its Disorders: Knowing the Difference between Disease and Sin.* Grand Rapids: Zondervan, 1991.

Wolters, Albert M. *Creation Regained: Biblical Basics for a Reformational Worldview.* 2d ed. with a postscript coauthored by Michael W. Goheen. Grand Rapids: Eerdmans, 2005.

Zylstra, Bernard. Introduction to *Contours of a Christian Philosophy: An Introduction to Herman Dooyeweerd's Thought,* by L. Kalsbeek, 14–33. Toronto: Wedge, 1975.

General Index

Scripture Index